T0330029

Ethical Value Networks in International Trade

Ethical Value Networks in International Trade

Social Justice, Sustainability and Provenance in the Global South

Edited by

Warwick E. Murray

Professor of Human Geography and Development Studies, Victoria University of Wellington, Aotearoa New Zealand

John Overton

Professor of Development Studies, Victoria University of Wellington, Aotearoa New Zealand

Kelle Howson

Postdoctoral Researcher, Oxford Internet Institute, University of Oxford, UK

Cheltenham, UK • Northampton, MA, USA

Published by
Edward Elgar Publishing Limited
The Lypiatts
15 Lansdown Road
Cheltenham
Glos GL50 2JA
UK

Edward Elgar Publishing, Inc.
William Pratt House
9 Dewey Court
Northampton
Massachusetts 01060
USA

A catalogue record for this book
is available from the British Library

This book is available electronically in the **Elgar**online
Geography, Planning and Tourism subject collection
http://dx.doi.org/10.4337/9781800374508

ISBN 978 1 80037 449 2 (cased)
ISBN 978 1 80037 450 8 (eBook)

Printed and bound by CPI Group (UK) Ltd, Croydon, CR0 4YY

Contents

Contributors

EDITORS

Professor Warwick E. Murray, Victoria University of Wellington, New Zealand

Professor John Overton, Victoria University of Wellington, New Zealand

Dr Kelle Howson, University of Oxford, United Kingdom

CONTRIBUTING AUTHORS

Dr Simon Bidwell, Victoria University of Wellington, New Zealand

Dr Nora Lanari, Coventry University, United Kingdom

Professor Johannes Rehner, Pontificia Universidad Católica de Chile, Chile

Dr Navé Wald, University of Otago, New Zealand

Theresa Sila Wikaningtyas, Victoria University of Wellington, New Zealand

Dr Peter B.F. Williams, Victoria University of Wellington, New Zealand

Acknowledgements

We gratefully acknowledge the support of the New Zealand Royal Society Te Apārangi Marsden Fund which allowed the editors to undertake the research project upon which this book is based. The grant funded much of the doctoral and masters work contained here, as well as fieldwork, international conference presentations and other activities associated with the work.

The editors would like to thank all of the research students that took part in the project for their excellent ideas, dedicated work and good-humoured company. All of the authors pay a special thanks to primary research participants and others that helped support them in the field. Gratitude is extended to members of geography and development studies departments at Universidad Católica de Chile, Universidad Católica de Peru, Bergen University (Norway), University of Cambridge (UK), University of the South Pacific, and Stellenbosch University (South Africa).

Warwick E. Murray and John Overton, *Te Whanganui-a-Tara/Wellington*, Aotearoa New Zealand and Kelle Howson, *Cape Town*, South Africa

PART I

Context and theory

1 The rise of ethical value in global trade networks

Warwick E. Murray, Kelle Howson and John Overton

INTRODUCTION

Consumers in supermarkets, local stores and produce markets, and on a plethora of online virtual stores, are faced with a bewildering array of foods and beverages on offer from producers across the globe. Significant globalisation and liberalisation of trade over the past three decades has greatly increased the range of fresh and processed foodstuffs available just as it has often lowered the price of such goods. Consumers have been linked to places and systems of production through complex chains and networks that span the globe. Some are small and local linkages, as in local produce markets where growers sell direct to consumers; others are very large and complex, combining agro-commodities from different places, in sometimes large-scale industrial manufacturing processes where the origin and nature of raw materials becomes anonymised. In many cases, it is these latter Fordist systems of food and beverage production that have come to dominate, providing cheap, uniform products with brand names and characteristics recognisable and available worldwide.

Yet many consumers have eschewed these global products and brands, having become aware of their often-deleterious effects on human and environmental well-being, and been motivated to seek healthy, safe and clean alternatives. They seek virtuous products – ethical products – those that don't harm the environment, don't exploit workers and come from particular identifiable places and communities. However, this is no simple task. How can a potential buyer of a bottle of wine, or a bunch of asparagus, or a bag of apples, be assured of where they come from, how and by whom they have been produced and what remains in the product in the form of chemical residues or additives? As a result, many products come with claims and certification of their authenticity of origin, method of production and integrity of contents – their ethicality. These claims – often but not always supported by robust regulatory and auditing systems – serve to link consumer decisions to imaginaries of production, involving combinations of people, cultures, communities, environments, places, traditions and techniques. Ethicality is proclaimed, valued and incorporated in practice and often reflected in (higher) price. What is thus linked in the minds of consumers is mirrored by real – and often highly complex – networks of production, processing, transport, wholesaling and retailing. Throughout these networks, value is created, traded, augmented and appropriated by a wide variety of institutions and individuals.

This book is concerned with these networks, the way they are constructed, regulated and operated. We are also focused on the idea of value, particularly in the way value moves through the networks, hopefully creating increased returns and incentives for particular producers, systems of production and places. And we are fundamentally interested in the notion of ethics – how ethical production is perceived, enacted and traded. We propose and adopt the concept of Ethical Value Networks (EVeNs). The book describes and theorises the rise of EVeNs and provides a range of case studies at the national and local scales which investigate the detail of the evolution, construction and outcomes of these networks.

This chapter introduces the collection and sets out the purpose and rationale for the work. We start by outlining the concept of EVeNs before tracing the rise of ethical consumption. The uneven and highly asymmetric global agri-food economy is briefly outlined – that which sees capture of value in the core among large-scale TNCs (trans-national corporations) in many globalised sectors. The rise of EVeNs in response has been led by a consumer movement and labelling effort where Northern purchasers 'vote' with their demand decisions. This has led to a burgeoning of market-based movements that seek to incorporate an ethical dimension in trade patterns, such as fair trade, organic production and Geographical Indications (GIs). Following these introductory remarks, we raise several questions with regard to these processes that inform the chapters which follow.

ETHICAL VALUE NETWORKS

There has been a significant rise in ethically-labelled primary product trade. This has been led in part by shifting taste and behaviours among consumers in the West. Concerned with the rise of uneven and unsustainable trade, there has been a growth in the marketing of agro-commodities that trade on the ethicality of production and delivery. Our concept of EVeNs – these varied and expanding networks of production and trade – builds on work in economic geography and related disciplines on commodity chains, global value chains and global production networks. Ethical value networks are globalised systems that integrate various nodes of productive, distributive and consumption activity across the globe in which, at some stage, a claim for 'ethicality' is certified and labelled as such. EVeNs are both a tool of analysis and an aspiration. They have the potential to identify some of the more unjust and non-sustainable aspects of global agri-food networks as the value added is traced through the nodes, flows and relations that comprise the global economy (Bidwell et al., 2018a, 2018b).

Constellations of Ethical Trade

EVeNs aim to augment the value of commodities through the addition of an 'ethical premium', which seeks to establish, regulate and certify a link between producers and consumers that assures authenticity, social justice and environmental sustainability. In part, EVeNs indicate a greater concern on the part of consumers for equity, environmental protection, food safety and 'authentic', localised production. At the same time, they reflect shifts in the agri-food regime away from Fordist mass-produced commodities towards niche-based export production that emphasises diversification, quality and provenance (Gereffi et al., 2005; Hughes, 2005; Ponte & Ewert, 2009). In short, EVeNs can be seen as an attempt to re-embed production, or at least to counter-act the disembeddedness that characterises neoliberal globalisation in the first two decades of the 21st century.

Critically, we see EVeNs as part of a strategy to construct narratives and regulatory frameworks that appeal to consumer tastes and which – perhaps paradoxically – help renew and make profitable neoliberal regimes of accumulation. EVeNs help particular commodities to gain a foothold in global markets by creating and exploiting niches that appeal to discerning consumers in search of ethical, sustainable and place-specific products. Marketeers seek to compete on the basis of factors such as quality, virtue and provenance rather than merely on price. An objective in the construction of ethical value chains and networks is for rural producers to gain a premium for their products and a stable and more just return on their labour as the higher prices paid by ethical consumers supposedly flow back down the chains and networks (McCarthy, 2006; Raynolds, 2012; Raynolds et al., 2007). However, despite these attempts to find alternative food networks and to provide more just, sustainable and supposedly authentic systems of production and trade, we will see that neoliberal processes of appropriation and accumulation continue and have significantly penetrated and even dominated these networks.

The notion that individuals can contribute to social and environmental justice through the exercise of consumer choice has become thoroughly rooted in the Western public imagination. The availability of products with certified normative qualities has grown at an order of magnitude over the past two decades to meet the demand of an expanding base of ethically-minded consumers. The free-market hegemony that emerged in the 1980s has accelerated the transformation of agricultural systems, drawing small farmers into expanded networks of trade in which value and power is increasingly retained at the buying end, and commodity producers are subject to extreme price fluctuations, dependence and insecurity. A consequence of this process has been the intensified fetishisation of food products, which become disembedded from their geographical and social origins, effectively concealing producers from consumers, and rendering unseen the effects of commodity dependence and trade injustice. The asymmetric gains and regional inequalities heralded by globalisation have prompted a transnational mobilisation of loosely organised actors seeking more equitable trade relationships and wealth distribution in commodity networks. This can be conceived as a global social movement, known as the ethical trade movement. Yet whilst this movement in its many different guises is frequently strongly critical of neoliberalism's excesses, proponents often adhere to certain tenets of neoliberalism – namely individualism, consumerism and the ineffectiveness of states in affecting just change. In the case studies that follow in this book, we will see this confused relationship between ethical trade and neoliberalism percolating through many of the resulting EVeNs that are created.

We identify three constellations of ethical trade – social justice, sustainability and authenticity – that comprise a broader universe of EVeNs. The former refers to cases where elements of justice are claimed within networks – most notably involving fair trade. This constellation of EVeNs has grown rapidly in the recent past particularly in products such as coffee, cocoa and bananas, and especially sourced from Latin America. The 'sustainability' constellation refers to EVeNs where environmental imperatives are prioritised, though it can also impinge upon social and cultural notions of health, stability and resilience that allow production and consumption systems to survive well into the future. The rise of organic farming globally and its labelling is central in this regard. We have witnessed an almost bewildering array of labelling efforts in this sector and a sharp rise in consumption of such products, most especially in European markets. Finally, there has been an increase in efforts to capture and protect the authenticity of production – assurances of the place of origin of products. This has been based in part on European models of '*terroir*' applied to and codified in the wine sector as *Denomination of Origin* and broader geographic indications legislation. This concept has spread across the world including to the Global South. In Latin America, for example, we have witnessed a significant rise in the evolution of GI legislation and regulation. Yet we will also see the idea of provenance more broadly than just a guarantee of the place of origin. It can be understood as a fundamental concept that underpins ethicality, including justice and sustainability, in the way it seeks to construct and present narratives about the way certain agro-commodities are produced across time and space. There has been a significant rise in the amount of products traded within these three constellations and each of these has seen the rise of systems of labelling and auditing.

The establishment of EVeNs is especially pertinent in resource peripheries. These are national, regional or local economies that have had to compete in an increasingly globalised world market by increasing production of resource-based commodities and seeking low-cost high-volume modes of production. We focus on three broad regions (South Africa, Latin America and South East Asia) that have both varied histories as resource peripheries and similar contemporary experiences seeking alternative trading strategies. Interestingly, these regions remain in competition with one another in exporting many resource-based commodities – they are competitive niches – yet they also have a shared interest in promoting consumer awareness and discrimination.

Our concept of ethical value networks builds on the now extensive literature on global value chains and networks (Bair, 2009; Coe & Yeung, 2009; Gereffi, 1996, 2014; Gibbon, 2001; Neilson et al., 2014). This work has identified key issues such as governance (Gibbon et al., 2008; Ponte & Gibbon, 2005) and the way chains are controlled by certain agencies and enterprises within them (Palpacuer, 2008; Pietrobelli & Saliola, 2008). There has also been research on commodity chains involving fair trade, organics, sustainable production and geographical indications, and some authors have linked value chains to issues of development (Bolwig et al., 2010; Ponte & Richey, 2014). Yet there is a dearth of research that has tied these various commodity chains together and identified their common foundation in ethical trade and consumer demand. No one has adequately explored the ways such chains are constructed.

However, while gaps remain in our understanding of EVeNs, ethical trade certifications are the subject of a robust discipline-straddling academic literature. Scholars from such diverse fields as business(Beckett & Nayak, 2008; Brei & Böhm, 2011; Gendron et al., 2008), anthropology (Fridell et al., 2008; Lyon, 2006), psychology (Bratanova et al., 2015), and geography (Bek et al., 2012; Hughes, 2005; Hughes et al., 2008; McEwan & Bek, 2009; Mutersbaugh, 2005) have grappled with defining, theorising and evaluating ethical trade. A number of key critiques have emerged from these endeavours. Some of these are grounded in empirical case-study findings and focus on practical limitations to the effectiveness of ethical certifications in protecting vulnerable producers and workers. These limitations include structural barriers to entry which have seen the poorest excluded from ethical networks (Lyon, 2006; Neilson & Pritchard, 2010), and the difficulties of reconciling conflicting interests within governance structures (Klooster, 2005; Taylor et al., 2005). Some researchers have observed that the increasing standardisation of ethical certifications renders them less able to respond to the subtleties of local contexts and that they constitute a top-down model of development (Freidberg, 2004;

Mutersbaugh et al., 2005). Other scholarly approaches are concerned with continued asymmetric power and profit distribution within ethically-certified networks, and question which parties are best able to appropriate the 'symbolic capital' generated by certification (Guthman, 2007; Heynen & Robbins, 2005). It is pointed out that ethical trade initiatives almost inevitably fall subject to the diluting forces of corporate co-optation or appropriation (Fridell et al., 2008; Jaffee & Howard, 2010). A more theoretical subset of the literature questions the political economy and vision of certification initiatives and points out the fundamental paradoxes of market-led social justice (Fridell, 2006, 2007; Guthman, 2007; Modelo, 2014). These writers raise questions as to the ability of the ethical trade movement to transform neoliberal globalisation.

CENTRAL QUESTIONS OF THIS BOOK

Although there has been an increase in the volume of research on fair trade, organic production and GIs, and some research on their putative ethical dimensions as noted, very little has been reported on multiple countries and sectors. The literature also fails to address a number of questions relating to the operation of EVeNs at various scales. In this regard, some of the principal questions this work seeks to answer are brought together below. We do not seek to answer the questions definitively or in great depth; rather we provide theoretical and empirical arguments and examples that might facilitate their answering in the future.

1. What is meant by the term 'ethical' when EVeNs are constructed?
2. How are such claims codified and inserted into value chains?
3. What are the impacts of the evolution of EVeNs on the ground?
4. What are the factors driving the adoption of EVeNs at various nodes in the production network?
5. To what extent do the benefits of EVeNs flow to the intended recipients, namely producers in the Global South?
6. Linked to the above, are the local impacts of EVeNs truly ethical as the certification and marketing rhetoric suggests?
7. To what extent can the rise of EVeNs address asymmetric power relations existent in the global agri-food network?
8. How can we conceptualise EVeNs and how do they relate to broader literature concerning chains and networks?
9. How can EVeNs be criticised?
10. What components should be emphasised in further work which seeks to understand the evolution and impact of EVeNs?

This work has both policy implications as well as theoretical dimensions. Little is known of the comparative impacts of the rise of EVeNs in the Southern Hemisphere, although such knowledge is crucial as demand grows in the expanding global middle class. It has long been accepted that countries outside the cores of the global economy struggle to gain sustainable bases for economic development when they remain largely dependent on the export of primary commodities. Countries in the resource periphery have attempted to develop new export strategies that are more secure and lucrative. It is important that policymakers in the Global South understand better the complexities and possible contradictions within different EVeNs so that more effective regulation or facilitation of ethical production and trade can lead to better desired social and environmental outcomes. In this sense, the book is at once descriptive, analytical and aspirational.

OUTLINE OF THE BOOK

The first part of the book is theoretical and contextual. Chapter 2 provides a review of the rise of ethical-labelled production focusing on the three constellations – social justice, sustainability and authenticity – as introduced previously. In order to do this we trace the rise of the sectors both at the global level and at lower scales focusing on links between the constellations and the challenges they face. In Chapter 3 we provide a brief overview and analysis of work in economic geography on commodity chains, global value chains, as well as global value networks and identify the gaps which we believe ethical networks can fill. In Chapter 4, we contextualise and theorise ethical value networks and how they might be described, analysed and applied. We reflect on the role of convention theory as well as other concepts that help us to understand the rise of ethical trade focusing on certification. Chapter 5 presents a brief overview of the critiques of ethical trade that have appeared in the literature. These serve to warn us of the potential problems and pitfalls in the implementation of EVeNs and to provide a critical frame of reference for the case studies that follow.

In the second part of the book a range of local case studies based on primary fieldwork is provided. These case studies are based on the research work of Masters and PhD students of the editors, as well as their own primary fieldwork, undertaken as part of the project that underpins this collection.[1] These case studies are drawn from Latin America, Africa and Southeast Asia and deal with a range of sectors, including wine, fruit, cinnamon, coffee, and water (see Figure 1.1). Although not intended to be exhaustive, this thematic and geographical range is unique to the literature. The case studies illustrate a wide range of outcomes – cases where ethical-labelling and EVeNs have worked in the favour of producers and labourers and others where they have clearly not.

At the general level, we make the conclusion that the evolution, construction and outcomes of EVeNs are highly differentiated and context-specific. We make a call for more sensitive geographies of ethicality in this regard. A critical component in future studies is locality studies that pay attention to the specific political economy of the places under consideration and the agents at work, whilst not losing sight of the co-deterministic structure of capital and the power that plays an important conditioning role on outcomes on the ground. These 'whole network' geographies have been largely ignored in the ethical trade literature to date.

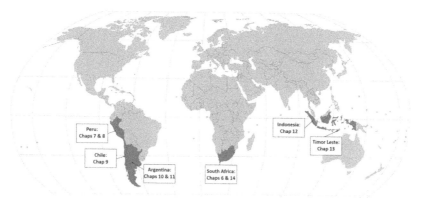

Figure 1.1   Location of case studies

In the third part of the book we draw together the challenges and gaps that exist in terms of the evolution and application of EVeNs approaches. We reflect on the role of virtue as it relates to authenticity and provenance as a unifying theme for future geographies of ethicality, tracing out the conceptual challenges faced in the evolution and application of EVeNs theory and policy. We conclude with a review of commonalities, critical issues and remaining questions for the analysis and construction of socially just, sustainable and authentic value networks that place ethical trade at the centre.

NOTE

1. This book builds in large part from a 4-year research grant (2015–2018 inclusive) entitled 'Re-placing Commodity Dependence: Alternative Sustainable and Ethical Value Chains in the Resource Periphery', led by Professors Warwick Murray and John Overton and also involving Professors Johannes Rehner and Jonathan Barton of Pontificia Universidad Católica, Chile. PhDs by Kelle Howson, Peter Williams and Simon Bidwell as well as numerous Masters theses resulted from this project. Many of the thesis findings appear in this collection as well as broader related

work by the project leaders and others beyond the immediate group. We gratefully acknowledge the generous financial support of the New Zealand Marsden Fund administered by the Royal Society of New Zealand. We also thank staff in the Research Office at Victoria University of Wellington as well as administrative staff at SGEES at Victoria University of Wellington for their invaluable support.

REFERENCES

Bair, J. (2009). Global commodity chains. In J. Bair (Ed.), *Frontiers of commodity chain research* (pp. 1–34). Stanford University Press.

Beckett, A., & Nayak, A. (2008). The reflexive consumer. *Marketing Theory*, *8*(3), 299–317.

Bek, D., McEwan, C., & Binns, T. (2012). The South African wine industry: Meeting the challenges of structural and ethical transformation. In P. H. Dougherty (Ed.), *The geography of wine* (pp. 137–157). Springer.

Bidwell, S., Murray, W. E., & Overton, J. (2018a). Ethical agro-food networks in global peripheries, Part I: The rise and recommodification of fair trade and organics. *Geography Compass*, *12*(4) online DOI: 10.1111/gec3.12366 11pp

Bidwell, S., Murray, W. E., & Overton, J. (2018b). Ethical agro-food networks in global peripheries, Part II: Re-placing commodity dependence. *Geography Compass*, *12*(4) online DOI: 10.1111/gec3.12365 11pp

Bolwig, S., Ponte, S., Du Toit, A., Riisgaard, L., & Halberg, N. (2010). Integrating poverty and environmental concerns into value-chain analysis: A conceptual framework. *Development Policy Review*, *28*(2), 173–194.

Bratanova, B., Vauclair, C.-M., Kervyn, N., Schumann, S., Wood, R., & Klein, O. (2015). Savouring morality. Moral satisfaction renders food of ethical origin subjectively tastier. *Appetite*, *91*, 137–149.

Brei, V., & Böhm, S. (2011). Corporate social responsibility as cultural meaning management: a critique of the marketing of 'ethical' bottled water. *Business Ethics: A European Review, 20*(3), 233-252.

Coe, N. M., & Yeung, H. W. C. (2019). Global production networks: Mapping recent conceptual developments. *Journal of Economic Geography*, *19*(4), 775–801.

Freidberg, S. (2004). The ethical complex of corporate food power. *Environment and Planning D: Society and Space*, *22*(4), 513–531.

Fridell, G. (2006). Fair trade and neoliberalism: Assessing emerging perspectives. *Latin American Perspectives*, *33*(6), 8–28.

Fridell, G. (2007). *Fair trade coffee: The prospects and pitfalls of market-driven social justice*. University of Toronto Press.

Fridell, M., Hudson, I., & Hudson, M. (2008). With friends like these: The corporate response to fair trade coffee. *Review of Radical Political Economics*, *40*(1), 8–34.

Gendron, C., Bisaillon, V., & Rance, A. I. O. (2008). The institutionalization of fair trade: More than just a degraded form of social action. *Journal of Business Ethics*, *86*(1), 63–79.

Gereffi, G. (1996). Global commodity chains: new forms of coordination and control among nations and firms in international industries. *Competition and Change*, *1*(4), 427–439.

Gereffi, G. (2014). Global value chains in a post-Washington Consensus world. *Review of International Political Economy*, *21*(1), 9–37.

Gereffi, G., Humphrey, J., & Sturgeon, T. (2005). The governance of global value chains. *Review of International Political Economy*, *12*(1), 78–104.

Gibbon, P. (2001). Upgrading primary production: A global commodity chain approach. *World Development*, *29*(2), 345–363.

Gibbon, P., Bair, J., & Ponte, S. (2008). Governing global value chains: An introduction. *Economy and Society*, *37*(3), 315–338.

Guthman, J, (2007). The Polanyian way? Voluntary food labels as neoliberal governance. *Antipode*, *39*(3), 456–478.

Heynen, N., & Robbins, P. (2005). The neoliberalization of nature: Governance, privatization, enclosure and valuation. *Capitalism Nature Socialism*, *16*(1), 5–8.

Hughes, A. (2005). Geographies of exchange and circulation: Alternative trading spaces. *Progress in Human Geography*, *29*(4), 496–504.

Hughes, A., Wrigley, N., & Buttle, M. (2008). Global production networks, ethical campaigning, and the embeddedness of responsible governance. *Journal of Economic Geography*, *8*(3), 345–367.

Jaffee, D., & Howard, P. (2010). Corporate co-optation of organic and fair trade standards. *Agriculture and Human Values*, *27*, 387–399.

Klooster, D. (2005). Environmental certification of forests: The evolution of environmental governance in a commodity network. *Journal of Rural Studies*, *21*(4), 403–417.

Lyon, S. (2006). Evaluating fair trade consumption: Politics, defetishization and producer participation. *International Journal of Consumer Studies*, *30*(5), 452–464.

McCarthy, J. (2006). Rural geography: alternative rural economies – the search for alterity in forests, fisheries, food, and fair trade. *Progress in Human Geography*, *30*(6), 803–811.

McEwan, C., & Bek, D. (2009). The political economy of alternative trade: Social and environmental certification in the South African wine industry. *Journal of Rural Studies*, *25*(3), 255–266.

Modelo, M. (2014). The paradox of fair trade. *Stanford Social Innovation Review*. Retrieved from http://ssir.org/articles/entry/the_paradox_of_fair_trade

Mutersbaugh, T. (2005). Just-in-space: Certified rural products, labor of quality, and regulatory spaces. *Journal of Rural Studies*, *21*(4), 389–402.

Mutersbaugh, T., Klooster, D., Renard, M.-C., & Taylor, P. (2005). Certifying rural spaces: Quality-certified products and rural governance. *Journal of Rural Studies*, *21*(4), 381–388.

Neilson, J., & Pritchard, B. (2010). Fairness and ethicality in their place: The regional dynamics of fair trade and ethical sourcing agendas in the plantation districts of South India. *Environment and Planning A*, *42*(8), 1833–1851.

Neilson, J., Pritchard, B., & Yeung, H. W. C. (2014). Global value chains and global production networks in the changing international political economy: An introduction. *Review of International Political Economy*, *21*(1), 1–8.

Palpacuer, F. (2008). Bringing the social context back in: Governance and wealth distribution in global commodity chains. *Economy and Society*, *37*(3), 393–419.

Pietrobelli, C., & Saliola, F. (2008). Power relationships along the value chain: Multinational firms, global buyers and performance of local suppliers. *Cambridge Journal of Economics*, *32*(6), 947–962.

Ponte, S., & Ewert, J. (2009). Which way is 'up' in upgrading? Trajectories of change in the value chain for South African wine. *World Development*, *37*(10), 1637–1650.

Ponte, S., & Gibbon, P. (2005). Quality standards, conventions and the governance of global value chains. *Economy and Society*, *34*(1), 1–31.

Ponte, S. & Richey, L. A. (2014) Buying into development? Brand aid forms of cause-related marketing. *Third World Quarterly*, *35*(1), 65–87.

Raynolds, L. T. (2012). Fair trade: Social regulation in global food markets. *Journal of Rural Studies*, *28*, 276–287.

Raynolds, L. T., Murray, D., & Heller, A., (2007). Regulating sustainability in the coffee sector: A comparative analysis of third party environmental and social certification initiatives. *Agriculture and Human Values*, *24*(2), 147–163.

Taylor, P. L., Murray, D. L., & Raynolds, L. T. (2005). Keeping trade fair: Governance challenges in the fair trade coffee initiative. *Sustainable Development*, *13*(3), 199–208.

2   Constellations of ethical trade

John Overton, Simon Bidwell, Kelle Howson and Warwick E. Murray

INTRODUCTION

This book focuses on the notion of ethical value in agri-food products, value which is created in production and marketing processes and validated through consumption choices. But what are the moral principles that underpin this ethical value, and where do they come from? How have they evolved over time and space and can we discern patterns, linkages and genealogies in what appears to be a very diverse range of ethics?

At first sight, we see a universe of production and consumption populated by a plethora of regulatory regimes and social movements espousing ethics and concepts as diverse as food miles, biodiversity protection and *appellation d'origine contrôlée*. However, within this crowded ethical agri-food landscape, we suggest that there are several 'constellations', discernible patterns and commonalities amongst the complexity.

An important integrating concept that links these constellations is provenance. This term relates to where something comes from,[1] but in fields such as art or antiques its use is somewhat broader than its place of origin, encompassing wider accounts of how it was produced, by whom, and its history of ownership. Provenance therefore provides a useful concept for interrogating agri-food systems and chains, allowing us to question "the spatial and social history of [food]" (Morgan et al., 2006, p.185). In this book, we use provenance in this broader way, spanning as it does our three suggested constellations, though it retains a particular resonance for examining place of origin (Overton et al., 2019).

Thinking about the provenance of a product leads us to seek information and reassurances from producers and sellers regarding production systems and marketing chains, but the desire for such assurances, often associated with added value, also opens possibilities for manipulation and obfuscation. 'Origin stories' become an important facet of marketing strategies to create and exploit opportunities for a price premium. Provenance, then, is not a simple matter of the 'facts' of origin; it involves – as we will see – strategic and deliberate ways to narrate products in ways that convince consumers that they have ethical value. In this sense 'provenance' is a process to create 'spatial and social histories' just as much as it is text, recording of place and method of production.

Provenance links to another meta concept, that of integrity. Integrity implies that there is honesty behind the claims to ethical value; that claims can be verified; and that the claims themselves appeal to sets of shared values. These values, we suggest, orbit in three (overlapping) constellations around key questions relating to the social, environmental and geographical life histories of products. In this sense it can be interpreted in part as a cultural and economic response to the disembeddedness and commodity fetishism embodied in the process of agri-food globalisation. In a geographical sense, provenance and authenticity become important underpinning concepts due to the opacity of large scale global agri-food networks.

These concepts above then translate to three broad categories of ethical value and potential regulation. First, there is *social justice*, which focuses on the human relationships involved in the production and exchange of foods. Movements and networks within this constellation emphasise fairness and transparency, and they seek to empower (economically, socially and even politically) small producers and workers, particularly those who have been historically marginalised and exploited. Second, we see a broad field of *sustainability*, which encompasses two main ethical principles: a concern for human health, particularly with regard to inputs (chemicals and other artificial and harmful additives to production and processing); and a desire to reduce or eliminate environmental damage in production and marketing (through harmful land and water use, resource depletion, carbon emissions, etc.). It may also include concerns for animal welfare and means to facilitate its flourishing. Third, there is *authenticity*.[2] This constellation covers concern with respect to the geographical origin of a product, which may not only be treated as an indication of quality, but also evoke the special environmental, social and cultural characteristics (assumed to be) associated with particular places. In geographical terms, differentiating, valuing and specifying authenticity in this way can be seen a process of 're-embedding' (Murray and Overton, 2015).

In this chapter we examine each of these three constellations in turn. We investigate the ethical foundations and complexities of each before asking how they have evolved, how they are manifested, contested and regulated in various ethical schemes, and how they might be moulded or manipulated throughout their value chains and networks. The aim is to establish a range of broad issues and questions that will be examined in greater depth in the case study chapters which follow.

SOCIAL JUSTICE: FAIR TRADE AND EMPOWERMENT

Within the agri-food sector, the social justice constellation is closely associated with the spectrum of networks and movements grouped under the banner of 'fair trade'.[3] Contemporary fair trade can be conceptualised as deriving from two distinct sources: first, the network of direct exchange relationships that grew up from the 1950s between solidarity and faith-based alternative trade organisations (ATOs) in the Global North, and artisan producers in the South (Fridell, 2007; Tallontire, 2007); and, second, the state-led and multilateral attempts to regulate North–South trade in tropical food commodities. These included the International Coffee Agreement, which operated between 1962 and 1989, and other market access agreements between European countries and their former colonies (Fridell, 2007; Moberg, 2014; Raynolds, 2008).

The direct exchange and the market regulation aspects of fair trade began to merge in the 1980s. On the one hand, bolstering sales of ethically sourced coffee became key to the strategies of North–South solidarity networks such as those formed with post-revolutionary Nicaragua and indigenous movements in Mexico (Bacon, 2013; Fridell, 2007). On the other, the collapse of commodity agreements following neoliberal deregulation of global trade left small producers facing increased vulnerability, while at the same time new market niches were generated by growing consumer interest in quality, equity and sustainability (Bidwell et al., 2018a; Fridell, 2007; Raynolds et al., 2004).

In 1988, the Max Havelaar movement in the Netherlands pioneered a key fair trade innovation – a certification and labelling regime that would allow fairly traded products to be sold through mainstream retailers. (Fridell, 2007; Renard, 2005). Similar initiatives in other countries quickly followed, and by the late 1990s there were 17 national certification and labelling organisations in Europe, North America and Japan (Lyon, 2006; Raynolds et al., 2004). In 1997, the national organisations formed the umbrella group Fairtrade Labelling Organizations (FLO). In 2002, FLO launched the Fairtrade Mark to provide a single and easily recognisable fair trade brand. In 2004, FLO split into Fairtrade International (FI), a standards setting and producer advocacy organisation, and Flo-cert, a for-profit certification body (Raynolds, 2012).

Fairtrade certification thus grew out of a primary focus on supporting small producers of 'traditional' tropical commodities such as coffee, bananas and cacao. To obtain certification, these small producers were required to organise themselves into democratic cooperatives and to pursue environmental sustainability goals. To use the Fairtrade label, importers were required to contract directly with a certified cooperative, offer contracts extending beyond a single harvest, and pay a defined minimum price as well as a premium to be used by the producer associations for community development or business investment. Later, standards were also developed to allow fair trade to be extended to products primarily grown on plantations, such as tea, sugar and cotton. In these cases, the plantation was required to conform to International Labour Organization (ILO) labour standards, with the cooperative replaced by a democratically organised committee of worker and manager representatives, which allocates the Fairtrade premium (Fridell, 2007; Lyon, 2006). This was a controversial and significant development in the history of Fairtrade. FI initially resisted plantation standards, leading Fairtrade USA to splinter off. Eventually FI added 'standards for hired labour' too – a move which some commentators saw as the ultimate co-optation of the movement, conceived to protect smallholder farmers.

In the 30 years since its entrance into the mainstream, fair trade has grown and diversified in both geographical and product terms. In addition to traditional products such as coffee, cacao and bananas, trade certification and labelling is now applied to cotton, flowers, fresh fruit, honey, juices, rice, spices and herbs, sugar, tea and wine, and it has been extended beyond food products to sports balls, gold and carbon credits among other things (Fair Trade International, 2020).

In 2003, total international Fairtrade sales were estimated at around $500 million (Raynolds et al., 2004), with growth accelerating to $7 billion by 2012 (Fair Trade International, 2013), then levelling out to approximately $9.5 billion by 2018 (Fair Trade International, 2019). A key factor has been the adoption of Fairtrade-certified products by major retailers, including supermarket chains in Europe, which has seen the United Kingdom become the single largest fair trade market. Direct exchange networks have also grown and diversified, with a cursory review of speciality markets in New Zealand showing numerous self-proclaimed 'real trade' arrangements for coffee, cacao and 'superfoods' such as maca. However, direct exchange is now quantitatively dwarfed by mainstream, certification-based trade.

In 2020, Fairtrade International comprised 1822 certified producer organisations representing 1.7 million farmers and workers in 72 countries (Fairtrade International, 2020).[4] The number of Fairtrade certified producers has grown significantly over the past decade, from 827 organisations in 60 countries in 2009–2010 (Fairtrade International, 2013). From 2005 to 2018, retail sales of Fairtrade International certified products increased from just over €1 billion, to €9.8 billion, of which farmers received a premium of €178 million in 2018 (Fairtrade International, 2019). In terms of producer premium earned in 2020, coffee continued to represent the largest share of Fairtrade International products, followed by cocoa, bananas, sugar, flowers and plants, and tea (Fairtrade International, 2020).

The Promise and Challenges of Fair Trade in the Global South

In theory, fair trade promises economic, environmental and social benefits for small producers and workers. Its advocates argue that fair trade is part of a "network of international solidarity" (Raynolds, 2008, p. 180), which aims to ensure that the ethical premium paid by consumers is used to support production under "socially and environmentally healthy conditions" (Shreck, 2002, p. 13). The extent to which fair trade lives up this promise has been subject to an increasing volume of academic research over the past three decades. Key themes include the impacts on producer and community livelihoods, the balance of power and distribution of benefits in networks and value chains, and the overall place of fair trade within the evolution of global capitalism.

Benefits of fair trade for small producers in the South have been reported to include higher and stable market prices, quality improvement, improved organisational capacity and access to credit, as well as collective benefits for communities from the Fairtrade premium (Dragusanu et al., 2014; Fridell, 2007; Lyon, 2006; Raynolds et al., 2004; Shreck, 2002; Utting-Chamorro, 2005). A particularly notable impact was the stabilisation of prices received by small coffee producers in 2000–2004 when the Fairtrade price was up to three times higher than the market price (Fridell, 2007; Pay, 2009). Some researchers have also described a virtuous circle of livelihood protection, product quality improvement and social organisation arising from the closer and more empathetic relationships that developed between Northern coffee importers and roasters and Latin American small farmers, as the former sought consistent supplies of high-quality coffee and became interested in the production and livelihood challenges of the latter (Bacon, 2013; Bidwell et al., 2018a; Lyon, 2006; Utting-Chamorro, 2005).

However, a number of factors have limited the impact of fair trade. A fundamental challenge is the mismatch between demand and supply. Most producer cooperatives sell limited quantities on fair trade terms, ranging from 50% for long-established cooperatives and those that can maintain higher quality standards, to 20% or less in the case of newer entrants (Goodman et al., 2012; Raynolds & Bennett, 2015). In addition, importers who only buy a small percentage of fair trade can choose this based on quality, reducing the effective premium (Goodman et al., 2012). The Fairtrade minimum price has declined over time in real terms (Pay, 2009; Valkila, 2009) and, apart from periods such as 2000–2004, it has to be equal to or more than the market price. This may help explain why some comparative studies have not found significant effects of fair trade on producer incomes (Ruben & Fort, 2012), while in many cases the Fairtrade premium received is too small to make a significant contribution to local development projects (Jaffee, 2012; Utting-Chamorro, 2005).

Another factor is the highly uneven *access* to fair trade networks. A common finding is that successful involvement in such networks is associated with stable land tenancy and the ability to mobilise resources at the family level; and institutional capacity at the cooperative level (Arce, 2009; Fridell, 2007; Goodman et al., 2012; Neilson & Pritchard, 2010). This raises the question of whether these networks simply consolidate the position of relatively resilient 'small farmers', a term which, as Leutchford (2008) suggests, obscures the important differences between those with 5 to 10 hectares of land and those with one hectare or less. Researchers generally concur that few benefits reach unorganised farmers, those with insecure land tenure, or – at least until the adoption of plantation standards – landless workers (Ruben & Fort, 2012; Utting-Chamorro, 2005).

Concerns about uneven access have grown since the mid-2000s with what Goodman et al. (2012, p. 197) term the "turn to quality" in fair trade, involving efforts to target mainstream markets through a focus on quality and taste. This has further raised barriers to entry for the poorest producers, who, in addition to meeting governance requirements and paying the significant costs of certification, must deliver the quality standards demanded by mainstream buyers. Thus, a significant part of the growth in fair trade markets has occurred through expanded sales by larger, well-established producer cooperatives, often those with the longest history of NGO support (Goodman et al., 2012).

Other criticisms relate to the imbalance of power both in the institutional certification system and in the overall value chain. A common critique is that, in spite of the theoretical promise of fair trade for actors in global peripheries, the greatest share of material benefits is captured in the North. Small Southern producers generally have to meet Fairtrade certification requirements for all their production, while contractors, buyers and retailers can choose how much they buy and may have opposing practices in other branches of their business (González & Nigh, 2005; Williams, 2019). Powerful buyers such as super-markets have increasingly based access to their Fairtrade niches on stringent quality standards, reducing the real margin for producers, while reaping the benefits of consumer willingness to pay more for ethical products (Dolan, 2008; Freidberg, 2003; Lyon, 2006; Ponte, 2009; Raynolds et al., 2007; Valkila et al. 2010).

Researchers have also criticised the power relations between the Northern consumers, social movements and certifiers who lead the construction of fair trade networks, and the Southern producers and workers who are ostensibly the main beneficiaries of these networks. They raise the question of who sets the 'fair' price and the participation by producers in defining the terms of cer-tification (Bacon, 2013; Lyon, 2006; Renard, 2005). While these points have most often been made with respect to the Fairtrade certification and labelling system, direct exchange networks are not necessarily immune from these criticisms.

A broader criticism of fair trade is that, at best, it offers palliative impacts without challenging the fundamental structures of globalisation. Critics underline this point by detailing the attempts by powerful interests to evade, weaken, or co-opt the standards of ethical regimes – not only in fair trade but also in other networks, such as certified organics (Fridell et al., 2008; Jaffee & Howard, 2010). First, these actors participate in ethical networks while ensuring they remain marginal ('fairwashing'). Second, they develop alternative, 'diluted' standards, such as Utz Kapeh/Rainforest Alliance or Starbucks' and Nestlé's private labelling initiatives, none of which include a binding minimum price (Raynolds et al., 2007). Third, they lobby to influence standards and frameworks that govern ethical regimes. Jaffee & Howard (2010) demonstrate how large coffee importers and retailers have promoted the Fairtrade certification of plantations, which is convenient for the supply chain practices of these actors but threatens to squeeze out smaller growers.

Thus, fair trade has grown into a movement now well-established in global markets. It has origins in a concern for social justice and its main certification system is based on explicit commitments to fair and stable returns for producers and just working conditions and pay for labourers. Yet significant concerns and questions have been raised with regard to the size and distribution of benefits, power relations within networks and whose interests they primarily serve. Much still needs to be investigated. Much of the work to date has focused on coffee, and further research is needed on other products in other geographical settings, particularly where fair trade standards are applied to a factory or plantation. We also need to examine more closely the relations of production, rather than just exchange (Raynolds, 2012; Raynolds & Bennett, 2015).

SUSTAINABILITY: HUMAN HEALTH AND ENVIRONMENTAL PROTECTION

The sustainability constellation is arguably the most diverse of the three examined in this book, both in terms of its historical origins and its ethical and philosophical concerns. At first glance, it seems that this constellation is too diffuse to be considered a single set of ethics. It has a strong and seemingly quite coherent focus on one hand to do with the way harmful substances enter the food chain and affect human health and contribute to diet-related diseases such as the obesity epidemic (Morgan et al., 2006). We can also see a strong and emerging concern for animal welfare and, indeed, branches which are opposed to the consumption of any animal products. Then there is a wide array of concerns relating to the environmental impacts of food production and consumption, ranging from water and soil quality, through carbon-neutral production to food miles. However, they share some common elements, linked by a concern with the impact of food systems on long-term human and environmental wellbeing. We use the broad concept of sustainability to encompass these ethical concerns for, whilst they may call for radical changes in behaviour, they seek to maintain both human and environmental health now and for future generations.

The publication of Rachel Carson's *Silent Spring* in 1962 is often regarded as a key moment in the modern environmental movement and it provides a key foundation stone for the sustainability movement. This strong exposé of the way agriculture in the USA was using harmful chemicals in the form of pesticides and herbicides was important because not only did it outline the dangers to birdlife, insects and plant life in the wider environment – the 'silencing' of the countryside – but it also pointed to the way residues from such chemicals entered the food chain and were consumed – unwittingly – by humans. Ecological damage and human sickness were linked to a common cause: 'modern' high-input agricultural systems that used artificial additives to increase production.

Another key foundation stone – and one with earlier origins – was laid by Rudolf Steiner who proposed the concept of biodynamic agriculture in the 1920s. At one level, this has been seen as a call to avoid the use of artificial fertilisers and chemicals and instead use composts and manures within a farming system. In this, it can be regarded as one of the first organic farming movements. Yet, at another level, it added a spiritual and philosophical dimension, arguing that astrological forces influenced soil and human health. Its quasi- or pseudo-scientific approach has attracted much scepticism but it remains influential as a global movement and it maintains strict codes of practice and certification (Sansavini and Wollesen, 1992).

A third foundational element for sustainability can be traced to the modern environmental movement and, more specifically to the *Limits to Growth* warnings of the Club of Rome in the early 1970s (Meadows et al., 1972). This work, and much since, has pointed to the dangers of resource depletion, increasing pollution and environmental degradation, and both population and economic growth. More recently, these concerns have grown and sharpened, with a focus on carbon emissions and climate change. Within this approach we see strong concerns for planetary ecology: for soil fertility and carrying capacity, for deforestation, for air and water pollution, and for the accelerated use of non-renewable resources – and the ways these affect, and are affected by, modern food production systems.

Over the past five decades, the issue of sustainability in food production has become much more prominent, though in many ways more diffuse. Steiner's and Carson's early concerns over the use of chemicals in agriculture have grown – as industrial agriculture itself has expanded greatly – and have expanded from the use of chemical additives in production to those in processing. There have been consequent pressures to make food labelling much more explicit with regard to chemical residues in food and, in recent years, campaigns to eliminate or at least make clear, the use of genetically-engineered ingredients in food. In many ways, the field of food sustainability has coalesced around the organic agriculture movement. This, as we will see, has come to encompass both health and environmental concerns. It does not necessarily accommodate all aspects or movements in this category (some aspects of animal welfare for example) and it perhaps underplays the issue of climate change (in concepts such as food miles), yet it is a global phenomenon that has considerable presence in global markets.

Organic Agriculture – Promise and Challenges

The concept of organic agriculture was developed by disparate movements in Europe, Australia and the USA in the early 20th century (of which Steiner's biodynamic movement has claims to being the first). These movements had a common focus on maintaining and improving the health and vitality of the soil in order to address problems such as erosion and decline in the quality and quantity of crop yields (Kuepper, 2010; Sansavini & Wollesen, 1992). In the 1960s, interest in sustainable farming practices was energised by countercultural movements that aimed to enact ecologically and socially kinder alternatives to industrialised food production and distribution (González & Nigh, 2005; Goodman et al., 2012).

Various factors have contributed to the growing awareness and popularity of organic agriculture, including increasing scientific respectability through the development of agroecology as a discipline (Gliessman, 1998) and periodic crises of conventional agriculture. The International Federation of Organic Agriculture Movements (IFOAM) was founded in 1972, and the first certification schemes were developed shortly after. Legislation regulating organic production was passed in various European countries during the 1980s (Sansavini and Wollesen, 1992) while a EU-wide resolution on organic agriculture was promulgated in 1991 and, following legislation originally passed in 1990, organic standards were eventually implemented in the USA in 2002.

During the 1980s and 1990s, demand for organic food rose rapidly in response to consumer concerns about inputs to industrial agriculture including chemical fertilisers, hormones, antibiotics and genetic modification (Daviron & Vagneron, 2011; Raynolds, 2008). Consumer surveys suggest that the most important motivations for people buying organic food are personal health – particularly relating to the absence of pesticide residue – and more general concerns about the environment (Biasetti, 2014; Idda et al., 2008; Pearson et al., 2011). Other motivations include taste, perceptions of quality and the desire to support local farmers, suggesting that organics overlaps and links with movements in the social justice and authenticity constellations (Hinrichs, 2000, 2003; Winter, 2003).

The growth of the organic industry has been rapid, with global sales increasing from almost nothing in 1980 to $20 billion in 2000 and $97 billion in 2017 (Willer & Lernoud, 2019). The USA represents approximately 46% of the global organic market and Germany a further 11% (Willer & Lernoud, 2019). Certified organic agriculture has also expanded quickly in the Global South since the 1990s, with Latin America and the Caribbean a leading region. International NGOs and aid agencies were promoting organic approaches by the early 1980s as part of rural development and appropriate technology programmes (Raynolds, 2008). The promotion of export opportunities followed rapidly, as Western demand for organics expanded to include out-of-season fruit and vegetables and exotic tropical products (Bidwell, 2020; IFAD, 2003; Raynolds, 2008).

The Global South and Organic Agriculture

Experiences in the South with organics in many ways overlap with and mirror fair trade. On the one hand, there were initial successes for early adopters that transitioned to certified organic production, especially for small farmers already producing in near-organic ways, with studies showing evidence of price premiums, net income gains and health and environmental benefits (Bidwell, 2020; Bidwell et al., 2018a; IFAD, 2003; Raynolds, 2008). Increasing demand for organic products – linked to the growth of quality niches – has had a measurable impact on the global division of labour. For example, Latin American countries dominate the organic and heirloom cacao market, despite their relatively small footprint in conventional production. Mexico and Peru are easily the largest exporters of organic coffee (and place 12th and 13th respectively in total organic exports) while the presence of conventional powers such as Brazil and Colombia in this niche has been marginal (Willer & Lernoud, 2019). In Peru in particular, organic coffee is the domain of small producers working under cooperative structures.

On the other hand, as Laura Raynolds notes, "as organic commodities become more mainstream, they are shaped increasingly by mainstream market pressures" (2008, p. 181). Small farmers whose traditional practices are close to those espoused by the organic movement have seen their initial competitive advantages eroded by a combination of increasing costs of certification, quality demands of buyers, and the growing involvement of medium and large producers in organic markets. For example, Raynolds (2008) notes that the share of organic banana exports held by small farmers in the Dominican Republic dropped from 90% to 50% as large exporters began to vertically

integrate by growing their own produce. A further issue is that to obtain certification, producers in the South have to conform to international standards that
are developed in temperate countries and may be inappropriate for tropical
agriculture (González and Nigh, 2005).

Up until the late 1970s, organic movements included a spectrum of attitudes
and practices which included occasional and judicious use of chemical inputs
(Kuepper, 2010). The transition to a definition based on complete exclusion of
synthetic chemicals came with the rise of certification schemes and national
standards in the 1980s, and arguably reflects the growing importance of
consumer concerns in the movement. The shift of focus from soil health to
excluding chemicals has seen the organic appellation applied to a range of
non-soil-based products such as fish, shellfish and hydroponics.

Standards developed to regulate organic production have thus largely
focused on defining permissible inputs, which in turn have been subject to
concerted lobbying by agribusiness (see Jaffee & Howard, 2010). Globally
dominant standards have few requirements about overall environmental
impact, limited provisions for animal welfare and none at all for the social relations of production (Daviron & Vagneron, 2011; González and Nigh, 2005).
Certification may nevertheless be too onerous or expensive for small farmers
who do follow wider organic principles. Thus, some authors have identified a
'bifurcation' of organics between a 'movement-oriented' stream committed
to principles of social and ecological sustainability, and a 'market-oriented'
stream focused on input substitution (Goodman et al., 2012; Guthman, 2004).
Movement-oriented actors have fought back by promoting their own 'beyond
organic' standards (for example, the tight regulations for biodynamic agriculture maintained by the Demeter organisation, which date back to the 1920s);
and by developing alternative participatory guarantee systems (PGS) based on
farmer peer review for organic production aimed at local markets (Willer &
Lernoud, 2019).

Beyond Organics

Alongside the debates and attempts to regulate what is passed as 'organic'
there has been a proliferation of related narratives and regulatory frameworks
for other aspects of healthy and sustainable food production and trade. We can
also see a wide variety of labelling, largely unregulated, which uses terms such
as 'carbon neutral' or 'local' which appeal to the wider narratives of sustainability, but which lack coherence or substance without strong standards, certification or monitoring. Furthermore, whilst there might be some legislative
action to enforce the integrity of food labelling, regarding some food additives
or chemical residues (as in the EU), there are in many parts of the world a lack

of legal requirements to specify product origins, production methods (such as the use of GE inputs), or related claims to be 'natural' or 'sustainable'.

Further clouding this constellation has been a range of other health and welfare narratives which have gained awareness and some market traction. Vegetarianism and veganism, in many respects, are separate movements which have led to their own value networks but they have had a more general impact on wider food networks by giving added impetus to the demand for clearer food labelling and more transparent supply chains so that animal products can be identified and separated in food chains. Environmental and health concerns are often cited as motivations for vegetarianism and veganism, but, as with consumer resistance to chemical residues, the emphasis on complete exclusion of animal products only connects partially with movements focused on ecological balance and sustainability. As global consumer movements, vegetarianism and veganism arguably belong in the social justice constellation, with concerns about welfare being extended from humans to non-humans. They also have connections with much older religious traditions that prohibit consumption of (all or some) animal products for a mix of philosophical and pragmatic or symbolic reasons.

Similarly, 'sustainability' has been widened as a concept in globalised agri-food networks. Early organic agriculture concerns for soils at farm-level – and some schemes to protect local biodiversity next to agriculture – have been joined by more global-level fears regarding climate change and resource depletion. This is manifested in several forms, ranging from food-miles campaigns to promote locally-produced foods rather than those transported over long distances, to carbon-zero or carbon-neutral schemes which, in addition to transport, also factor in carbon use in production, processing and waste generation.

Given such a diversity of concerns and narratives, we can see this ethical constellation as being particularly fraught with obfuscation and confusion. Although there are subsets within the constellation, such as biodynamics, which are tightly specified and regulated, in total there is little that can assure consumers of the human, animal or planetary health costs and benefits of agri-products we consume. Instead, we see a wide menu of provenance stories (some with their own certification schemes) that producers and retailers can choose from to establish some claim to health and sustainability benefits. It becomes very difficult for a consumer, say in the UK, to choose between locally produced vegetables (using chemical fertilisers and herbicides but with minimal food miles) and those transported from low-input or organic producers in Latin America. The overall term 'sustainable' or 'sustainably-produced', often used, is a weak and imprecise guide. Given this confusion, there is scope for various agents along the value chain to employ different narratives and claims in ways which appeal to broad general sustainability virtues but which act to further confuse consumers and thus dilute the ethical basis – and ethical premium – of products that have clear and acceptable provenance.

AUTHENTICITY: GEOGRAPHICAL INDICATIONS AND PLACE OF ORIGIN

Geographical Indications (GIs) are "place-based names that convey the geographical origin, as well as the cultural and historical identity of agricultural products" (Bowen, 2010, p. 1). The use of place names and claims or assurances regarding the origin of agri-food products is well established in global markets. Significant numbers of consumers want to know where their food comes from and many associate the place identity of a product with particular taste characteristics, links to culture and tradition, and imaginations of 'quality'. In these ways, GIs provide not only an assurance of origin but also a framework for constructing narratives about distinctiveness. Their ethical foundation, then, is based upon the idea that place is a proxy for quality and authenticity.

To a large extent, the emergence of geographical origin as the basis for an ethical constellation was built upon wine and the notion that particular places – distinct physical and cultural environments – bestow certain qualities on wine (Howson et al., 2020). Climate, soils, aspect, and even underlying geology, some argue, determine the fruit flavours and thus the taste of wine (Fanet, 2004; Overton & Murray, 2017; Wilson, 1998). Furthermore, the qualitative characteristics of wine are further shaped by viticultural and vinicultural practices embedded in place through generations of winemaking traditions (Moran, 2001). This relation between place and quality is encapsulated in the concept of *terroir*, the way that 'the land'/place/environment is reflected in the taste of a wine. *Terroir,* in turn, is strongly bound to cultures of wine production and consumption (Demossier, 2010; Trubek, 2008). Places – Champagne, Bordeaux, Rioja and Chianti – are fixed to particular styles, and perceived qualities, of wine to the point where the wines carrying these place names are better known than the regions they come from.

It is a short step from the idea that *terroir* provides wine with distinctive characteristics to claims that some wines (and some wine regions) are 'better' than others. Place becomes a surrogate for quality. Thus, some places are favoured; their wines cost more than wines from other places; and place has demonstrable value as part of a brand. Value in place then requires that place brands are regulated and protected to prevent producers from other regions from appropriating (and diluting) the value of using a favoured place name, such as Champagne or Burgundy for wines produced elsewhere.

While legal defences of product-place identities date back at least to port in the 17th century (Josling, 2006), the best-known geographical indications are the systems of wine appellations in European countries such as France, Italy and Spain. The French *appellation d'origine contrôlée* (AOC) system began in the early 20th century, when regulations were made to combat fraud, but it evolved over time into a comprehensive approach to overseeing product provenance, production methods and quality (Bowen, 2010; Trubek, 2008). Although wine has been at the vanguard of efforts to protect place names, as regulatory systems developed, they dispersed in space and also spread to cover other products. At an international level, protections for 'indications of source' were included in the Paris Convention for the Protection of Industrial Property of 1883, which was updated in 1967, while geographical indications were also covered by the General Agreement on Tariffs and Trade (GATT) in 1947 (Yeung & Kerr, 2011). The Lisbon Union, which was negotiated in 1958 and revised in 1967, established an international approach to registering appellations of origin, but the agreement only has 26 members and does not include the USA, the EU or Japan (Giovannucci et al., 2009; Josling, 2006).

In 1992, the EU established a framework for GIs with broad aims including promoting rural development and protecting traditional culture and knowledge embedded in artisanal production methods (Giovannucci et al., 2009). There are two different categories under this framework:

(1) *Protected Designation of Origin* (PDO) – a product must be produced and processed in a defined geographical area and its quality, reputation and characteristics must be essentially due to that area.
(2) *Protected Geographical Indication* (PGI) – a product must be produced or processed in a geographical area, and its quality, reputation or characteristics must be attributable to that area (raw materials do not need to be from the area).

Meanwhile, the USA has historically recognised GIs through its trademark system, which allows any private entity to register a place name as part of a mark as long as it is not misleading as to the product origin. The USA also provides for collective marks or certification marks, with the latter being similar in some respects to the EU's system, in that they allow the mark's owner to set quality and other standards while requiring open access to any producer who meets these standards. A number of international products have gained protection under certification marks in the US, including Darjeeling tea and Jamaica Blue Mountain coffee (Giovannucci et al., 2009).

During the Uruguay round of World Trade Organisation (WTO) negotiations in 1994, GIs were added to the agreement on Trade-related Intellectual Aspects of Property (TRIPS). It is significant that, in the adoption of GIs in global trade agreements, the basis for the acceptance of the designation and protection of place names was not a *terroir*-based argument (that places define unique characteristics of a product) but rather that place names are a form of intellectual property (Moran, 1993); place names embody generations of tradition and cultural value that should not be appropriated freely by others.

The TRIPS agreement defines GIs as applying "where a given quality, reputation or other characteristic of [a] good is essentially attributable to its geographical origin" and obliges signatory parties to provide the means of defending them. Although the general provisions only cover cases of misrepresentation or consumer deception, Article 23 offers a higher level of protection for wines and spirits, in that non-origin producers may not use terms protected by GIs even where the product origin is made clear. By 2007, 111 countries had developed *sui generis* systems for protecting GIs (Giovannucci et al., 2009). Countries to follow the USA in relying on a trademark system and consumer protection law have included Japan, South Africa, Australia and New Zealand but almost all of these (including the US) now have at least some form of geographical indications framework for wine.

As GIs have been consolidated within their traditional stronghold of the EU and expanded globally, they have become the subject of considerable debate and negotiation in international forums. Primarily, this reflects the different philosophies underlying the respective approaches of the EU and the USA/ New World. Under the USA approach, the state provides a framework for companies and other organised groups to develop and protect intellectual property, prioritising innovation, competition and consumer benefit, while Europe envisages a more interventionist role for the state and places greater emphasis on public benefits and responsibilities such as the protection of culture and tradition. There have been tensions relating to the mutual accessibility of the respective systems, as well as disputes about the attempts of European producer interests to 'claw back' the use of product names that some argue have become generic and have developed their own tradition in New World countries, including feta, champagne and prosciutto, among others (Giovannucci et al., 2009; Josling, 2006). Both the EU and the USA have sought to advance their approaches through bilateral trade deals (Giovannucci et al., 2009), while the EU has led a movement to expand the TRIPS protections for wine and spirits to other products.

Impacts of GIs in the Global North and South

A body of theoretical debate on GIs pitches those who argue that they provide an accurate signal of quality that reduces search costs for the consumer and appropriately rewards producers, against those who maintain they allow established producer interests to capture economic rents and restrict innovation and competition through bureaucratic rigidity (Battaglene, 2005; Josling, 2006; Rangnekar, 2004). In parallel, case study-based research has explored the extent to which GIs provide benefits to small producers and to the wider community and region of which they are a part. Studies in the EU have suggested that GI-protected products can obtain significant price premiums and may be associated with conservation of environmental and cultural diversity (Belletti et al., 2017; Giovannucci et al., 2009; Rangnekar, 2004). This has led researchers to explore whether similar results might be seen in the Global South (Belletti et al., 2017; Biénabe & Marie-Vivien, 2017; Bramley & Kirsten, 2007; Jena & Grote, 2012; Wilkinson et al., 2017).

Studies suggest that the impacts of GIs turn on two key factors. First, is the way in which relationships between place and product are constructed. This includes the scale of the GI area and the extent to which quality and reputation are linked to locally specific factors such as traditional production techniques, local knowledge and biocultural diversity. Explicit links between quality and *terroir* can help ensure that ecological and cultural diversity is valued and protected, while emphasis on technical, standardised measures can actually reduce diversity and may allow the elimination of local actors from the supply chain (Bowen, 2010; Galtier et al., 2013; Giovannucci et al., 2009; Mancini, 2013). A case in point is tequila, where a large, undifferentiated GI area and technical specifications have allowed the value chain to be dominated by bottling interests based in North America, promoted large-scale monoculture, and provided little benefit for small agave growers in rural Mexico (Bowen, 2010). In some cases of coffee GIs, debates about territorial boundaries have created significant tensions, while in other cases detailed, *terroir*-linked and inclusive systems of appellations have defused some of these tensions (Galtier et al., 2013; Giovannucci et al., 2009; Mancini, 2013; Wilkinson et al., 2017).

For wine, similar issues with regard to the malleability of GI boundaries have been noted in several studies (for example Banks & Sharpe, 2006; Overton & Murray, 2017). We have gone further to suggest that there are active processes of place-making that seek to construct narratives and definitions of wine regions – 'fictive places' – so that economic value is made, protected and appropriated by certain wine producers (Overton & Murray, 2016). This is an industrial strategy of a 'race to place' – securing and protecting place names in order to gain a market premium – as opposed to a 'race to the bottom', maximising profit through economies of scale and minimising costs. A variety of enterprises may pursue such strategies. Small producers make use of their fixed location in favoured regions to charge more for their bottles of wine and survive alongside cheaper mass-produced products. Yet large corporate beverage producers also make use of GIs, both to promote higher-priced brands in their portfolio, and to build the image of wine in general as one linked to quality claims (using region of origin, vintage and grape variety) for nearly all but their cheapest bulk brands of wine.

A second key factor is the nature of the institutional governance arrangements for the GI, in particular, whether they allow equitable representation of all value chain participants (Belletti et al., 2017; Bowen, 2010; Mancini, 2013; Wilkinson et al., 2017). This affects whether "local participants are able to resist the appropriation of locally embedded supply chains by extralocal actors" (Bowen, 2010, p. 237). A crucial factor is the involvement of the State: on the one hand in creating a coherent GI regime that empowers producers while maintaining appropriate quality checks (Bowen, 2010); and on the other, in its general policies towards agriculture and rural development such as supporting small producers, disseminating information and appropriate technology, and facilitating social organisation. The state's failure to perform these key roles is cited as one reason for the relatively disappointing results of GI regimes in the South, such as tequila and mescal in Mexico and Chontaleño cheese in Nicaragua (Bowen, 2010; Giovannucci et al., 2009; Mancini, 2013). Bowen goes so far as to say that "in the absence of some social and environmental protections from the state, it is unlikely that GIs will be able to make substantial contributions to rural development" (2010, p. 237).

Experience with GIs may also be influenced by product-specific factors. For example, the intrinsic scarcity of some GI products, such as Blue Mountain or Kona coffee helps maintain their premium value (Giovannucci et al., 2009). Jena and Grote (2012) report that small farmers in India have obtained a relatively reliable income premium for Basmati rice because the distinctiveness that is directly attributable to the raw grain gives it 'GI-like' characteristics, even in the absence of formal GI protections. On the other hand, products that depend on further processing may be more vulnerable to having the value captured by actors outside the area of origin. An example is Darjeeling tea, where there has been a sustained (and costly) state-led strategy to defend the denomination of origin in international markets, but the tea market is dominated by a few large players and most tea is sold as a blend under brand names rather by origin; thus, most value is captured at the retail end of the value chain (Das, 2006; Giovannucci et al., 2009).

Overall, the impact of GIs in the South has been somewhat disappointing. In a few cases, GIs have cemented existing product identities, especially for coffee. They have also helped coalesce resistance to appropriation of emblematic product names and renewed local interest in these products – as shown by the cases of Rooibos tea in South Africa (Biénabe & Marie-Vivien, 2017) and pisco in Peru (Williams, 2019). However, where products do not already have a high profile, there is little evidence that GIs can generate price premiums (Bidwell, 2020; Yeung & Kerr, 2011). A key point is that successful GIs in Europe usually have a strong base in local markets, and their protection only places a formal seal on longstanding traditions of spatially clustered production, processing and consumption (Bowen & Mutersbaugh, 2014; Sanz Cañada

& Muchnik, 2016). As Bidwell et al. (2018b) argue, more research is needed on the role of place identities in maintaining or regenerating local production–consumption networks in the South.

Ethicality, Authenticity and the 'Local'

A broader debate relevant to GIs is whether the push for localisation in the agri-food industry is inherently ethical. The interest in place and provenance is frequently associated with concerns about quality, sustainability and equity, but these assumed relationships have been questioned by a number of scholars (e.g. Goodman et al., 2012; Hinrichs, 2003; Winter, 2003). These authors criticise the assumption that 'more local' production–consumption relations will be more likely to support desired social and environmental outcomes, noting that reactive support for 'local' production can strengthen elites and obfuscate questions about the actual environmental conditions in which food is produced.

The variability in social and environmental outcomes under different GI regimes reinforces the warning not to "conflate spatial relations with social relations" (Bowen, 2010, p. 213).[5] For example, herbicide use is significantly lower in the Comté cheese PDO area than in the surrounding region of France (Giovannucci et al., 2009), while, conversely, the growth of demand for tequila has driven more intensive agave cultivation, which has resulted in soil erosion and ground water pollution (Bowen, 2010). Likewise, preserving and raising the profile of local traditions is often cited as a benefit of GIs, but by standardising the contested notion of 'local', GI regimes can actually reduce cultural diversity. This is seen in the cases of tequila, mezcal and Chontaleño cheese where official standards have resulted in the exclusion of artisanal producers and idiosyncratic varieties valued by connoisseurs (Bowen, 2011; Giovannucci et al., 2009; Mancini, 2013).

Thus, the growth and diffusion of GIs both spatially to different parts of the world and into different agro-commodities has been rapid and relatively recent. What may be seen – in wine – as an initial attempt to protect certain 'Old World' regions from competition and place-appropriation, has broadened considerably to become a global phenomenon. It has an international regulatory framework, through the recognition of GIs in trade agreements, and it has led to sets of regulations in many different countries covering a wide range of products and defining large sets of place names. However, many issues remain to be understood, particularly with regard to the way different enterprises and producers, large and small, can engage in and benefit from GI schemes. Of particular concern for us in this volume is the 'ethical' question of whether and to what extent can GIs provide a means for small-scale producers both to protect their places, traditions, lifestyles and production methods, and to gain some sort of competitive advantage in markets where otherwise they would struggle to survive.

CONCLUSION

The past three decades have seen the rise to prominence of a variety of movements to reconnect the production and consumption of food with specific places, cultures, practices and social relations. On the one hand, these movements are driven by the concerns of consumers about the quality, origins and impacts of the products they eat; on the other, they represent efforts by producers to escape from a 'race to the bottom' of mass commodity production and differentiate their products in order to access higher-value niche markets (Bidwell et al., 2018a; Murray & Overton, 2015).

This chapter has provided an overview of three constellations of networks and movements organised around the overlapping ethical principles of social justice, sustainability and authenticity. The chapter has shown how the emblematic movements within these constellations have their origin in the search for 'ethical' alternatives to profit maximisation and narrowly-defined utility: fair trade seeks to make relations of market exchange more equitable for marginalised participants; organic agriculture envisages a long-term, symbiotic relationship between environmental and human health and food production; while geographical indications are designed to protect the unique web of geographical and cultural characteristics represented by a particular *terroir*. Over the past three decades, these ethical movements and principles have become embedded to varying degrees in global production and trading networks, although their relative role in agri-food networks remains very small overall (and certainly no more than 3% of the total value of trade). Their growing popularity among consumers has raised hopes that market-led strategies can help maintain quality and diversity in food production, promote environmental sustainability, protect the livelihoods of small farmers, and offer opportunities for producers in developing countries to access more lucrative markets.

However, the very popularity of these movements generates new problems and paradoxes. The additional value conferred on a product labelled as fair trade, organic, or of particular provenance represents a kind of symbolic capital, which raises questions about who is able to appropriate this capital. The threat of misrepresentation and need to define and defend 'what counts' as organic or fair trade has led to increasingly bureaucratic processes of certification and standards setting, culminating in government regulation at national and international levels. There is also a diverse range of parties involved – NGOs, state agencies and private companies – often with different or competing interests and motivations. These processes risk undermining the original philosophies of the movements: shared values and common under-standing may be replaced by technical measures and standards, which in turn may permit increased power for market participants (such as large producers and supermarkets) that do not share the value and motivations of the ethical movement as a whole.

Across the three constellations, we can see a degree of mutual interest in promoting these alternative food networks. Fair trade and organic production are often seen together, evidence of place of origin can support claims about organic or fair production, and retailers can see value in offering a strong range of ethical products on their shelves as part of their own branding strategies. But there are also potential tensions. The local food/food miles approaches can conflict with efforts to promote the products of distant fair trade producers; the dominant low-tech narratives of organic agriculture can contrast with new high-tech solutions to move from animal proteins to artificial meat; and the use of globally-recognised, stringent and expensive certification schemes can undermine benefits flowing to the most marginalised producers.

Finally, within this complex and fluid landscape of ethical production and trading, and associated multiplicity of schemes, competing interests and diverse geographies, we can discern that provenance, whilst of growing importance, is a highly malleable concept in practice. Histories of place and production are actively constructed, and sometimes contested, in order to promote particular narratives of provenance that aim to secure a premium position in markets and appeal to the moral preferences of consumers. It is this process of 'provenancing' across the ethical market landscape that we develop as a central theme of this book.

NOTES

1. From the Latin *provenire* and French *provenir* – to come forth.
2. This refers to authenticity pertaining to a place. In other words assurance that the geographical origin is specified, differentiated, and valued.
3. Other networks and movements within the social justice constellations include the sweat-free movement and associated certifications in clothing and apparel and conflict-free assurances for precious metals and jewellery, among others.
4. Fairtrade International (previously Fairtrade Labelling Organisations or FLO) is the most prominent fair trade certification system, recognisable by the familiar green and blue mark. Other fair trade labelling organisations include Fair Trade USA (formerly TransFair USA), the World Fair Trade Organisation (WFTO) and Fair For Life. These systems vary slightly in terms of standards and certification methodologies, but each follow the basic tenets of the fair trade movement.
5. Giovannucci et al. (2009, p. 118) warn that: "Poorly managed GIs can even stimulate inappropriate practices that destroy competition, traditional cultural practices or biodiversity."

REFERENCES

Arce, A. (2009). Living in times of solidarity: Fair trade and the fractured life worlds of Guatemalan coffee farmers. *Journal of International Development*, 21, 1031–1041.

Bacon, C. (2013). Quality revolutions, solidarity networks, and sustainability innovations: Following Fair Trade coffee from Nicaragua to California. *Journal of Political Ecology*, 20(1), 98–115.

Banks, G., & Sharpe, S. (2006). Wine, regions and the geographic imperative: The Coonawarra example. *New Zealand Geographer*, 62(3), 173-184.

Battaglene, T. (2005). The Australian wine industry position on Geographical Indications. Presentation to the Worldwide Symposium on Geographical Indications. Parma (Italy), June 27–29, 2005.

Belletti, G., Marescotti, A., & Touzard, J. M. (2017). Geographical indications, public goods, and sustainable development: The roles of actors' strategies and public policies. *World Development*, 98, 45–57.

Biasetti, D. (2014). Italy organic agriculture update 2014. GAIN Report IT1412, Global Agricultural Information Network, USDA Foreign Agricultural Service.

Bidwell, S. (2020). *Cultivating what is ours: Local agro-food heritage as a development strategy in the Peruvian Andes*. PhD thesis, Victoria University of Wellington.

Bidwell, S., Murray, W. E., & Overton, J. (2018a). Ethical agro-food networks in global peripheries, Part I: The rise and recommodification of fair trade and organics. *Geography Compass*, 12(4) online DOI: 10.1111/gec3.12366 11pp.

Bidwell, S., Murray, W. E., & Overton, J. (2018b). Ethical agro-food networks in global peripheries, Part II: Re-placing commodity dependence. *Geography Compass*, 12(4) online DOI: 10.1111/gec3.12365 11pp.

Biénabe, E., & Marie-Vivien, D. (2017). Institutionalizing geographical indications in southern countries: Lessons learned from basmati and rooibos. *World Development*, 98(1), 58–67.

Bowen, S. (2010). Embedding local places in global spaces: Geographical indications as a territorial development strategy. *Rural Sociology*, 75(2), 209–243.

Bowen, S. (2011). The importance of place: Re-territorializing embeddedness. *Sociologia Ruralis*, 51(4), 325–348.

Bowen, S., & Mutersbaugh, T. (2014). Local or localized? Exploring the contributions of Franco-Mediterranean agrifood theory to alternative food research. *Agriculture and Human Values*, 31, 201–213.

Bramley, C., & Kirsten, J. F. (2007). Exploring the economic rationale for protecting geographical indicators in agriculture. *Agrekon*, 46, 47–71.

Carson, R. L. (1962). *Silent spring*. Houghton Mifflin.

Das, K., (2006). International protection of geographical indications with special reference to Darjeeling tea. *The Journal of World Intellectual Property*, 9(5), 459–495.

Daviron, B., & Vagneron, I. (2011). From commoditisation to de-commoditisation and back again: Discussing the role of sustainability standards for agricultural products. *Development Policy Review*, 29, 91–113.

Demossier, M. (2010). *Wine drinking in France: An anthropology of wine culture and consumption in France*. University of Wales Press.

Dolan, C. (2008). In the mists of development: Fairtrade in Kenyan tea fields. *Globalizations*, 5, 305–318.

Dragusanu, R. E., Giovannucci, D., & Nunn, N. (2014). The economics of fair trade. *NBER Working Paper* No. 20357.

Fairtrade International. (2013). Annual Report 2012-13. Retrieved from: http://www
.fairtrade.net/annual-reports.html, December 2014.
Fairtrade International. (2019). Choosing a fairer future through trade: Annual Report,
2018-19. Retrieved from: https://www.fairtrade.net/library/2018-19-annual-report
-choosing-a-fairer-future-through-trade
Fairtrade International. (2020). Innovation and resilience for a more sustainable world:
Annual Report, 2019-20. Retrieved from: https://www.fairtrade.net/library/2019
-2020-annual-report
Fanet, J. (2004). *Great wine terroirs* (translated from French by F. Brutton). University
of California Press.
Freidberg, S. (2003). Cleaning up down South: Supermarkets, ethical trade and African
horticulture. *Social and Cultural Geography*, 4(1), 27–43.
Fridell, G. (2007). *Fair trade coffee: The prospects and pitfalls of market-driven social
justice*. University of Toronto Press.
Fridell, M., Hudson, I., & Hudson, M. (2008). With friends like these: The corporate
response to fair trade coffee. *Review of Radical Political Economics*, 40(1), 8–34.
Galtier, F., Belletti, G., & Marescotti, A. (2013). Factors constraining building effective
and fair geographical indications for coffee: Insights from a Dominican case study.
Development Policy Review, *31*(5), 597–615.
Giovannucci, D., Josling, T., Kerr, W. A., O'Connor, B., & Yeung, M. T. (2009). *Guide
to geographical indications: Linking products and their origins*. International Trade
Centre.
Gliessman, S. R. (1998). *Agroecology: Ecological processes in sustainable agriculture*.
Ann Arbor Press.
González, A. A., & Nigh, R. (2005). Smallholder participation and certification of
organic farm products in Mexico. *Journal of Rural Studies*, 21, 449–460.
Goodman, D., DuPuis, E. M., & Goodman, M. K. (2012). *Alternative food networks:
Knowledge, practice, and politics*. Routledge.
Guthman, J. (2004). Back to the land: the paradox of organic food standards.
Environment and Planning A, 36(3), 511–528.
Hinrichs, C. C. (2000). Embeddedness and local food systems: Notes on two types of
direct agricultural markets. *Journal of Rural Studies* 16, 295–303.
Hinrichs, C. C. (2003). The practice and politics of food system localization. *Journal
of Rural Studies*, 19, 33–45.
Howson, K., Murray, W. E., & Overton, J. (2020). Certified utopia: Ethical branding
and the wine industry of South Africa. In J. Dutton & P. J. Howland (Eds.) *Wine,
terroir and utopia: Making new worlds* (pp. 145–162). Routledge.
Idda, L., Madau, F. A., & Pulina, P. (2008). The motivational profile of organic food
consumers: A survey of specialized stores customers in Italy. 12th Congress of the
European Association of Agricultural Economists.
International Fund for Agricultural Development (IFAD) (2003). *The adoption of
organic agriculture among small farmers in Latin America and the Caribbean:
Thematic evaluation*. Report no. 1337, IFAD.
Jaffee, D. (2012). Weak coffee: Certification and co-optation in the fair trade movement. *Social Problems*, 59(1), 94–116.
Jaffee, D., & Howard, P. (2010). Corporate co-optation of organic and fair trade stand-
ards. *Agriculture and Human Values*, 27, 387–399.
Jena, P. R., & Grote, U. (2012). Impact evaluation of traditional Basmati rice cultivation in Uttarakhand State of Northern India: What implications does it hold for
geographical indications? *World Development*, 40(9), 1895–1907.

Josling, T. (2006). The war on *terroir*: Geographical indications as a transatlantic trade conflict. *Journal of Agricultural Economics*, 57(3), 337–363.

Kuepper, G. (2010). *A brief overview of the history and philosophy of organic agriculture*. Kerr Centre for Sustainable Agriculture.

Leutchford, P. (2008). *Fair trade and a global commodity: Coffee in Costa Rica*. Pluto Press.

Lyon, S. (2006). Evaluating fair trade consumption: Politics, defetishization and producer participation. *International Journal of Consumer Studies*, 30(5), 452–464.

Mancini M. C. (2013). Geographical indications in Latin America value chains: A "branding from below" strategy or a mechanism excluding the poorest? *Journal of Rural Studies*, 32, 295–306.

Meadows, D. H., Meadows D. L., & Randers J. B. W. W. (1972). *The limits to growth: A report for the Club of Rome's project on the predicament of mankind*. Potomac Associates.

Moberg, M. (2014). Certification and neoliberal governance: Moral economies of fair trade in the Eastern Caribbean. *American Anthropologist*, 116, 8–22.

Moran, W. (1993). Rural space as intellectual property. *Political Geography*, 12(3), 263–277.

Moran, W. (2001). Terroir – the human factor. *Australian and New Zealand Wine Industry Journal*, 16, 32–51.

Morgan, K., Marsden, T., & Murdoch, J. (2006). *Worlds of food: Place, power, and provenance in the Food Chain*. Oxford University Press.

Murray, W. E., & Overton, J. (2015). *Geographies of globalization* (2nd ed.). Routledge.

Neilson, J., & Pritchard, B. (2010). Fairness and ethicality in their place: The regional dynamics of fair trade and ethical sourcing agendas in the plantation districts of South India. *Environment and Planning A*, 42(8), 1833–1851.

Overton, J., & Murray W. E. (2016). Fictive place. *Progress in Human Geography*, 40(6), 794–809.

Overton J., & Murray W. E. (2017). GI Blues: Geographical indications and wine in New Zealand. In W. van Caenegem & J. Cleary (Eds.) *The importance of place: Geographical indications as a tool for local and regional development* (pp. 197–220). Springer.

Overton, J., Murray, W. E., & Howson, K. (2019). Doing good by drinking wine? Ethical value networks and upscaling of wine production in Australia, New Zealand and South Africa. *European Planning Studies*, 27(12), 2431–2449.

Pay, E. (2009). *The market for organic and fair-trade coffee*. Trade and Markets Division, Food and Agriculture Organization of the United Nations.

Pearson, D., Henryks, J., & Jones, H. (2011). Organic food: What we know (and do not know) about consumers. *Renewable Agriculture and Food Systems*, 26(2), 171–177.

Ponte, S. (2009). Governing through quality: Conventions and supply relations in the value chain for South African wine. *Sociologia Ruralis*, 49(3), 236–257.

Rangnekar D. (2004). *The socio-economics of geographical indications: A review of empirical evidence from Europe*. Issue Paper No. 8. ICTSD, UNCTAD.

Raynolds, L. T. (2008). The organic agro-export boom in the Dominican Republic: maintaining tradition or fostering transformation? *Latin American Research Review*, 43(1), 161–184.

Raynolds, L. T. (2012). Fair trade: Social regulation in global food markets. *Journal of Rural Studies*, 28, 276–287.

Raynolds, L. T & Bennett, E. A. (Eds.) (2015). *The handbook of research on fair trade.* Edward Elgar.

Raynolds, L. T., Murray, D., & Heller, A. (2007). Regulating sustainability in the coffee sector: A comparative analysis of third party environmental and social certification initiatives. *Agriculture and Human Values*, 24(2), 147–163.

Raynolds, L. T, Murray, D., & Taylor, P. L. (2004). Fair trade coffee: Building producer capacity via global networks. *Journal of International Development*, 16, 1109–1121.

Renard, M. C. (2005). Quality certification, regulation, and power in fair trade. *Journal of Rural Studies*, 21, 419–431.

Ruben, R., & Fort, R. (2012). The impact of fair trade certification for coffee farmers in Peru. *World Development*, 40(3), 570–582.

Sansavini, S., & Wollesen, J. (1992). The organic farming movement in Europe. Proceedings of the workshop on the history of the organic movement. *HortTechnology*, 2(2), 276–281.

Sanz Cañada, J., & Muchnik, J. (2016). Geographies of origin and proximity: Approaches to local agro-food systems. *Culture and History Digital Journal*, 5(1), e002.

Shreck, A. (2002). Just bananas? Fair trade banana production in the Dominican Republic. *International Journal of Sociology of Food and Agriculture*, 10, 25–52.

Tallontire, A. (2007). CSR and regulation: Towards a framework for understanding private standards initiatives in the agri-food chain. *Third World Quarterly*, 28(4), 775–791.

Trubek, A. (2008). *The taste of place: A cultural journey into terroir.* University of California Press.

Utting-Chamorro, K. (2005). Does fair trade make a difference? The case of small coffee producers in Nicaragua. *Development in Practice*, 15, 584–601.

Valkila, J. (2009). Fair trade organic coffee production in Nicaragua: Sustainable development or a poverty trap? *Ecological Economics*, 68, 3024.

Valkila, J., Haaparanta, P., & Niemi, N. (2010). Empowering coffee traders? The coffee value chain from Nicaraguan fair trade farmers to Finnish consumers. *Journal of Business Ethics*, 97, 264.

Wilkinson, J., Cerdan, C., & Dorigon, C. (2017). Geographical indications and 'origin' products in Brazil: The interplay of institutions and networks. *World Development*, 98, 82–92.

Willer, H., & Lernoud. J. (Eds.) (2019). *The world of organic agriculture: Statistics and emerging trends.* FiBL and IFOAM.

Williams, P. B. F. (2019). *Creating ethical markets or marketing ethics? A critical exploration of ethical value networks in Chilean and Peruvian viticulture and oenology.* PhD thesis, Victoria University of Wellington.

Wilson, J. E. (1998). *Terroir: The role of geology, climate, and culture in the making of French wine.* Mitchell Beazley.

Winter, M. (2003). Embeddedness, the new food economy and defensive localism. *Journal of Rural Studies*, 19(1), 23–32.

Yeung, M. T., & Kerr, W. A. (2011). Are geographical indications a wise strategy for developing country farmers? Greenfields, clawbacks and monopoly rents. *The Journal of World Intellectual Property*, 14(5), 353–367.

3 Uneven development: commodities, chains and networks

Kelle Howson, Warwick E. Murray and Johannes Rehner

This chapter[1] provides a brief overview of concepts from which ethical value networks (EVeNs) build. It discusses the early concepts of global commodity chains (GCCs) and the subsequent transformation analytically into global value chains (GVCs) and then global value networks (GVNs). In outlining this chronology it critiques the various concepts. Ultimately, it identifies a missing link in chains and network analysis – ethical value – laying the groundwork for the discussion of this novel concept in Chapter 4 of this book.

THEORETICAL FRAMEWORK: UNDERSTANDING UNEVEN DEVELOPMENT

This book draws on a number of complementary theoretical frameworks from the fields of political economy, development studies and economic geography. In the past two decades, in response to the perceived limitations of prior theories of economic development, economic and development geographers have worked at perfecting a heuristic framework that can reflect the increasing complexity of global economic organisation. The question of how to conceptualise 'the economy' itself from a geographic perspective; how to map its spatialities and temporalities, and what factors should and should not be considered to this end, remains unresolved, not least because 'it' is changing constantly.

Scholarly approaches to studying economies and their geographies may be separated (at risk of over-simplification) into two main strains. One is the Marxian approach with roots in 1970s and 1980s: scholarship which describes economies, and uneven development (Smith and Harvey, 1990) through an emphasis on structures, systems and institutions, characterised by Wallerstein's world systems theory. The second stems from a relational turn in the 1990s, which privileges considerations of the interrelations between places, people and things within economic constructions, and advocates a more nuanced approach, with a focus on agency and social processes, and a consciousness of epistemology (for discussion of this see Bathelt & Glückler, 2003; Boggs &

Rantisi, 2003). Ray Hudson (2004) characterises this discursive dichotomy as political-economy versus cultural-economy. The processes of production and distribution of commodities are increasingly diversified across territories, and are in a perpetual state of flux; continually changing in response to internal and external conditions (Coe et al., 2008). As relationships of economic exchange stretch, and new linkages and fragmentations occur, a flexible analytical framework is required that can situate these processes in space, and examine their consequences. Importantly for the study of regional development, such a framework must be able to account for the uneven geographic distribution of the gains of economic globalisation. The contested nature of globalisation carries with it implicitly political discourses. Conflicting ideas of what globalisation means and how it functions have implications for the direction of regulation, which itself generates political outcomes with inherent winners and losers (Dicken et al., 2001; Murray & Overton, 2015). The subsequent section outlines the major approaches in economic geography that conceptualise global economic organisation, and how they address the question of uneven development under neoliberal globalisation.

Early Global Economic Geography: World Systems, Structuralism and Dependency Theory

Immanuel Wallerstein's world systems theory provides a background for theories of chains and networks (Wallerstein, 1974, 2004) and can be used as a foundation for EVeNs. The focus on unevenness in global trade theorises the political issues of development and inequality as being tied up in globalised economic systems, which transcend the narrow scope of states and borders. This basic assumption derives from a fundamental turn in geography and geopolitics in the mid twentieth century, when new perspectives emerged on the interconnectedness of development and modernisation processes in different world regions – creating new theoretical space for understanding the linkages between the industrialised regions of Europe and North America, and the less industrialised world – Latin America, Africa and the Asia-Pacific. During this time the speed of globalisation and the integrating world economy resulted in the declining significance of nation-states as the primary agents of global change, replaced by *systems* which incorporated territorially protracted linkages of capitalists, labour, governments and other non-state actors. In response, world systems theory offered a framework for understanding uneven rates of development and industrialisation in different world regions, based on an integrated analysis of global linkages. World systems analysis aims to describe regional and global divisions of labour rooted in capitalist structures in which non-industrialised or *peripheral* economies produce raw resources, primary commodities, and low-skilled labour for supply to core economies which create and retain value through capital-intensive production of knowledge, technology, and value-added goods (Hayter et al., 2003).

World systems theory shares important commonalities with structuralist theory in development studies. First coined by Raul Prebisch and Hans Singer, the theory argued that the terms of global trade inherently disadvantaged peripheral countries, and that poor states were poor not because that was their traditional state, or because of internal deficiencies, nor were they poor because of global power relations. In fact, they were poor as a condition of their integration in the global economy (Amin, 1976; Prebisch, 1950; Singer, 1949). The structure of the global economy was such that producers of manufactured goods would always accumulate capital at the expense of producers of primary products, because of the relative decline in the terms of trade for primary products. The demand for manufactured goods is income-elastic relative to primary products, therefore – other things being equal – primary goods decline in price relative to manufactured goods as global income increases. Ultimately, this disadvantages economies that specialise in the export of unprocessed primary goods, and widens the gap between the core and the periphery. This perspective, known as the Prebisch–Singer hypothesis (Arezki et al., 2013; Harvey et al., 2010), emerged in response to the earlier dominance of modernisation theory, which stated that all economies followed the same path to industrialisation along a continuum, as described by Walt Rostow's (1959) 'five stages of growth' and the ideal of export-driven development based on the assumption of global free trade benefiting all participants, as derived from David Ricardo's trade model.

Structuralist thinking informed development policy and saw widespread implementation of import-substitution industrialisation (ISI) and land reform, particularly in Latin America. However, for some this did not go far enough to address the core problem, and a radical school of Marxist thought became popular in the 1970s which emphasised capitalist exploitation and class struggle within core–periphery structures, theorising the coercive dependence of developing countries on global capitalism. Dependency theory, promulgated by Frank (1967, 2018), Cardoso and Faletto (1979), and others argued that underdevelopment was created by neo-colonial relations present in flows of trade, aid, technology, capital and culture. This allowed wealthy countries to 'extract surplus', and Transnational corporations (TNCs) were often pointed to as key agents in this process. Dependency theory proponents argued that the flow of primary resources from peripheral to core regions meant surplus extraction and wealth accumulation would always occur in the core, denying opportunities for the sustained creation and retention of value in the periphery – that underdevelopment in the periphery was a condition of development in the core. This was viewed through the Marxist analytical framework of unequal exchange, as a feature of the irrationality and injustice of capitalism.

Dependency theory has declined in popularity in the policy world, in conjunction with the rise of neoliberalism. In academia it has been somewhat threatened by the paradigm shift to post-structuralism, which in development studies has given rise to post-development and anti-development. However, it remains influential, especially in Latin American and some African studies (Gudynas, 2018). World systems and dependency theories provide useful frameworks for analysis of the impact of systems of international trade on uneven patterns of development, and the consequent emergence of ethical value networks which purport to address these inequities. These theories are powerful tools for generating dynamic understandings of unequal exchange and uneven development between states, regions, and actors in global economic systems. They also allow for the evaluation of proposed solutions to core–periphery dependence, such as ethical certification.

The rise of Global Commodity Chains
Theoretical tools for describing the diverse linkages in world systems have become more sophisticated since the emergence of world systems theory. The Global Commodity Chains (GCC) framework developed primarily by Gary Gereffi was an extension of core/periphery models which accounted for and attempted to map the complexity of global economic organisation. This theory represented a significant innovation which explained observed changes in global economic organisation with a specific focus on firms as the key players. The chain metaphor refers to a series of interconnected parts, and evokes a useful visualisation of the linkages between various functions in the life of a commodity. These functions (also called segments, or nodes) may include *inter alia* research and design, production/manufacturing, packaging, distribution, marketing, and retail (Gereffi, 1999). The chain framework offers a blueprint for observers to connect spatially distant productive activities through the vector of an individual commodity, to better understand the multi-scalar mechanisms of globalising trade.

With GCCs, Gereffi proposed a theoretical basis for not only mapping global trade linkages, but for better understanding patterns of inequality in cross-border production relationships, through the concept of 'driven-ness' in economic exchange (Gereffi, 1994; Gereffi & Korzeniewicz, 1994). In GCC theory, chains are divided into two categories, depending on where in the chain the 'lead', or driving, firm is located – either at the buying end, or the production end. The buyer-/producer-driven dichotomy had a significant impact on the study of global economic organisation and regional development. It offered an empirically supported explanation for relatively novel phenomena – in particular the rapidly growing power of northern TNCs, and the increasing evidence of heightened commodity dependence and underdevelopment in the economic periphery, through (or despite) increased global economic integration.

Producer-driven chains are those in which manufacturers wield the defining power. Based on the observations of economic geographers in the 1980s and 1990s, these were most likely to be in industries with knowledge- and capital-intensive production, with a high level of functional integration, and where technological innovation determined value (Gereffi, 1999; Gereffi et al., 2001). The most prominent were the technology and automotive industries in the Global North. In the second type of commodity chain – the buyer-driven chain – large northern-based retailers (Walmart, Tesco's, Starbucks, etc.) captured the majority of value through the securing of monopsony power.[2] Although they were unlikely to own the factories or plantations that produced their goods (in other words their chains were not vertically integrated), they exerted price pressure on suppliers by demanding concessions for large volumes purchased, and they governed production activities through the requirement of compliance with technical codes (Bair, 2009; Gereffi, 1996). This downwards price pressure was inevitably passed on to the most vulnerable value chain participants – smallholders and workers in the periphery – and contributed enormously to insecurity in commodity-exporting regions. In buyer-driven chains which have reasonably basic production specifications that do not require advanced technical capacity, value is added through the activities of design and marketing, and is therefore more likely to be integrated into the functions of buying firms. Table 3.1 gives an overview of the characteristics of buyer- and producer-driven chains as described in Gereffi's framework.

Value Added: The Evolution of Global Value Networks

However, as the new millennium unfolded, the explanatory power of the GCC framework was quickly outgrown by the reality of the rapid evolution and ever-increasing complexity of economic geographies under globalisation. Industries increasingly failed to fit neatly into their buyer- or producer-driven designations. Knowledge-intensive manufacturing sectors were becoming de-verticalised as various production functions were outsourced, and complex knowledge increasingly transferred between functional nodes via advanced codification systems (Gereffi, 1996, 2001; Sturgeon, 2007). The static binary of driven-ness was no longer reflective of the dynamism of governance relationships. As the limitations of GCCs became more evident, scholars endeavoured to develop a more sensitive approach, which was empirically-informed enough to be applicable to real-world situations, and broad and adaptable enough to be industry-neutral and relevant to all types of production chains. From this effort emerged the global value chains (GVCs) framework (Gereffi

Table 3.1   Characteristics of producer- and buyer-driven commodity networks

	Producer-driven commodity chains	Buyer-driven commodity chains
Drivers of global commodity chains	Industrial capital	Commercial capital
Core competencies	Research and development, manufacturing/production	Design, marketing
Barriers to entry	Economies of scale	Economies of scope
Typical industries	Automobiles, computers, aircraft	Apparel, footwear, agri-food commodities
Ownership of manufacturing firms	Transnational firms	Local firms, mostly located in developing countries
Main network links	Investment-based	Trade-based
Predominant network structure	Vertical	Horizontal

Note: Adapted from Gereffi (1999, p. 9).

et al., 2001; Gereffi & Kaplinsky, 2001; Sturgeon, 2007). In order to better account for asymmetric distributions of power and profit in all types of chains, the new paradigm incorporated an emphasis on charting the *value added* at each point of the chain.

Actors are able to increase their representation and returns in GVCs through a process of 'upgrading'. This is the strategy whereby local development can take place in the South by way of more extensively participating in value chain activity beyond primary production. Producers can add value by integrating more vertical functions, such as marketing and distribution into the local production end of the chain . This can also be achieved through forms of horizontal industrial cooperation, as discussed in the industrial clustering literature, which examines the impact of cooperation of supply-end actors in strengthening local business and improving regional development outcomes (Bathelt et al., 2004; Fløysand & Jakobsen, 2011; Fløysand et al., 2012; Humphrey & Schmitz, 2000, 2002).

In response to criticism that the GVC approach was overly simplistic, Gereffi, Humphrey and Sturgeon (2005) promulgated a theory of value chain governance drawing on transaction cost economics (Williamson, 1989), in which three main variables determine the level of driven-ness in any given value chain. These are: (1) the complexity of transactions; (2) the codability of transactions; and (3) the level of capability in the supply base (Gereffi et al., 2005, p. 78). Where suppliers possess the knowledge and capacity to develop and carry out complex technical processes, value chains are more likely to be supplier-driven. Conversely, where suppliers do not have to perform complex

Table 3.2   *Types of value chain relations by level of lead firm governance*

Governance type	Complexity of transactions	Ability to codify transactions	Capabilities in the supply-base	Degree of driven-ness and power asymmetry
Market	Low	High	High	Low
Modular	High	High	High	
Relational	High	Low	High	
Captive	High	High	Low	
Hierarchy	High	Low	Low	High

Note: Adapted from Gereffi et al. (2005, p. 87).

functions, or are delivering to strict codes set by buying firms, value chains are buyer-driven with profitability at the top. Within this model, the authors identify five types of governance relationships, along a spectrum of driven-ness: market, modular, relational, captive, and hierarchical (Gereffi et al., 2005; Sturgeon, 2007) (see Table 3.2).

By identifying the type of governance relationship in a global value chain as an expression of the level of vertical integration and coordination, and a determinant of the extent of the asymmetry of power and profit within the chain, researchers and policymakers are able to generate clear lessons about the potential for upgrading and development.

Global Production Networks – Creating Theoretical Space for Non-firm Actors

A significant school of economic geography contends that GVCs do not go far enough in acknowledging the spatio-temporal contingency of the construction and coordination of economic linkages. In the early 2000s, a group of scholars, including Neil Coe, Peter Dicken, Jeffrey Henderson, Martin Hess and Henry Wai-Chung Yeung, formulated an alternative approach to analysing global economic processes which moved beyond the linearity of the firm-focused GVC, and beyond static notions of permanent core–periphery dependency, to encompass the multi-dimensional, complex and evolving *networks* involved in production and trade (Coe et al., 2004, 2008; Coe & Yeung, 2015; Dicken et al., 2001; Henderson et al., 2002). Dicken et al. (2001, p. 92) characterised this theoretical change as a "microscale retreat from macroscale processes". However, although the analytical approach may have changed, Dicken and colleagues insist that the network itself is not novel, and that it has always been fundamental to economic organisation. Drawing on actor-network theory

(ANT) (Latour, 1996, 2005), this framework emphasises the relationality of production networks, and the agency of a wide range of actors in influencing trade outcomes. Global Production Networks (GPNs) take into account the role of non-firm actors including labour, civil society organisations (CSOs), states, international regulatory bodies, and consumers, to demonstrate that production networks are deeply relational, and their coordination is influenced by myriad internal and external factors which may be cultural, political or economic (Coe et al., 2008). In addition, networks spanning multiple geographic scales are territorially embedded in numerous places, and may comprise diverse organisational forms (Dicken et al., 2001).

GPN approaches emphasise the multi-scalar nature of the trade processes that determine development (Coe et al., 2004). GPN theorists attempt to better link processes of globalisation with regional (sub-national) development processes, to demonstrate the influence of local territorial formations on development outcomes within global networks (Coe et al., 2004). Dicken and colleagues (2001) argue that this is a critical mission, as the privileging of one scale, the global or the local, in analysis is inherently political: "a particular constellation of power relations [is] implicit in any understanding of the global economy" (p. 88). GPN theorists avoid focusing on any one geographical scale or organisational form as the centre of global economic analysis, giving equal weight to all scales and forms that make up networks (Dicken et al., 2001).

GPN analysis also takes into account the evolutionary nature of economic coordination – paying attention to history in analysis of the development of network configuration and the geographical contingency of network manifestations. Approaches of evolutionary economic geography enable this aspect of GPN analysis. Evolutionary economic geography (EEG) is an emerging project in economic geography which aims to situate industrial dynamics within their spatial-temporalities to understand how institutions, clusters and industries develop and innovate in particular directions based on the evolving make-up of networks (Boschma & Frenken, 2006, 2011; Fløysand & Jakobsen, 2016; Frenken & Boschma, 2007; Martin & Sunley, 2006). EEG draws on Darwinian concepts to theorise the economic landscape as an adaptive system (Martin & Sunley, 2007). In short, EEG attempts to demonstrate that *past* and *place* matter in economic organisation, and that industrial dynamics are products of the spaces they inhabit, the actors and institutions they involve, and the pathways they have followed.

GPNs provide a method for describing the fluidity and complexity of global economic relationships and their development outcomes. However, they can result in convoluted network visualisations, and have been critiqued for a diminished explanatory power due to their preoccupation with complexity at the expense of universally applicable theory-building. Additionally, GPNs as well as GCC/GVC approaches have attracted recent criticism for paying insufficient attention to labour (Selwyn, 2013), an absence that was first addressed in GPN work in the mid-2010s (Barrientos, 2013; Barrientos & Smith, 2007; see also Coe & Hess, 2013). A particularly useful feature of GPN analysis for this book is its emphasis on the geographical contingency of network structure and development outcomes, i.e. economic or social 'upgrading'. In this sense GPNs provide a more contextually sensitive method for interpreting trade and development processes than GVCs, allowing for analysis of the dynamic relations between the local and the global.[3]

Notwithstanding this promise, there has been critique of GPNs from a development point of view (see McGrath, 2018). Phelps et al. (2018, p. 240) argue "the GPN paradigm far from increasingly embracing uneven development seems to have lost touch with its [political economy] roots" and indeed has "succumbed to the lure of a decidedly flat ontology in which the unevenness of development has receded from view". In this regard and drawing on critiques from other areas in economic geography, particularly by McGrath (2018), Coe and Yeung (2019, p. 792) make the point that that GPN 2.0 theory has an 'impoverished understanding' of development on three levels:

> First, by bracketing-off economic development from the social, cultural and environmental dimensions it is only offering a partial window onto what constitutes development in the round. Secondly, by focusing on 'little d' development at the expense of 'big D' development, it downplays the connections between the two and the associated distributional struggles over the value created in global production networks. Thirdly, prioritization of the material over the discursive realm is argued to narrow again the perspective unproductively. McGrath argues for a perspective that foregrounds the ways in which the operation of global production networks functions through borders and bordering practices, discursive constructions and practices of gendering and racialization.

Mapping Chains and Networks

Both GVCs and GPNs offer 'mapping' methodologies to assist researchers in visualising actors, functions, territories, and profit and governance flows. In GVC analysis, this is represented as a linear chain of firms, functions and value involved from conception to consumption (as in Figure 3.1). Value chain analysis involves four analytical components which can be undertaken in a mapping activity (Gereffi & Fernandez-Stark, 2011): *input–output structure* – identifying the material inputs and outputs of a value chain's geographic make-up; how value chains are distributed across *space and scale* through local, national, regional and global functions; *governance* – identifying the level and direction of explicit coordination and patterns of power and wealth accumulation; and *institutional context* – the identification of the range of institutions (firms or otherwise) involved in value chain activities.

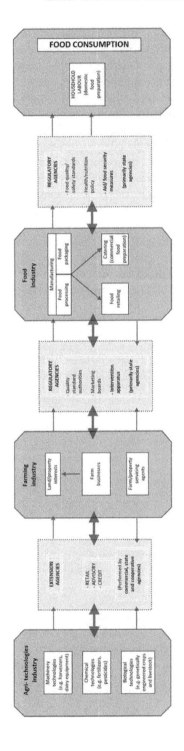

Source: Adapted from Whatmore (2009, p. 18).

Figure 3.1   Agribusiness commodity chain

However, chain/network maps can include myriad components beyond actors and materials (see for example Dicken, 2015). Maps may include an explicit focus on the territorial distribution of actors, functions and materials. This allows for a visualisation of the influence of network construction and coordination on core–periphery relationships and regional development (Coe et al., 2004). For example, Figure 3.2 illustrates the geographic distribution of the BMW production network, with a concentration of investment and technology in the Global North, with lower-value functions such as assembly taking place in the Global South. This visualisation indicates this to be a producer-driven network in which governance flows from the lead producing firm and value is captured in the core, while still displaying the intra-regional core/periphery structures which make up the network, i.e. Rayong/Samutprakam represents the core area of the peripheral region. In GPN mapping especially, non-firm stakeholders and institutions (both formal and informal) may be included. This can encompass regulatory bodies and standards, and cultural structures.

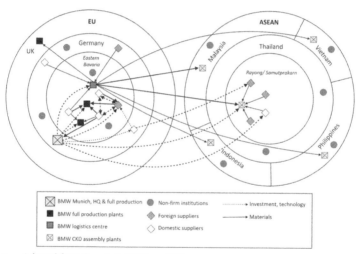

Source: Adapted from Coe et al. (2004, p. 481).

Figure 3.2   *Regional distribution of the BMW production networks*

Network maps that avoid linearity and do not take progressive value chain segments such as production, processing, retail and consumption as their backbone can become extremely complex and, in many cases, difficult to decipher meaning from. In practice, many of the examples of GPN mapping that we have found in the literature struggle to do justice to GPN's theory of the complexity, fluidity and multifaceted nature of economic organisation, and, as such, we believe using GPNs as an analytical framework does not easily lend itself to mapping methodologies (see Bridge, 2008, for an exception).

Although, in reality, economic organisation and exchange is a fluid cycle with no start point or end point, we agree with GVC proponents, such as Sturgeon (2007), that is it important for researchers and policymakers to have a widely applicable theoretical toolkit that can "bring some order to this complexity" (p. 27). As such, in analysing chains and networks in this book, we will utilise, in different ways in various case studies, the methodology of first identifying the chain of value chain segments, then their territorial distributions, and finally formal and informal institutional influences, power and governance flows, which influence value creation and capture.

CONCLUSION

This chapter has traced the emergence of the Global Value Networks (GVNs) framework, seeing it as progressively adding complexity to foundational concepts of uneven development, production chains and value networks. GVNs have clear spatial and social dimensions, touching down in different ways in different parts of the world and affecting different socio-economic classes and communities in varying ways. The framework also raises key questions regarding governance and regulation of the networks and asks us to consider how value is created in different parts of the network and crucially who gets to capture this value.

However, we contend in the face of the rise of ethical consumerism, that there is a missing link in value network analysis. That link concerns the manner in which 'value' should be understood more broadly and in particular the way that ethical value is created, designated, certified, captured, distributed and traded. Based on the ethical constellations discussed in Chapter 2, the concept of value needs to be seen not just in terms of economic value derived from race-to-the-bottom strategies to minimise costs and maximise profits. Rather, we argue the focus should be on the premium consumers will be prepared to pay for goods they judge to be more ethically-produced. This requires the use of an enhanced framework – EVeNs – to which we turn to in the following chapter.

NOTES

1. This chapter draws and builds significantly on Howson's PhD thesis (Howson, 2019).
2. 'Monopsony' denotes a market whereby one actor possesses singular buying-power for a given commodity. This is as opposed to monopoly, which refers to a system in which there is only one supplier of a product to a market. This book will also use 'oligopsony' – in which buyer-power for a product is held by a small group (in

contrast to oligopoly, in which there is a small group of suppliers of a product in a market).

3. For the state-of-the-art review of global production literature over the recent past see Coe and Yeung (2019).

REFERENCES

Amin, S. (1976). *Unequal development: An essay on the social formations of peripheral capitalism* (translated B. Pierce). Monthly Review Press.

Arezki, M.R., Hadri, M.K., Loungani, M.P., & Rao, M.Y. (2013). *Testing the Prebisch-Singer hypothesis since 1650: Evidence from panel techniques that allow for multiple breaks*. International Monetary Fund.

Bair, J. (2009). Global commodity chains. In J. Bair (Ed.) *Frontiers of commodity chain research* (pp. 1–34). Stanford University Press.

Barrientos, S. (2013). Labour chains: Analysing the role of labour contractors in global production networks. *Journal of Development Studies, 49*(8), 1058–1071.

Barrientos, S. & Smith, S. (2007). Do workers benefit from ethical trade? Assessing codes of labour practice in global production systems. *Third World Quarterly, 28*(4), 713–729.

Bathelt, H., & Glückler, J. (2003). Toward a relational economic geography. *Journal of Economic Geography, 3*(2), 117–144.

Bathelt, H., Malmberg, A., & Maskell, P. (2004). Clusters and knowledge: Local buzz, global pipelines and the process of knowledge creation. *Progress in Human Geography, 28*(1), 31–56.

Boggs, J.S., & Rantisi, N.M. (2003). The 'relational turn' in economic geography. *Journal of Economic Geography, 3*(2), 109–116.

Boschma, R., & Frenken, K. (2006). Why is economic geography not an evolutionary science? Towards an evolutionary economic geography. *Journal of Economic Geography, 6*(3), 273–302.

Boschma, R., & Frenken, K. (2011). The emerging empirics of evolutionary economic geography. *Journal of Economic Geography, 11*(2), 295–307.

Bridge, G. (2008). Global production networks and the extractive sector: Governing resource-based development. *Journal of Economic Geography, 8*(3), 389–419.

Cardoso, F.H., & Faletto, E. (1979). *Dependency and development in Latin America* (translated M.M. Urquidi). University of California Press.

Coe, N.M., & Dicken, P., & Hess, M. (2008). Global production networks: Realizing the potential. *Journal of Economic Geography, 8*(3), 271–295.

Coe, N.M. & Hess, M. (2013). Global production networks, labour and development. *Geoforum 44*, 4–9.

Coe, N.M., Hess, M., Yeung, H.W-C., Dicken, P., & Henderson, J. (2004). 'Globalizing' regional development: A global production networks perspective. *Transactions of the Institute of British Geographers, 29*(4), 468–484.

Coe, N.M., & Yeung, H. W-C. (2015). *Global production networks: Theorizing economic development in an interconnected world*. Oxford University Press.

Coe, N.M., & Yeung, H. W-C. (2019). Global production networks: Mapping recent conceptual developments. *Journal of Economic Geography, 19*(4), 775–801.

Dicken, P. (2015). *Global shift. Mapping the changing contours of the world economy* (7th ed.). SAGE.

Dicken, P., Kelly, P.F., Olds, K., & Yeung, H.W-C. (2001). Chains and networks, territories and scales: Towards a relational framework for analysing the global economy. *Global Networks*, *1*(2), 89–112.

Fløysand, A., & Jakobsen, S.-E. (2011). The complexity of innovation: A relational turn. *Progress in Human Geography*, *35*(3), 328–344.

Fløysand, A., & Jakobsen, S.-E. (2016). In the footprints of evolutionary economic geography. *Norsk Geografisk Tidsskrift – Norwegian Journal of Geography*, *70*(3), 137–139.

Fløysand, A., Jakobsen, S.-E., & Bjarnar, O. (2012). The dynamism of clustering: Interweaving material and discursive processes. *Geoforum*, *43*(5), 948–958.

Frank, A.G. (1967). *Capitalism and underdevelopment in Latin America*. Monthly Review Press.

Frank, A.G. (2018). The development of underdevelopment. In P.F. Klarén (Ed.), *Promise of development* (pp. 111–123). Routledge.

Frenken, K., & Boschma, R. (2007). A theoretical framework for evolutionary economic geography: Industrial dynamics and urban growth as a branching process. *Journal of Economic Geography*, *7*(5), 635–649.

Gereffi, G. (1994). The organization of buyer-driven global commodity chains: How US retailers shape overseas production networks. In G. Gereffi & M. Korzeniewicz (Eds.), *Commodity chains and global capitalism* (pp. 95–122). Praeger.

Gereffi, G. (1996). Global commodity chains: New forms of coordination and control among nations and firms in international industries. *Competition & Change*, *1*(4), 427–439.

Gereffi, G. (1999). A commodity chains framework for analyzing global industries. http://citeseerx.ist.psu.edu/viewdoc/download?doi=10.1.1.608.812&rep=rep1&type=pdf

Gereffi, G. (2001). Shifting governance structures in global commodity chains, with special reference to the internet. *American Behavioral Scientist*, *44*(10), 1616–1637.

Gereffi, G., & Fernandez-Stark, K. (2011). *Global value chain analysis: A primer*. Center on Globalization, Governance & Competitiveness (CGGC), Duke University.

Gereffi, G., Humphrey, J., & Kaplinsky, R. (2001). Introduction: Globalisation, value chains and development. *IDS Bulletin*, *32*(3), 1–8.

Gereffi, G., Humphrey, J., & Sturgeon, T. (2005). The governance of global value chains. *Review of International Political Economy*, *12*(1), 78–104.

Gereffi, G., & Kaplinsky, R. (Eds.) (2001). The value of value chains: Spreading the gains from globalisation. *Institute of Development Studies*, *32*(3).

Gereffi, G. & Korzeniewicz, M. (Eds.) (1994). *Commodity chains and global capitalism*. Praeger.

Gudynas, E. (2018). Extractivisms. Tendencies and consequences. In R. Munck & R. Delgado Wise (Eds.), *Reframing Latin American Development* (pp. 61–76). Routledge.

Harvey, D., Kellard, N.M., Madsen, J.B., & Wohar, M.E. (2010). The Prebisch-Singer hypothesis: Four centuries of evidence. *The Review of Economics and Statistics*, *92*(2), 367–377.

Hayter, R., Barnes, T., & Bradshaw, M. (2003). Relocating resource peripheries to the core of economic geography's theorizing: Rationale and agenda. *Area*, *35*, 15–23.

Henderson, J., Dicken, P., Hess, M., Coe, N., & Yeung, H.W.-C. (2002). Global production networks and the analysis of economic development. *Review of International Political Economy*, *9*(3), 436–464.

Howson, K. (2019). *Bottling the colonial unconscious: Ethical value networks and the commodification of fairness in the South African wine industry.* PhD thesis, Victoria University of Wellington.

Hudson, R. (2004). Conceptualizing economies and their geographies: Spaces, flows and circuits. *Progress in Human Geography, 28*(4), 447–471.

Humphrey, J., & Schmitz, H. (2000). *Governance and upgrading: Linking industrial cluster and global value chain research.* Institute of Development Studies.

Humphrey, J., & Schmitz, H. (2002). How does insertion in global value chains affect upgrading in industrial clusters? *Regional Studies, 36*(9), 1017–1027.

Latour, B. (1996). On actor-network theory: A few clarifications. *Soziale welt, 47*(4), 369–381.

Latour, B. (2005). *Reassembling the social: An introduction to actor-network-theory.* Oxford University Press.

Martin, R., & Sunley, P. (2006). Path dependence and regional economic evolution. *Journal of Economic Geography, 6*(4), 395–437.

Martin, R., & Sunley, P. (2007). Complexity thinking and evolutionary economic geography. *Journal of Economic Geography, 7*(5), 573–601.

McGrath, S. (2018). Dis/articulations and the interrogation of development in GPN research. *Progress in Human Geography, 42*(4), 509–528.

Murray, W.E., & Overton, J. (2015). *Geographies of globalization* (2nd ed.). Routledge.

Phelps, N.A., Atienza, M., & Arias, M. (2018). An invitation to the dark side of economic geography. *Environment and Planning A: Economy and Space, 50*(1), 236–244.

Prebisch, R. (1950). *The economic development of Latin America and its principal problems.* Economic Commission for Latin America, United Nations.

Rostow, W.W. (1959). The stages of economic growth. *The Economic History Review, 12*(1), 1–16.

Selwyn, B. (2013). Social upgrading and labour in global production networks: A critique and an alternative conception. *Competition and Change, 17*(1), 75–90.

Singer, H. (1949). Economic progress in underdeveloped countries. *Social Research: An International Quarterly of Political and Social Science, 16*(1), 1–11.

Smith, N., & Harvey, D. (1990). *Uneven development: Nature, capital, and the production of space.* University of Georgia Press.

Sturgeon, T.J. (2007). From commodity chains to value chains: Interdisciplinary theory building in an age of globalization. *ITEC Working Paper Series, 28*(7).

Wallerstein, I. (1974). The rise and future demise of the world capitalist system: Concepts for comparative analysis. *Comparative Studies in Society and History, 16*(4), 387–415.

Wallerstein, I. (2004). *World systems analysis: An introduction*: Duke University Press.

Whatmore, S. (2009). Agricultural geography. In D. Gregory, R. Johnston, G. Pratt, M.J. Watts & S. Whatmore (Eds.,) *The Dictionary of Human Geography* (pp. 17–19). Wiley-Blackwell.

Williamson, O.E. (1989). Transaction cost economics. In R. Schmalensee & R. Willig (Eds.,) *Handbook of industrial organization* (Vol. 1, pp. 135–182). Elsevier.

4 Ethical value networks

Warwick E. Murray, Kelle Howson, Simon Bidwell, John Overton, Johannes Rehner and Peter B.F. Williams

INTRODUCTION

In this chapter we explore the concept of ethical value networks. The purpose is to move towards a theoretical elaboration of Ethical Value Networks (EVeNs) in the context of the broader chain and network frameworks discussed in Chapter 3. In order to provide the context for this we first look at the impact of globalising agriculture, the rise of ethical consumerism as response and resistance, and the consequent evolution of ethical trade as a form of dealing with unjust consequences. We pay special attention to certification as a means of codifying and convention theory in the context of ethical trade networks. In the second half of the chapter we conceptualise EVeNs and offer an idealised framework for analysis.

GLOBALISATION, AGRI-FOOD AND ETHICS AS RE-EMBEDDING

Following the turmoil wrought by the economic shocks of the 1970s, a new ideological hegemony of global trade emerged to replace the Fordist New International Division of Labour. Rooted in the Western enlightenment-derived values of individualism, modernisation and accumulation, a largely unchallenged neoliberalism has overwhelmingly determined the direction and impacts of globalisation for the last four decades. Beginning in the late 1970s, proponents of this new regime – including economists (such as Milton Friedman and the 'Chicago Boys'), and powerful politicians (notably Margaret Thatcher and Ronald Reagan) – advocated the removal of barriers to international flows of goods, services and capital, arguing that unhampered global economic integration would benefit developed and developing nations alike. States were encouraged to dismantle protectionist policies and remove tariffs. Structural adjustment conditions on development loans or debt relief handed down by the International Monetary Fund (IMF) or the World Bank required developing nations to privatise industry, deregulate their economies and adopt the Washington Consensus' prescription for development. At the heart of neo-liberalism is a distrust of states as distributive instruments, and their declining significance has given way to the increased supremacy of transnational corporations (TNCs) in global configurations of wealth and power.

The uneven impacts of globalisation have been particularly evident in the agri-food sector, drastically impacting agrarian areas in developing countries. Over the course of a century, agricultural production has transitioned from small-scale farming for local markets, to complex global agri-food systems dominated by TNCs (LeHeron, 1993; Whatmore, 2002). A number of factors combine to make globalised agriculture particularly precarious for small farmers and workers. A central factor is that much of the world's agri-food production takes place in 'developing' economies. Many primary food commodities – and the majority of those exported – are produced in marginalized countries, where climatic conditions favour tropical goods such as tea, coffee, cacao, sugar and fresh fruit. Additionally, much of the consumer base for these products is located in the North. The South-to-North trade pattern of such commodities serves to perpetuate a core–periphery dependency model (Talbot, 2002). Furthermore, in much of the developing world, land and labour costs are lower, environmental standards are weaker, and producing in the Global South means fresh goods can be supplied out of season for Northern hemisphere consumers. Following trade liberalisation and the entry of TNCs, diversified rural livelihoods have often been displaced by monocultures of primary commodity production. As large proportions of rural populations in developing countries have become dependent on primary product exports for their livelihoods, market fluctuations in commodity prices can have disastrous effects on farming communities. Finally, small-scale farmers who have escaped displacement and proletarianisation have been subsumed into export-oriented networks in which value-adding functions such as processing, packaging, marketing and distribution are removed from primary production. This often means the amount of value primary producers retain from the end retail price is extremely limited.

The concept of commodity fetishism, originating with Karl Marx's *Capital* (Marx et al., 1990), describes the process by which capitalism obscures the human origins and inputs of a given product, reducing its value to a pure materialism and hiding the social relations of its production, thereby disconnecting the product itself from the capitalist exploitation in which it is rooted. The related Polanyian concept of embeddedness is used in geography to refer conversely to the extent to which economic products are grounded in the territorial, institutional, social and cultural contexts in which they are produced (Hess, 2004). Scholars such as Anthony Giddens (1990) argue that globalisation has meant the 'disembedding' of products from their environmental and social origins, and the diminishing relevance of the 'place of food' (Feagan, 2007). Critics argue that one consequence of globalisation's fetishisation and disembedding of food products has been a concealment of production circumstances, labour conditions and environmental impacts of agri-food systems from consumers (De Neve et al., 2008; Wilk, 2001).

As argued earlier in this book, a countervailing trend has arisen, in which the discourse of ethical trade can be situated. A growing emphasis on *re*localisation, or *re*spatialisation of food systems represents a response to globalisation's 'disembedding mechanisms' (Feagan, 2007). Provenance and normative concerns regarding conditions of production have re-entered discourses of food quality, and are becoming increasingly mainstream. This shift can be identified in diverse literatures and encompasses a number of scholarly terms, including post-productivism (Mather et al., 2006; Wilson, 2001), the quality turn (M.K. Goodman, 2004), the third food regime, alternative food networks (Goodman & Goodman, 2009; Renting et al., 2003), and local food systems. Broadly, this new 'political ecological imaginary' amongst consumers in developed countries, represents a redefinition of what constitutes quality, and an insertion of 'ethical' concerns alongside the market functions of price, material quality and demand. Many writers emphasise the theoretical importance of Polanyian 'embeddedness' theories in understanding contemporary alternative food movements (Hudson & Hudson, 2003).

This shift has purported benefits for producers, who are able to profit from product differentiation and market niches, and thus escape primary commodity dependence and a 'race to the bottom'. It also holds advantages for consumers, who may benefit from increased variety, healthier choices, and more information about food origin and production (Sánchez-Hernández et al., 2010). Further, it is hoped by development practitioners and observers that these changes in producer-consumer relations will have positive impacts in rural development and the empowerment of producing communities in developing countries (Higgins et al., 2008). As Rosol (2020, p. 68) says: "They build alternatives that address exigent circumstances and try to de-commodify food and land. Crucially, they are also engaged in processes and networks that seek to change the dominant food system and its political regulation."

Ethical Consumerism

The concept of the 'reflexive consumer' (Beckett & Nayak, 2008) has arisen as a way of understanding changing value chain relationships and the transforming role of consumers in the governance of economic activity. Rather than being confined to simply being 'sovereign choosers', the role of the consumer has been theoretically expanded to include active participation in economic coordination. Reflexive consumers exert influence in the governance of value networks and play a central role in the ongoing 'creative destruction' (Schumpeter, 1942) of industrial norms and conventions. Reflexive consumption is closely associated with morality. Sen (1977) advocates for an expansion of ideas of individual consumer preferences to incorporate ethical considerations. Orthodox, particularly neoclassical, economics assumes that consumers will behave 'rationally', and narrowly defines rationality as self-interest. However, Sen and others contend that definitions of rationality should not be incompatible with utilitarian or altruistic behaviour, and that rational individuals will often take their relationships with others, including distant others, into account in their consumer choices (Sobel, 2005).

Moral reflexive consumerism, being concerned with intangible or extrinsic qualities, relies on the ability of suppliers to communicate a lot of information about a product within a relatively restricted format. M.K. Goodman (2004) illustrates that this type of communication entails the connection of consumers with producers over expanded spatial and temporal distances (an embedding process). Importantly for Goodman, the information being communicated is not technical specifications, but images, symbols and narratives – a type of closely managed *cultural meaning*. Goodman terms this 'semiotic shouting': the commoditisation of meaning in order to transmit it over a "material and discursive 'scale jump'" (M.K. Goodman, 2004, p. 893). To extend the shouting metaphor, it follows that clarity and detail must be sacrificed in service of volume. As a number of authors have pointed out with regard to reflexive consumerism, because of limitations on the amount of technical information consumers can access and understand about a given product, ethical value networks rely on the important element of consumers' *trust* in certifications (Castaldo et al., 2009).

Although reflexive consumerism has driven a reorientation towards civic, domestic and ecological production conventions, studies regularly find a surprising lack of correlation between the ratio of consumers who identify as ethical, and actual ethical consumption patterns (see Auger & Devinney, 2007). In a 2005 study, Futerra found that while 30% of consumers claimed to be ethically motivated, only 3% followed through in their purchasing decisions (Futerra, 2009, in Carrington et al., 2010, p. 139). While consumers consistently claim in surveys that the ethical reputation of a brand significantly informs their choices, evidentially they do not always 'walk their talk' at the supermarket counter. The so-called 'intention-behaviour gap' in ethical consumption generates concerns about the real potential of reflexive consumers to drive sustainable ethical change. Cluley and Dunne (2012) undertake an interesting exploration of this intention–behaviour gap in order to position it within the Marxist theory of commodity fetishism. They argue that even informed consumers, when selecting a conventionally-produced product over an ethically-certified counterpart, will in fact "act as if we did not know what we know only all too well about the various uncomfortable facts about production" (Cluley & Dunne, 2012, p. 255). This type of self-deception or "disavowal of the hidden world of production" (p. 255), is in fact a type of wilful commodity fetishism, which the authors term 'commodity narcissism'.

Studies show that the psychological reward of feeling oneself to be moral is an important motivation for ethical consumers (Sobel, 2005). This is reminiscent of Parkin's (1968) claim in *Middle Class Radicalism* that middle class activists enjoy an emotional reward from their contribution. In addition to the emotional benefits of ethical consumption, a recent psychological study of ethical consumers found that ethical consumption choices yielded physical rewards, in that they made food products literally taste better. Bratanova and colleagues (2015) undertook three studies with organic, Fairtrade, and locally-produced foods respectively, and found that in each case, consumers' 'moral satisfaction' with their consumption choices enhanced taste experiences. The authors drew the conclusion that this taste reward acted as a feedback loop which reinforced consumers' willingness to pay a higher price for ethically-certified products in the future.

Some commentators have lamented the 'individualisation of responsibility' signalled by the rise of ethical consumerism as a mainstream avenue for trade equity and sustainable development. Maniates (2001) sees this as an impediment to meaningful collective action on issues of trade justice, arguing that it obscures real issues of the nature of institutionally-situated power in influencing global trade. Sarah Lyon also points out an important limitation of individualist consumerism in envisioning and implementing trade justice. She notes that it underscores inequalities even in wealthy societies, where not everyone has the equal ability to participate: "Voting with our dollars marks not only the inequities in the global arena but also those at home: while we all have the same number of votes, we do not all possess the same number of dollars" (Lyon, 2006, p. 452).

ETHICAL TRADE AND ETHICAL CERTIFICATION: MANIFESTATIONS AND DEFINITIONS

So far, this book has used both 'ethical trade' and 'ethical certification' to describe similar concepts. However, to proceed it is important to draw distinctions between these activities. Many claims are made to 'ethical trade', referencing variously environmental sustainability, labour rights, the protection of smallholder livelihoods and the legal protection of origin. Discourses of 'corporate social responsibility' (CSR) and 'ethical sourcing' are now practically ubiquitous in the policy and marketing of agri-food TNCs (see Luhmann & Theuvsen, 2016 for a review of CSR in agri-food networks). Within these claims are varying standards of ethicality, involving different levels of commitment and verification. 'Trade' itself is a multi-scalar process, comprising activities of production, distribution, manufacturing and retailing. However, 'ethical trade' claims often refer more narrowly to practices taking place within selected value chain nodes, most often at the production end. They may or may not imply consideration of the relationships and terms of trade between value chain actors. Little precedent exists in literature and practice as to a widely accepted definition of ethical trade. Notably, as a consequence, large manufacturers and retailers benefit from this lack of clarity, which enables them to exploit consumers' confusion over competing ethical claims to generate definitions of ethicality which suit their interests.

'Ethical trade' and 'ethical certification' are the most common descriptors used (often interchangeably) for the myriad trade practices claiming to be ethical. However, both have limitations. The former is a loosely-defined catch-all, given to both the social movement driven by activists, NGOs and consumers to address the negative impacts of globalised trade on local people and places – the ethical trade movement; and, to the ethical social and environmental sourcing practices of large companies (Ethical Trading Initiative, 2017). The latter refers nominally to trade practices which are verified against codes or standards, set either by lead firms in the value chain, or by external bodies such as NGOs or industry boards. In this book, the term *ethical value networks* refers to the relational structures of global trade that include value created by alignment with ethical conventions, gathered in constellations (see Chapter 2) and usually (though not exclusively) indicated through ethical certification. The following paragraphs will provide some context pertaining to manifestations of certification.

Ethical Certification: Proliferation and Convergence

While Fairtrade is arguably the most well-known example of ethical certification, such schemes have proliferated in both the social and environmental spheres (many covering both), and often come into direct competition for market share. Dual processes of proliferation and convergence have taken place, as more and more ethical trade claims crowd the market, but individual certifications have expanded to address separate issues of development, labour rights and environmental protection simultaneously (Smith & Barrientos, 2005). This has been the case with certifications which were originally developed in the social sphere – exemplified by Fairtrade's expansion first into organic certification, and then into hired labour – and with certifications which emerged in the environmental sphere, such as IMO Organic's development of the Fair for Life social and labour standards, and the conservation certification Rainforest Alliance's forthcoming merger with the labour-rights focused UTZ certified (formerly UTZ Kapeh) (see Bennett, 2018 for a general critique). While some certifications, such as UTZ certified, and Rainforest Alliance are established and monitored by independent non-profits, others, such as Mondelez International's recently announced 'Cocoa Life' scheme, and Sainsbury's (also recently announced) 'Fairly Traded' programme, are established by lead firms, which set standards for compliance in-house, and engage a dedicated monitoring company to carry out their auditing. Such programmes may or may not include product labels to signify certification to consumers, or the payment of a social premium to producers. Certifications also vary significantly in monitoring methodologies, some requiring regular on-the-ground audits, and some consisting simply of self-reviews.

It is possible to loosely categorise ethical certification claims along a spectrum from unverified statements aimed at marketing products, to progressive development-focused interventions which are rigorously independently monitored. Table 4.1 gives an overview of the varying levels of assurance in ethical value networks.

This confusing landscape of products with ethical labels conceals different levels of ethical standards and assurances. As Table 4.1 indicates, ethical claims may or may not be supported by certification systems. They may or may not involve third-party monitoring, and they may or may not address entire chains. As ethically-labelled products proliferate, and ethical claims become broader and vaguer, consumers will naturally find it more difficult to navigate ethical markets, and trust in the ethical claims of the array of ethical labels available could suffer as a consequence. Furthermore, though '100%' alternative trade systems such as Worldshops emerged at the top of the table of ethical legitimacy, the question must be asked even of them: *does it work?* A high level of 'ethical assurance' does not necessarily indicate highly favourable outcomes for producing communities. Given these vagaries, scholars have grappled with the question of whether market-driven ethical certification is able to foster ethical sustainable development in the Global South.

Theorising Ethical Certification: Convention Theory

In order to situate ethical certification within academic theory, we explore convention literature in this section. Convention theory provides an innovative basis by which to understand economic coordination based on ethical values and extrinsic qualities.

Any form of coordination among different actors needs a set of practices, rules or conventions participants agree on – the global food system for instance is characterised by particular conventions regarding safety and quality, but is also related to culture and identity (Morgan et al., 2006, p. 19). Ethical labelling systems depend fundamentally on communicating information about

Table 4.1   *Levels of assurance within ethical certification schemes*

Level of ethical assurance		Examples
LOW	References to ethicality on packaging and marketing materials	Use of terms 'eco' 'green' 'fair' etc.
	+ Standards established for ethical practices by lead firms	Corporate codes of conduct Corporate social responsibility strategies
	+ Independent monitoring of lead firms' ethical standards*	Mondelez International's 'Cocoa Life' 'Starbucks' 'C.A.F.E practices' Sainsbury's 'Fairly Traded'
	Ethical standards established and monitored by independent body	ISO 26000 Ethical Trade Initiative (ETI)
	+ Official label guarantees ethical compliance to consumers	UTZ certified/Rainforest Alliance** Organics, i.e. Biogro, USDA organic Geographical indications
	+ Ethical standards include minimum price and social premium to producers	Fairtrade Fair Trade USA Fair For Life
	+ Retailers required to trade in 100% certified products	World Fair Trade Organisation (WFTO)
HIGH	+ Importing and retailing functions integrated	Worldshops Trade Aid

Notes: * A large amount of variation exists in monitoring practices. Monitoring can involve regular on-site audits (i.e. UTZ certified), or reviews of member companies' reporting by boards (i.e. ETI). ** UTZ certified and Rainforest Alliance merged in 2018.
Source: Howson (2019).

production process or quality to consumers that is often extrinsic to the products themselves. Many ethically-labelled products are materially identical to their conventional counterparts. How, then, can they be imbued with additional value, and how is that value measured? One explanation originates in a French institutionalist approach with the theory of sociologists Boltanski and Thévenot (1991). Their work, *On Justification: The Economies of Worth*, proposed a series of criteria by which agents evaluate their actions and those of others. In Boltanski and Thévenot's view, these criteria or 'orders' (commonly called conventions) become established norms only through a social process of negotiation and contention, which incorporates the various values and priorities of diverse actors.

Salais and Storper, also seminal contributors to the theory of conventions, elaborated on how such norms become institutionalised in configurations of production and consumption, and come to dictate what they call 'worlds of production' (Storper & Salais, 1997). They define conventions as "practices, routines, agreements, and their associated informal and institutional forms which binds acts together through mutual expectations" (Salais & Storper, 1993, p. 174). As Wilkinson (1997) notes, convention theory draws from actor-network theory in that it "has the actor as its analytical starting point" (p. 306). An important meaning of this focus on actors is that because conventions are determined through ongoing processes of mutual agreement, they are subject to constant change and revision. They are at once established modes, and critiques of what is confirmed. "They are both guides for action and collective systems to legitimise those actions that can be submitted to testing and discussion" (Ponte, 2009, p. 239). It is this reflexive process of negotiation of standards for conduct that is particularly relevant to explaining emerging forms of private trade regulation based on normative values.

Convention theory offers a number of orders by which a product's worth can be measured, and by which production networks are organised. These convention categories are: market (supply and demand); industrial (technical functioning); domestic (embeddedness – attached to place); public (brand reputation); civic (the impact of industrial activity on people's wellbeing); and ecological (environmental impact). A single value network, or 'world of production' can incorporate one or many of these sets of conventions. For example, a consumer may choose which petrol station to refill their car at simply based on a market convention of price, whereas they might choose a coffee brand on the basis of a complex combination of each of the conventions listed above. Through their decision-making, that reflexive consumer contributes to the process of defining and refining the balance of conventions governing a value network. From the convention theory perspective, we might make the point that quality conventions are a key aspect of fair trade agricultural markets, but they also produce barriers and exclusions: "the standardization and verification of certifications guaranteeing 'quality' of multiple sorts ensures premiums but also creates rents, imposes costs on producers, and excludes many potential beneficiaries" (McCarthy, 2006, p. 808). In Table 4.2 we reproduce a set of conventions in the wine industry to illustrate the nature of these sets of processes (Howson, 2019).

Convention theory's dissemination into Anglophone scholarship remains fairly limited, though some authors have found it useful for describing the regulation of agri-food networks through the establishment of norms, particularly where embeddedness and quality are emphasised. McEwan and Bek (2009) have used it to talk about indicators of quality for wine (as adapted in Table 4.2). A small cohort of scholars are adopting aspects of convention theory to better understand the world of ethical certification (see Raynolds, 2014). Broadly, the theory demonstrates that ethical certification is an instrument for foregrounding the domestic, civic and ecological conventions in economic decision-making, and also a process by which the expectations and parameters

Table 4.2   Quality conventions in the wine industry

Quality convention	How 'quality' is measured in general	Indicator of 'quality' in wine
Inspiration	Personality	Unique wine, cult winemaker
Domestic	Proximity, trust, repetition	Varietal, terroir, geographical indication
Opinion	External expert judgement	Endorsement by critic/publication, medal/award
Civic	Social impact	Labels and certifications
Ecological	Environmental impact	Labels and certifications
Market	Price	Price
Industrial	External objective measurement	Laboratory tests, codification of processes

Source: Adapted from McEwan and Bek (2009, p. 257).

for certification are continually created and reinforced by all network participants, including consumers. The theory allows us to better understand the mechanics of value chain governance and regulation, and the ways in which power is consolidated and challenged.

PLACING THE ETHICAL IN VALUE NETWORKS

No single theory has described in an integrated way the manner in which ethical qualities are agreed-upon, codified and measured in different global economic networks. Moreover, scholars have yet to theorise how those qualities are translated into value through transactions. While we have theories and vocabularies to describe the complex networks and relations of global production and consumption, as well as mature research methodologies to trace the creation, distribution and accumulation of value, and its intersections with the distributions of power, much of that value is generally derived from intrinsic or visible product qualities and characteristics, relative to other similar products.

However, as noted, recent decades have witnessed the normalisation of 'ethical' quality as a determinant of value in global production networks. By what mechanism and means is that value determined, monetised, and conveyed amongst territorially dispersed actors? One aspect of this process is deeply relational. It involves negotiation, norm-setting and contestation over beliefs about what is 'good'. Some have argued, using vegan food production as a case study, that "ethics are not just something folded back through the production process from the consumption end but are at the heart of how value is formed within it" (Mouat et al., 2018, p. 136). However, to counteract the relational and messy creation and destruction of ethical conventions that underpins the generation of ethical value, actors have developed a sophisticated certification infrastructure in order to capture and codify ethical qualities – to allow them to be valorised. Ethical value, in short, is the volatile marriage of a fragile consensus about what is good at any given time, and methodologies of compliance and surveillance characteristic of supply chain traceability and auditing. It is these linkages, and the monetary and informational flows that enable ethical value to be created and distributed, that we term ethical value networks (EVeNs).

EVeNs are useful partly to draw attention to the common premise of claims to ethical trade: that they 'even' the social, environmental and geographical score. This explicit focus on even or uneven outcomes in networks, encourages a programme of research which centres environmental and social justice in investigations of global networks that circulate ethical value. However, we also want to advance the concept of ethical value networks because researchers simply lack a conceptual touchstone for such networks, which clearly comprise a distinct and growing subset of global production networks.

EVeNs, Chains and Networks

In defining and understanding EVeNs, GVC/GPN is our clear starting point. This well-established field provides the predominant conceptual framework for understanding cross-border processes of production and consumption, and the myriad activities, transactions and relationships that comprise them. GVC/GPN shows us that there are often multiple points in this network where power is exercised, and one party emerges a 'winner'. They provide a clear framework for studying unequal or unjust outcomes in the global economy, through the lenses of value, embeddedness and governance. Drawing on earlier theories of world systems and dependency, GVC/GPN helps us to elucidate the structural underpinnings of geographical unevenness in global economic exchange. Research in this tradition has helped to demonstrate how inequitable outcomes for participants in economic peripheries and the Global South follows on from neo-colonial processes of extraction, disembeddedness and commodity fetishism. Some researchers have made the point that ethical consumption campaigns (for example, as in cause-related marketing), in spite of being globally interconnected and part of global practices, are also contextual and situated in particular places (Hawkins, 2015, p. 180).

It is precisely the concept of disembedded globalised agri-food networks, laid bare in consumer imaginaries thanks to the language and tools of GVC/GPN, that the advent of ethical trade initiatives and ethical labelling respond to and attempt to counter. Not only has GVC/GPN theory provided the tools for identifying this development and tracing its impacts, it has directly contributed to the evolution of the movement itself. It is through GVC/GPN theory and its Marxist structuralist predecessors that we have gained a more detailed understanding of the connections between geographically distant consumers and producers, and how injustice is produced and reproduced through these connections (Wilson & Jackson, 2016). Ethical trade movements begin from a place of understanding of the mechanisms and outcomes of GVC/GPNs, and the strategy of leveraging knowledge about them, to produce fairer outcomes (for an early attempt at this see Hughes et al., 2008). However, reviews of the literature and our own research experiences show us that both GVC and GPN approaches have limitations when it comes to describing the increasing focus on ethical qualities in global networks. Below we discuss these shortcomings.

The limits of Global Value Chains and Global Production Networks in analysing 'ethical value'

For those with a critical approach, the value chain analysis serves to uncover how power structures operate in global market relationships and how participation in these markets can perpetuate or even increase the marginalisation of less powerful actors. Such scholars and others (see Mook & Overdevest, 2018, for example) have pointed to the limitations of value chains as an analytic framework for alternative movements in food and agriculture. First, they have been argued to be overly economistic, with power structures shown to develop almost mechanically based on market relations and economies of scale. This can overlook the extent to which all economic relations are socially embedded and the ways in which the institutional or political context can influence how value chains 'touch down' in particular places.

Second, the GVC framework operates at a macro- or mesoscale and its units of analysis tend to be firms or categories of producers. Discussions of organics, fair trade or geographical indications often focus on the relative position of 'small producers' or 'family farms' and initiatives are considered to be successful when the position of these producers is strengthened. This can overlook differentiation between these producers and the very important differences between a farmer with ten hectares of land and one with one hectare or less, for example (Luetchford, 2008).

A further criticism is that value chains, like dependency analyses, work with a 'Smithian' model of economics that emphasises exchange over production, failing to consider the imperatives of the capitalist mode of production that underlie the behaviour of all market participants (Fridell, 2007). These criticisms may be valid and point to the need to complement value chain analyses with micro-level studies of livelihoods and production relations, evaluation of national political and institutional contexts, and wider historical-structural analysis of the evolution of capitalism. There are further criticisms that can be levelled at GVCs: they centre power as the focus of analysis, but in the preoccupation with prescriptive structures they do not pay enough attention to relational and contingent processes of value creation – negotiation, norm-making, consensus building. We also argue that GPNs do not account as well for the neo-colonial directionality of driven-ness and extraction that we witness across the global economy.

Conceptualising Ethical Value Networks

The term EVeN refers to global production networks that make a claim for, label and certify ethical value. While the concept can be used as a descriptor for any network that has some aspect of ethical certification, it should also be seen as aspirational: the objective of ethical certification is to *realise* ethical value, or networks that are just, sustainable and authentic. Thus, the study of EVeNs necessitates a critical approach to determining the contribution of ethical certification to the realisation of ethical trade and ethical development. The literatures and concepts which make up EVeNs are detailed in Table 4.3.

The use of EVeNs as a framework allows for a more integrated analysis of varying forms of 'ethical' regulation in international trade. By incorporating aspects of network theories, EVeNs also allow for the treatment of ethical certification bodies, NGOs and labourers as active influencers in the governance of economic activity, allowing for a deeper discussion of the role of ethics in market relations. The 'network' approach mandates consideration of local geographical contexts, including history, institutional makeup, culture and discourse in influencing the configuration and outcomes of trade relations. Network studies also include explicit attention to epistemology, which mitigates against narrow or politically-imbued understandings of the purpose and nature of global economic exchange. However, in incorporating aspects of value chains theory, retaining an emphasis on material outcomes and identifying the value that is added and captured within networks, EVeNs mandate structural analysis of distributions of capital and wealth, and provide a method of identifying transformations in the balance of power and profit in trade networks with ethical certification.

The mapping methodology of GVCs and GPNs, as discussed in Chapter 3, though limited in the linearity of the former and complexity of the latter, still assists in identifying the impact of ethical certification on profit and power distribution, particularly if used in conjunction with more relational approaches. Finally, EVeNs can be explicitly concerned with inclusive, egalitarian development. In this focus, EVeNs research has an explicitly political standpoint, and a critical and even sceptical approach to corporate claims to ethicality. Ethical certification is in large part an attempt to 'capture the gains', or retain value for more disadvantaged value chain participants at the supply end. So, by conceiving of ethical value networks, we can more easily talk about whether, and how, the 'gains' of ethical certification are distributed more

Table 4.3   *Key literature and concepts contributing to the model of*
                EVeNs

Ethical (E)	Value (Ve)	Network (N)
• *Ethical certifications*	• World systems/Dependency theory	
• *Alternative development*	• Global value chains	• Global production networks
• *Convention theory*	• Material focus	• Relationality
• *New social movements*	• Mapping	• Inclusion of non-firm actors
• *Embeddedness*	• Driven-ness	• Geographical contingency and
• *Ethical consumerism*	• Value creation, enhance-	local context
• *Sustainability*	ment and capture	
• *Participatory development*	• Unequal exchange	
• *Empowerment*	• Upgrading	
• *Reflexivity*	• Governance	

Source: Adapted from Howson (2019).

evenly amongst value chain participants or otherwise (see also Grabs & Ponte, 2019; Lund-Thomsen & Lindgreen, 2018).

ETHICAL VALUE NETWORKS: A CONCEPTUAL FRAMEWORK

In Figure 4.1 we have drawn an idealised conceptual framework for an ethical value network. This framework allows us to map a set of nodes and linkages that trace the source, location, regulation, distribution and flow of production, distribution and consumption through the network. It is important to note that this is an idealised version which presents a range of possibilities to which different examples of EVeNs can be 'plugged' into. Our concern is largely with flows between producers working in ethical networks in the Global South and consumers that purchase ethical products in the Global North. In this idealised model, we draw on our earlier reviews of value chains and networks and the work of Coe et al. (2004) (see Figures 3.1 and 3.2).

In the framework we see the Global South and North represented in different hemispheres connected through flows of profit, products and information. Ethical consumers are connected to ethical producers through a series of industrial nodes covering intermediary (buying, storage and processing), wholesaling (including branding, promotion and distribution) and retailing functions. In both major parts of the network there are three main conditioning elements that have a bearing on the eventual shape and nature of the EVeN. Civil society organisations and movements may play a role both through explicit and active involvement and also through awareness campaigns and other activities associated with promoting EVeNs. Industrial organisation is a second conditioning factor whereby the nature and/or structure of the sector has a bearing on the flow and distribution of prices and profits. These agencies have a key role in the networks at nearly all levels, often through complex trading relationships such as contracting, spot markets or direct supervision of production methods. Finally, state regulation can regulate and incentivise, or otherwise, different forms of ethical trade. Each of these elements will be important in all networks but they may have a different level of influence in any specific case. For example, as we will see, state regulation may be important in the case of GI legislation, while civil society activity may be more important in some forms of fair trade.

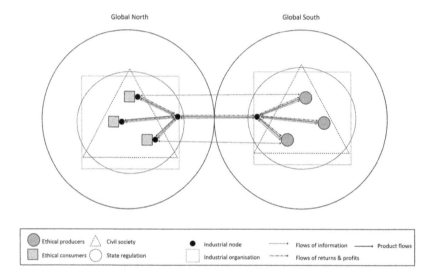

Figure 4.1   An idealised conceptual model for an ethical value network

We conceive of three types of flow. Product flows move from the producer to the consumers in a chain-like fashion through intermediaries, wholesalers and retailers, where they are subject to various forms of processing, packaging, branding and promotion. By contrast, we suggest that information flows move both ways, conveying market signals and consumer preferences from markets to intermediaries and producers; and relaying stories of origin and production back to consumers in ways that make claims to ethicality. Information flows are often mediated through both industry and civil society organisations.

Finally, returns and profits in theory flow back from the point of sale eventually to producers, though marketing, transport and processing costs and profits are realised along the way. We argue that, more often than not, in practice (through such intermediary costs and profits) value tends to accrue towards the consumption part of the network and away from producers.

This conceptualisation depicts a simplified and idealised model of the structures, agencies and flows within EVeNs. Following analyses of case studies in this volume, we return to this model in Chapter 16 to show how it is reshaped in practice in each of the different constellations and how different forms of organisation, relationships, power structures and flows are manifested in varied ways.

We can also begin to conceptualise *ethical value accumulation profiles*. Of critical importance is the distribution and realisation of ethical value throughout the network. Ethical value is created through the cultivation of consumer preferences and their willingness to pay more for 'virtuous' products that they believe have elements of ethicality. In theory, this ethical premium flows back to producers, particularly as ethical value networks make claims to increase the proportion of total value that ends up in the hands of primary producers. However, as noted above, we suggest that value is accrued in practice towards the retail and wholesaling parts of the network – though this need not necessarily be the case and there can be a range of profiles mapping how ethical value accrues across different parts of the networks. In order to trace this component we have drawn a number of hypothetical ethical accumulation diagrams in Figures 4.2 to 4.7. These map the value added at each point in the network (producers and the various nodes) in a relative sense – an approximation of the amount of the ethical value created that accrues at different stages and to different network actors. This should be seen as a proxy measure for the realisation of ethical value – ideally it would be useful to isolate that value which accrues due to claims of ethicality, and this remains a research challenge for the future.

In Figures 4.2 to 4.7 we draw idealised profiles of value accumulation at four points in the network: producer, intermediary, wholesaler and retailer. This can be more complex in reality with further stages and nodes (e.g. processing, transport/storage) and, on the other hand, some profiles may be simpler (e.g. short direct chains between growers and local consumers). However, these profiles allow for some conceptualisation of various general accumulation profiles. At each point value, accumulation is represented by a bar, with the production component of the network located on the right of the chart and the retail towards the left – echoing the location of the Global South and North respectively in Figure 4.1. The relative size of the bar (small/ medium or large) indicates the hypothetical relative proportion of the ethical value that is captured at each point.

An ethical value network that was fulfilling its ethical claims would see higher or at least equal value realised at the producer node – either individualised through prices to producers or realised through social external benefits associated with social premium distribution. This outcome is represented in Figure 4.2, which we term the *hyper-ethical* accumulation profile, where a greater proportion of the final market value flows directly to producers as in some form of direct trade and short networks. In this network we leave out two stages in the middle of the network, representing a direct link with producers and the retailer/consumer. A second possibility – an *ethical accumulation profile* is illustrated in Figure 4.3 where there is relatively greater proportion of value flowing to the producer but the network is more complex and involves production, intermediary, wholesale and retail nodes. These two profiles together represent ideal outcomes in terms of the proposed progressive benefits of EVeNs. We might see examples of these profiles in some fair trade chains that directly link producers, retailers and consumers through relationships mediated through civil society organisations.

In Figure 4.4 we illustrate a possibility where value shares are equal at each of the four nodes in the network – what we term an *equitable* accumulation profile. This would see ethical value accruing to all agents in roughly equal proportion along the chain. It may fulfil the criterion of increasing returns (and decreasing their variability) to producers but recognises that other agents are necessary if the network is to function effectively in competitive markets. This profile is unlikely in reality but it acts as a control for the other five profiles hypothesised here.

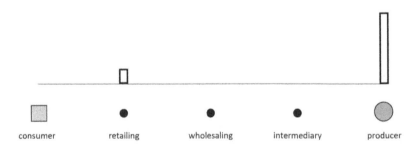

Figure 4.2   *Hyper-ethical accumulation profile*

In Figure 4.5 we draw what we term a *Southern capital capture accumulation profile* where intermediaries capture a disproportionate amount of the benefits. This might occur where medium or large-scale firms coordinate and control ethical trade systems and gather produce in large amounts. In these instances, local companies with strong buying power are able to dominate the supply chain and attach ethical claims to products they assemble, process and on-sell. We will see examples of this in fair trade wine, where large established local wine companies include fair trade brands in their product portfolios. Local grape producers may get an enhanced price but the overall profile is driven by commercial imperatives and by commercial enterprises in the South.

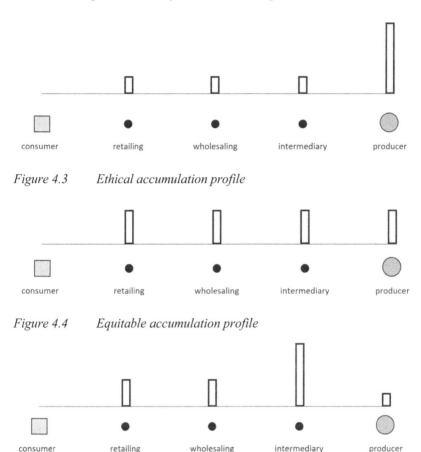

Figure 4.3   *Ethical accumulation profile*

Figure 4.4   *Equitable accumulation profile*

Figure 4.5   *Southern capital capture accumulation profile*

Two final options are presented in Figure 4.6 *Northern Wholesale Capital Capture* and Figure 4.7 *Northern Retail Capital Capture.* In the case of the former, oligopsonistic wholesalers control imports and accrue a disproportionate amount of the value. Here we see large companies engaged in processing, branding and promoting certain ethical products (fair trade coffee, region of origin wines or organic fruit) alongside their other product lines which are distributed through their established marketing channels. In the latter, supermarkets control the concentrated market for imported ethical products. Here these large and powerful retailing firms are able to exercise their buying power, often buying direct from intermediaries in the Global South and, as with the wholesalers and processors, selling and profiting from ethical brands alongside their parallel products. Both wholesaler and retail capital capture profiles may well involve these agents developing and promoting their own ethical certifications and claims in competition with those emanating from civil society initiatives. We argue later in this book on the basis of case study evidence, that most value networks – even those deemed ethical – are characterised by some version of these two profiles. It is a hypothesis for further research that the accrual of benefits towards the Northern part of the network is less pronounced in ethical value networks than it is in conventional ones.

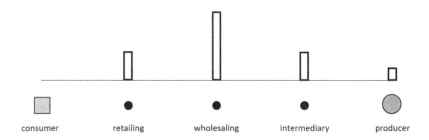

Figure 4.6   Northern wholesale capture accumulation profile

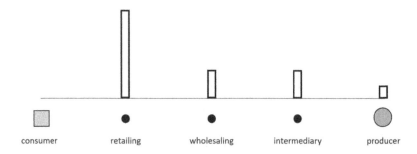

Figure 4.7   Northern retail capture accumulation profile

We are aware that such profiles provide only a rough measure of the distribution of value. They do not take costs into account (other than implicitly). Furthermore, the issue of social premium and its distribution in communities where fair trade is practised would also have to be factored in. This framework says very little about how ethical values are distributed within the producer domain, within communities and households or across gender, age and ethnic lines, for we know power relations and forms of appropriation and coercion may be evident across the whole network. There is also much research and typological design to be done to more accurately capture the private and social externalities – in terms of both costs and benefits – that accrue throughout the chain. In Chapter 16, we will revisit the issue of the distribution of ethical value and also raise a number of issues for further research that will allow us to elaborate upon this framework.

CONCLUSION

In this chapter we have discussed globalised agriculture and the resistive rise of ethical consumerism and trade. We considered the evolution of certification and utilised convention theory to throw light upon this movement. In our idealised EVeN conceptual framework and in the value accumulation profiles we provide a framework for the mapping and analysis of the creation, regulation, flow and distribution of ethical value. By adopting an EVeN approach, we can explicitly shift the focus of our ethical trade research to a wider geographical scale, while retaining case study parameters concerning a particular product from a unique production context. The usage of the acronym EVeN itself refers to this objective – and the question of the ability of ethical certification to promote evenness in global trade. As such, EVeNs provide a consolidated and holistic framework for approaching ethical certifications. It is to locality studies, which allow us to get inside such EVeNs, that much of the remainder of this book turns.

REFERENCES

Auger, P., & Devinney, T.M. (2007). Do what consumers say matter? The misalignment of preferences with unconstrained ethical intentions. *Journal of Business Ethics, 76*(4), 361–383.

Beckett, A., & Nayak, A. (2008). The reflexive consumer. *Marketing Theory, 8*(3), 299–317.

Bennett, E.A. (2018). Voluntary sustainability standards: A squandered opportunity to improve workers' wages. *Sustainable Development, 26*, 65–82.

Boltanski, L., & Thévenot, L. (1991). *De la justification les économies de la grandeur.* Gallimard.

Bratanova, B., Vauclair, C.-M., Kervyn, N., Schumann, S., Wood, R., & Klein, O. (2015). Savouring morality. Moral satisfaction renders food of ethical origin subjectively tastier. *Appetite, 91*, 137–149.

Carrington, M.J., Neville, B.A., & Whitwell, G.J. (2010). Why ethical consumers don't walk their talk: Towards a framework for understanding the gap between the ethical purchase intentions and actual buying behaviour of ethically minded consumers. *Journal of Business Ethics, 97*(1), 139–158

Castaldo, S., Perrini, F., Misani, N., & Tencati, A. (2009). The missing link between corporate social responsibility and consumer trust: The case of fair trade products. *Journal of Business Ethics, 84*(1), 1–15.

Cluley, R., & Dunne, S. (2012). From commodity fetishism to commodity narcissism. *Marketing Theory, 12*(3), 251–265.

Coe, N.M., Hess, M., Yeung, H.W.-C., Dicken, P., & Henderson, J. (2004). Globalizing regional development: A global production networks perspective. *Transactions of the Institute of British Geographers, 29*(4), 468–484.

De Neve, G., Luetchford, P., & Pratt, J. (2008). Introduction: Revealing the hidden hands of global market exchange. In G. De Neve, P. Luetchford, & J. Pratt (Eds.), *Hidden hands in the market: Ethnographies of fair trade, ethical consumption, and corporate social responsibility* (pp. 1–30). Emerald Group Publishing.

Ethical Trading Initiative (2017). Is ethical trade just for large companies? Retrieved 22 August, from http://www.ethicaltrade.org/faq/ethical-trade-just-large-companies

Feagan, R. (2007). The place of food: Mapping out the 'local' in local food systems. *Progress in Human Geography, 31*(1), 23–42.

Fridell, G. (2007). Fair-trade coffee and commodity fetishism: The limits of market-driven social justice. *Historical Materialism, 15*(4), 79–104.

Futerra, S.C.L. (2005). *The rules of the game: The principles of climate change communication.* Department for Environment, Food and Rural Affairs.

Giddens, A. (1990). *The consequences of modernity.* Stanford University Press.

Goodman, D. (2004). Rural Europe redux? Reflections on alternative agri-food networks and paradigm change. *Sociologia Ruralis, 44*, 3–16.

Goodman, M.K. (2004). Reading fair trade: Political ecological imaginary and the moral economy of fair trade foods. *Political Geography, 23*(7), 891–915.

Goodman, D., & Goodman, M.K. (2009). Alternative food networks. *International Encyclopedia of Human Geography, 3*, 208–220.

Grabs, J., & Ponte, S. (2019). The evolution of power in the global coffee value chain and production network. *Journal of Economic Geography, 19*, 803–828.

Hawkins, R. (2015). Shifting conceptualizations of ethical consumption: Cause-related marketing in India and the USA. *Geoforum, 67*, 172–182.

Hess, M. (2004). 'Spatial' relationships? Towards a reconceptualization of embeddedness. *Progress in Human Geography, 28*(2), 165–186.

Higgins, V., Dibden, J., & Cocklin, C. (2008). Building alternative agri-food networks: Certification, embeddedness and agri-environmental governance. *Journal of Rural Studies, 24*(1), 15–27.

Howson, K. (2019). *Bottling the colonial unconscious: Ethical value networks and the commodification of fairness in the South African wine industry.* PhD thesis, Victoria University of Wellington.

Hudson, I., & Hudson, M. (2003). Removing the veil? Commodity fetishism, fair trade, and the environment. *Organization & Environment, 16*(4), 413–430.

Hughes, A., Wrigley, N., & Buttle, M. (2008). Global production networks, ethical campaigning, and the embeddedness of responsible governance. *Journal of Economic Geography, 8*(3), 345–367.

LeHeron, R.B. (1993). *Globalized agriculture: Political choice.* Pergamon Press.

Luetchford, P. (2008). *Fair trade and a global commodity: Coffee in Costa Rica.* Pluto Press.

Luhmann, H., & Theuvsen, L. (2016). Corporate social responsibility in agribusiness. Literature review and future research directions. *Journal of Agricultural and Environmental Ethics*, *29*, 673–696.

Lund-Thomsen, P., & Lindgreen, A. (2018). Is there a sweet spot in ethical trade? A critical appraisal of the potential for aligning buyer, supplier and worker interests in global production networks. *Geoforum*, *90*, 84–90.

Lyon, S. (2006). Evaluating fair trade consumption: Politics, defetishization and producer participation. *International Journal of Consumer Studies*, *30*(5), 452–464.

Maniates, M.F. (2001). Individualization: Plant a tree, buy a bike, save the world? *Global Environmental Politics*, *1*(3), 31–52.

Marx, K., Engels, F., Mandel, E., & Fowkes, B. (1990). *Capital: A critique of political economy* (Vol. 1). Penguin in association with New Left Review.

Mather, A. S., Hill, G., & Nijnik, M. (2006). Post-productivism and rural land use: Cul de sac or challenge for theorization? *Journal of Rural Studies*, *22*(4), 441–455.

McCarthy, J. (2006). Rural geography: Alternative rural economies – the search for alterity in forests, fisheries, food, and fair trade. *Progress in Human Geography*, *30*(6), 803–811.

McEwan, C., & Bek, D. (2009). The political economy of alternative trade: Social and environmental certification in the South African wine industry. *Journal of Rural Studies*, *25*(3), 255–266.

Mook, A., & Overdevest, C. (2018). Does fairtrade certification meet producers' expectations related to participating in mainstream markets? An analysis of advertised benefits and perceived impact. *Sustainable Development*, *26*, 269–280.

Morgan, K., Marsden, T., & Murdoch, J. (2006). *Worlds of food: Place, power, and provenance in the food chain*. Oxford University Press.

Mouat, M.J., Prince, R., & Roche, M.M. (2018). Making value out of ethics: The emerging economic geography of lab-grown meat and other animal-free food products. *Economic Geography*, *95*(2), 136–158.

Parkin, F. (1968). *Middle class radicalism*. Manchester University Press.

Ponte, S. (2009). Governing through quality: Conventions and supply relations in the value chain for South African wine. *Sociologia Ruralis*, *49*(3), 236–257.

Raynolds, L.T. (2014). Fairtrade, certification, and labor: Global and local tensions in improving conditions for agricultural workers. *Agriculture and Human Values*, *31*(3), 499–511.

Renting, H., Marsden, T.K., & Banks, J. (2003). Understanding alternative food networks: Exploring the role of short food supply chains in rural development. *Environment and Planning A*, *35*(3), 393–411.

Rosol, M. (2020). On the significance of alternative economic practices: Reconceptualizing alterity in alternative food networks. *Economic Geography*, *96*(1), 52–76.

Salais, R., & Storper, M. (1993). *Les mondes de production*. Editions de I'EHEss.

Sánchez-Hernández, J.L., Aparicio-Amador, J., & Alonso-Santos, J.L. (2010). The shift between worlds of production as an innovative process in the wine industry in Castile and Leon (Spain). *Geoforum*, *41*(3), 469–478.

Schumpeter, J. (1942). *Capitalism, socialism and democracy*. Harper.

Sen, A. (1977). Rational fools: A critique of the behavioral foundations of economic theory. *Philosophy & Public Affairs*, *6*(4), 317–344.

Sobel, J. (2005). Interdependent preferences and reciprocity. *Journal of Economic Literature*, *43*(2), 392–436.

Smith, S., & Barrientos, S. (2005). Fair trade and ethical trade: Are there moves towards convergence? *Sustainable Development, 13*(3), 190–198.

Storper, M., & Salais, R. (1997). *Worlds of production: The action frameworks of the economy.* Harvard University Press.

Talbot, J.M. (2002). Tropical commodity chains, forward integration strategies and international inequality: Coffee, cocoa and tea. *Review of International Political Economy, 9*(4), 701–734.

Whatmore, S. (2002). From farming to agribusiness: global agri-food networks. In P.J. Taylor (Ed.,) *Geographies of global change* (pp. 57–67). Blackwell.

Wilk, R. (2001). Consuming morality. *Journal of Consumer Culture, 1*(2), 245–260.

Wilkinson, J. (1997). A new paradigm for economic analysis? Recent convergences in French social science and an exploration of the convention theory approach with a consideration of its application to the analysis of the agrofood system. *International Journal of Human Resource Management, 26*(3), 335–339.

Wilson, G.A. (2001). From productivism to post-productivism … and back again? Exploring the (un) changed natural and mental landscapes of European agriculture. *Transactions of the Institute of British Geographers, 26*(1), 77–102.

Wilson, M., & Jackson, P. (2016). Fairtrade bananas in the Caribbean: Towards a moral economy of recognition. *Geoforum, 70*, 11–21.

5 Critiques of ethical certification and trade

Kelle Howson

INTRODUCTION

EVeNs have gained significant economic and social importance in the last decade. The common factor between these different networks is an attempt to increase product values through the generation of an 'ethical premium'. This premium seeks to create a connection between Northern consumers and Southern producers. In addition to ethical and environmental concerns, EVeNs represent a shift from mass-produced agri-food systems to those of high-value niche production which emphasise quality, diversification, and place. Over recent decades agricultural products have increasingly been labelled and marketed to demonstrate how they have been produced, by who, where, and to what standards (Gereffi et al., 2005; Hughes, 2005; Ponte & Ewert, 2009). Each of these labels are associated with some form of EVeN.

EVeNs have become particularly important in the Global South. As discussed elsewhere in this collection, many countries there have become highly dependent on the export of agriculture and commodities through their integration into the global economy. In an attempt to counter increased competition due to market forces, these lower income countries have become progressively dependent on mass-production and low value-added commodities. It is suggested that the value-added offered by various ethical, sustainability and localised production labels may provide alternative models for easing the low-value commodity dependence of small-scale producers in the South (McCarthy, 2006; Raynolds, 2012).

The validity of EVeNs has, however, become the subject of debate. Academic interest has focused on the marketing and market spaces of some of the groups engaged in the diverse and growing EVeNs (Bowen, 2010; Renard, 2005). As mentioned, EVeNs are based on claims that appeal to global consumer concerns and demands for ethical, sustainable, localised or authentic production. Some critical exploration has illustrated that marketing groups utilise these ethical claims to establish and exploit the niche markets that appeal to these consumers (McCarthy, 2006; Raynolds, 2012). What remains unclear is which groups are truly benefiting from these ethical claims. The following sections will critically explore two important and distinct EVeNs: fair trade certification and geographical indication marks (GI), at a global and theoretical level. These two EVeNs have formed the central case studies of the research presented in this book.

Amidst the new international division of labour, there have been growing consumer concerns (predominantly emanating from Northern markets) about social justice, food quality and authenticity, environmental consequences, and impacts on human health in agricultural and commodity products (Hughes et al., 2008; Mutersbaugh, 2005). As a result, we are witnessing mounting levels of scepticism regarding how, where and to what standards food is being produced. It has been recognised that this scepticism and the changes in con-sumer preferences have evolved, in part, as a reactionary resistance to what has been labelled the 'placelessness' of global agri-food networks (Bowen & Mutersbaugh, 2014).

The global agri-food system is, therefore, experiencing a paradox. On the one hand, there has been a growing dominance of TNCs in agricultural pro-duction. This has accelerated and deepened the integration of Global South suppliers, creating mixed outcomes for exporting countries. On the other hand, however, Northern consumers have become more concerned with the negative impacts of the globalisation of agriculture. This is pressuring corporations to change how they operate and, more importantly, has created the demand for alternative food networks (Bowen & Mutersbaugh, 2014).

This chapter presents a literature review of research on ethical certifications in the 21st century. It provides a foundation for the exploration of ethical value networks in this volume, by outlining key debates since the emergence of ethical certifications, focusing in particular on the limitations to their ability to contribute to environmental, social and distributive justice.

CRITIQUES OF ETHICAL CERTIFICATION: WHO HAS THE POWER?

When ethical certification first emerged, it was treated with optimism by many scholars, who lauded its potential to harness the colossal power of wealthy socially- and environmentally-conscious consumers, circumventing the need for state regulation in upholding production standards, or filling the gaps in cross-border regulatory frameworks. However, as neoliberalism's shortfalls became more apparent, particularly growing inequality and the concentration of wealth, so too did the limitations of ethical consumption to create just and equitable trade. Although it has earned tentative praise from high profile figures, including Joseph Stiglitz (2007), commentators such as Raynolds

(2000) and Mutersbaugh (2005), have identified various practical limitations as demand for ethically-certified products increases and large market players enter into certification systems.

A reasonably predictable criticism has long been made by ethical labelling's detractors, who argue that certification results in market inefficiency, as it artificially rewards non-competitive enterprises, leading to oversupply, and lower quality products. Certification and premium payments have been theorised to encourage resource lock-in, and ultimately sustain primary commodity dependence (Griffiths, 2012). There is certainly evidence to support the notion that certification has led to an imbalance of supply and demand in some cases, and this has been the case in Fairtrade coffee (Sidwell, 2008). Overproduction of Fairtrade coffee has been shown to suppress the price of conventional coffee received by non-Fairtrade producers, and for Fairtrade producers attempting to sell their surplus to conventional markets. Fairtrade's right-of-centre critics may argue that producers receiving prices below the cost of production are being incentivised to diversify or transfer into more profitable types of production, higher value commodities or wage labour. However, such claims remain an oversimplification of the challenges and options faced by commodity producers in low income countries. The rest of this section will focus on the more widely debated critiques of ethical certification; namely mainstreaming, asymmetrical governance, barriers to entry, and lack of geographical sensitivity.

Mainstreaming and Corporate Co-optation

That ethical trade initiatives almost inevitably follow a mainstreaming path is widely accepted in the literature. To widen their reach, or in response to commercial pressure, many social and environmental certification schemes tend to shed their critical or oppositional credo (Auld et al., 2015; Child, 2015; Fridell et al., 2008; Jaffee & Howard, 2010). While this has been observed at different times across multiple market-based ethical initiatives, including forest stewardship (Klooster, 2005), organic agriculture and socially responsible investing (Child, 2015), it has been particularly contentious within the fair trade movement (see Jaffee, 2012; Jaffee & Howard, 2010; Raynolds, 2014).

A key feature of the mainstreaming of fair trade has been the development of rigid standards which, on the one hand, provide certification with credibility and universality, but, on the other, impose a top-down model of governance which serves to distance the movement from its grassroots 'partnership' rhetoric (Child, 2015). Critical voices within fair trade contend that the mainstreaming and codification of the movement has altered the balance of beneficiaries. While once consumer demand was a vehicle to facilitate development at supply-level, now in many cases consumer demand has become an end in itself. This 'metamorphosis', some claim, amounts to the transformation from fair trade as a vehicle for sustainable development, to fair trade as a marketing tool (Dalvai, 2017).

Corporate co-optation of ethical trade discourse and infrastructure is both a driving force and a consequence of the mainstreaming phenomenon. The process of contestation by which standards are negotiated and re-negotiated has become subject to corporate 'countermobilisation' (Fridell et al., 2008), or 'counter-reform' (Jaffee & Howard, 2010), as large commercial actors attempt to maintain their power and profitability in the face of increasing consumer awareness of the plight of producers in the Global South, and the sustainability of production. The concerted corporate response to the ethical consumerism movement has been to attempt to appropriate the symbolic value generated by ethical trade discourses while simultaneously working to "neutralise the transformative power of the standards" governing ethical trade (Jaffee & Howard, 2010, p. 389). These parallel objectives are achieved through a multifaceted approach which has included de-legitimisation, pre-emption through the adoption of ethical rhetoric accompanied by minimal practice reforms, appropriation of ethical identification systems, and attempts to exert pressure on fair trade institutions to weaken standards (Fridell et al., 2008). In reference to the final point, Jaffee and Howard (2010) termed the influence of powerful market actors over supposedly independent fair trade and organic standards 'regulatory capture' (p. 389). They argue that, contrary to the assumption that regulatory actors are strictly motivated by public interest considerations, individuals within regulatory bodies are likely to be sympathetic to the concerns of industry, and even to have backgrounds in the respective industry. In Jaffee and Howard's analysis, this 'revolving door' model has led to the over-representation of commercial agendas in ethical standards-setting institutions.

Jaffee and Howard identify specific outcomes of co-optation in both the United States Department of Agriculture (USDA) organic and Fairtrade movements. They show that regulatory capture has led to reduced democratic input on boards and in standards-setting processes and, in particular, an under-representation of small farmers within Fairtrade and US organic certifiers. Regulatory oversight has also decreased, with fewer site visits occurring, and fewer prosecutions of code violations. The authors point out that the FLO-Cert (the independent auditing body of Fairtrade) licensing fee structure disincentivises the strict oversight of high-volume producers (Jaffee & Howard, 2010). A 2015 study of the impact of ethical certifications on farmworkers, spanning 13 countries and eight commodities found that violations of ethical standards were widespread, and common in the realms of health and safety, freedom of association and collective bargaining, payment of a living wage, non-discrimination, and security of employment (van der Wal & Scheele, 2015). This finding supports the argument that the auditing systems of ethical certifications are not always sufficient to consistently enforce standards.

Dovetailing with declining producer representation and regulatory power, Jaffee and Howard also contend that mainstreaming and corporate co-optation has, since the emergence of the fair trade movement, exerted pressure to erode ethical standards. They cite numerous examples, such as Transfair USA's abandonment in 2000 of a standard that had required at least 5% of volume purchased to be certified in order for a manufacturer (i.e. coffee roaster) to carry the seal, allowing Starbucks' entry to the system with only 1% of its retail volume certified. In 2005, Nestlé unveiled a Fairtrade certified product, 'Partner's Blend', which represented less than 1% of its volume. The perceived tokenism of this corporate engagement with fair trade drew angry criticism, with the UK organisation, the World Development Movement, saying at the time:

> If Nestlé really believes in fair trade coffee, it will alter its business practices and lobbying strategies and radically overhaul its business to ensure that all coffee farmers get a fair return for their efforts. Until then, Nestlé will remain part of the problem, not the solution. (Quoted in Moberg & Lyon, 2010, p. 12)

The steady erosion of Fairtrade's standards can also be evidenced in a gradual decline in minimum coffee prices compared with inflation. The minimum Fairtrade price for coffee was established in 1988 and not pegged to inflation. Although there have been small upwards adjustments since then (in 2007 and 2011), the price has declined in real terms. In 1988, the Fairtrade floor price for washed Arabica coffee was US$1.26/lb, in 2017 it had risen to $1.60/lb. If the Fairtrade price had kept pace with inflation, it would now be $2.61/lb.[1] Although the floor price did protect farmers during an oversupply crisis in 2011, it has been well below the market price on average since 2007, and studies have indicated that Fairtrade farmgate prices have sometimes been below the cost of production (Howson, 2015). Weakened standards have also been observed in organics (Jaffee & Howard, 2010, p. 391).

Alongside the co-optation of existing movements, Fridell and colleagues (2008) identified other strategic phases in the early corporate response to ethical trade initiatives. In a study of the 'big four' coffee-buying oligopsony (consisting of Kraft, Procter and Gamble, Nestlé and Sara Lee), they illustrate that the initial corporate response to fair trade's increasing visibility was to deploy de-legitimising narratives. The corporate actors denounced fair trade's approach as naïve and ultimately damaging to farmers, as a price floor would result in oversupply and a downward trend in market prices. Instead, higher-cost producers should be incentivised to 'diversify' into other food production or into plantation models. The authors contended that this would mean large numbers of small farmers entering into the precarious informal urban economy (Fridell et al., 2008, p. 17). Fridell and colleagues also found that a common corporate counter-strategy was to adopt key signifiers of ethical development discourse in their messaging, in an effort to stave off calls for engagement with stringent third-party certifications. Discourses around social responsibility, partnership, and sustainability became rapidly incorporated into branding strategies from the 1990s onwards.

The coffee oligopsony began implementing philanthropic programmes in their supplier communities from the 2000s, and increased supply-chain monitoring measures (Fridell et al., 2008; Mutersbaugh, 2005). Some also implemented 'direct-buying' initiatives which follow a similar logic to that of the fair trade movement, in eliminating middle men to increase the profit-share returned to primary producers. Nestlé in particular has an extensive direct buying programme whereby growers can sell directly to the company's buying stations in their local area (Fridell et al., 2008). While such initiatives have the potential to positively impact the livelihoods of commodity-dependent communities, little third-party evaluation of their efficacy is available. Indeed, as Fridell and colleagues qualify: "The lack of independent, third-party veri-fication means that we must rely on Nestlé itself to quantify the benefits of its program" (2008, p. 20). This is the key limitation that distinguishes internal corporate ethical sourcing programmes from fair trade.

Multiple corporations have followed suit with in-house schemes that appro-priate the language of fair trade and environmental certification, but have less rigorous standards. In 2016, Mondelez International, the parent company of Cadbury, announced a new programme called 'Cocoa Life' to replace its Fairtrade certification (Stock, 2017). Confusingly, FLO-Cert (the independ-ent auditing body of Fairtrade) will be retained to carry out auditing against Mondelez's own standards, and in 2017 it was suggested that products might still carry Fairtrade's 'corporate logo', very similar to the official Fairtrade mark. This ongoing partnership with Fairtrade allows Mondelez to continue to benefit from the movement's credibility, even while replacing most of its standards and protections. Critics have argued that Cocoa Life's requirements are not as stringent as those of Fairtrade – lacking a minimum pricing structure, and that the new scheme creates confusion for consumers as to what is the most ethical standard.

As Fairtrade continues to diversify into new products, supermarkets are also looking for ways to gain more control over their ethical sourcing profiles. In June 2017, the UK supermarket giant Sainsbury, hitherto the world's largest retailer of Fairtrade products, announced plans to do away with the Fairtrade label on its own tea brand, replacing it with the phrase 'fairly traded'. This move has left the social premium which farmers had relied on in serious doubt. As various buyers implement in-house initiatives, which closely mimic established certifications, producers come under pressure to comply with not one, but multiple sets of standards, and to pay multiple certification and auditing fees. A further consequence of this new arena of competition and differentiation between large agri-food retailers is that the prohibitive costs of compliance with multiple certifications incentivises supplier loyalty and even network enclosure, as it makes it more difficult for suppliers to shop around between buyers.

Perhaps the most hotly debated outcome of Fairtrade's mainstreaming in the 2010s was the expansion of Fairtrade certification to hired labour plantations (Raynolds, 2017). This move was read by some as a signal of Fairtrade's commercialisation, and a concession to corporate stakeholders. Social certification emerged in the realm of smallholder production to protect farming livelihoods in low-income countries, and relied on the institution of a democratically managed cooperative to negotiate with buyers and oversee the allocation of social premiums. Although parallel ethical trade schemes had already emerged, which monitored working conditions in large-scale factory and plantation production, adherents of the fair trade movement saw plantations as antithetical to the goals of fair trade, and many continue to do so despite Fairtrade's adoption of a standard for hired labour in 2015. In response to these trends within the Fairtrade movement, a new ethical labelling initiative emerged, instigated by the Coordinating Body of Latin America and the Caribbean, the *Simbolo de Pequeños Productores* or Small Producers' Symbol (SPP) is a dedicated certification system for small producers governed by an NGO – the Foundation of Organised Small Producers. SPP standards include strict limits on the number of hired workers at a certified site, and also impose standards on buyers, including a commitment to annual volume growth of SPP certified products.

Power Imbalances and Certification as Neoliberal Governance

As the previous section has shown, the practice of ethical certification, both independent and corporate-controlled, has become increasingly focused on traceability, rather than partnership-driven development. Auld et al. (2015) describe certifications as existing along a continuum between the competing logics of *empowerment* and *control*. The authors argue that certifications usually begin by prioritising the logic of empowerment, and over time come to privilege the logic of control. This evolutionary-institutionalist interpretation is a useful starting point for understanding the extent to which certifications incorporate the interests of disadvantaged parties within their governance structures in order to effect empowerment. Where certifications prioritise a logic of control, they can serve as tools for lead firms to coordinate the activities of supply chain actors. Similarly, using global value chains analysis,

Ponte (2009), Guthman (2007), and others have argued that ethical certification is a tool of neoliberal governance. That is, ethical certification enables
lead firms to exercise power to control flows of profit in production networks.
A key insight from the empowerment/control framing is that each of these
logics facilitates different distributive outcomes (Cafaggi & Pistor, 2015). For
example, as Auld et al. (2015) show, the "control then empower" path may
increase wealth accumulation for producers but might not necessarily translate
to increased power and regulatory capabilities, whereas on the "empower then
control" path, the increased inclusion of quality conventions and corporate
retailers might shift the balance of power to the buying end of the value chain.

Certifications attempt to incorporate the concerns of a range of diverse
actors from non-profit, to cooperative, to corporate, and as such involve
myriad forms of interaction and contestation along a spectrum from partnership to conflict. Because they aim to foster areas of cooperation amongst
divergent interests, they are sites of conflict, negotiation, and power imbalance
(Mutersbaugh et al., 2005; Renard, 2005). Actors jostle to determine who
can access certification, who benefits from it, and who controls legitimacy.
In some instances, certification frameworks (especially those targeted at
larger-scale suppliers with no price incentive for participation) may allow lead
firms to 'drive' value chains by transmitting and monitoring technical and
quality requirements through the use of a third-party at little cost (Guthman,
2007; Heynen & Robbins, 2005; Ponte, 2009). As the costs of certification
and auditing are covered by suppliers, this is a method of codifying production
requirements, outsourcing the monitoring of compliance, and moving the costs
upstream, to the supply base (Mutersbaugh et al., 2005; Ponte, 2009).

While Fairtrade certification requires periodic auditing of the activities of
primary producers, distributors, and manufacturers, and imposes auditing fees
on those participants, it does not require retailers to comply with standards. As
Northern retailers remain the most powerful actors within agri-food networks,
this has been read as a concession to power, and the maintenance of top-down
governance structures. An implicit criticism of Fairtrade's lack of focus on
retailer conduct was reflected in the emergence of a competitor, the World
Fair Trade Organisation (WFTO), in 2007, to oversee a fair trade certification
system that incorporated the whole supply chain, and demanded that members
trade 100% in fair trade certified products. WFTO tends to certify smaller
speciality retailers more committed to direct trade relationships.

Organisational capacity, management experience, and education and lit-
eracy levels within producer cooperatives all have a significant influence
on the potential for certification to facilitate an equitable partnership across
production networks. Some Fairtrade impact studies over the past two decades,
including Shreck (2002) in Dominican bananas, Lyon (2006) in Guatemalan
coffee and Howson (2015) in East Timorese coffee, have documented a lack

of understanding of what fair trade means, amongst producers belonging to a certified cooperative. Shreck found that "Only half of the growers interviewed from [certified cooperatives] expressed knowledge of what Fair Trade was, and few seemed to understand how it worked" (p. 19). This is of course in contravention of most fair trade standards, which stipulate the implementation of training, organisational capacity building, access to resources about fair trade, and avenues for complaint or recourse for producers. However, the producers in Shreck's case study possessed a mean 2.5 years of formal education (p. 16), which would feasibly limit their ability to comprehensively participate in technical aspects of democratic cooperative management. Sarah Lyon's research in Guatemala reinforces and builds on Shreck's findings. Lyon found that out of 53 members of a fair trade certified coffee cooperative interviewed, only three were familiar with the term Fairtrade. To Lyon, this was indicative of a considerable power imbalance in the Fairtrade system.

In a related discussion, Cafaggi and Pistor (2015) distinguish between the concept of regulatory capacity, and that of regulatory capability. While the latter refers to the ability to advantageously *comply* with pre-existing regulatory regimes, as determined by the presence of relevant skill sets and access to information and resources, the former denotes the ability of constituencies to choose between governance options, and to participate in the rulemaking process. Regulatory capacity has been the focus of attention for development practitioners, who have aimed to improve the ability of marginalised actors to participate more effectively within 'regulatory regimes' such as gaining a better market position by implementing best-practice production standards. Cafaggi and Pistor call for a shift in attention away from regulatory compliance and towards regulatory capability, or the ability of farmers and workers to *choose* ethical certification, and to participate in standards-setting. This does not imply that capacity building is not of ongoing importance to development and empowerment, but rather that capacity-building activities should focus on improving the ability of marginalised actors to regulate, not simply to comply with, pre-set rules. True empowerment means the ability to participate in determining the rules that govern one's own life.

However, a well-documented power imbalance in many certification governance structures allows powerful actors the ability to direct the standards and implementation of certifications to their advantage. The mechanisms of certification are particularly appealing to Northern corporations as a way of outsourcing supply chain monitoring. Externalising monitoring systems at the cost of producers is one way buyers are able to appropriate the value generated by certification. One case study undertaken by Klooster (2005) emphasised this point, through analysis of the Forest Stewardship Council (FSC) environmental certification. In this case, increased market-driven regulation has not translated into increased bargaining power for small or medium-level producers in the Global South. Klooster highlighted that certification enhanced the capability of retailers to more effectively govern the value chain in a hands-off way. He concluded that in the case of the FSC, an activist concern about the sustainability of the industry has been transformed into a highly technical, buyer-driven instrument for sourcing large volumes of certified products, and that this model favours larger-scale production, due to the costs and requirements it imposes on suppliers. This trend also contributes to network enclosure and lock in – as suppliers' ability to contract with more than one buyer is diminished due to the financial and opportunity costs of complying with multiple certification schemes. In such cases we see ethical certification functioning as a tool of buyer-driven value chain governance, and a tool of control.

Beyond the empowerment/control debate, which remains focused on the *effectiveness* of ethical certification at bringing about empowerment within capitalist structures, a deeper question remains as to whether ethical certification itself legitimises exploitative structures. Ethical certification essentially relies on the market to define and implement justice and ethics in cross-border trade, by attaching ethical value to a commodity. This ethical value is only realised if consumers are willing to validate it, by choosing a product imbued with ethical value (certified) over a non-certified equivalent. Therefore, in the logic of ethical certification, it ultimately comes down to the individual consumer to decide what ethics mean in a given production network, or to at least valorise ethical signifiers. This is a fundamentally neoliberal logic. Here, ethics and justice are not the domain of state institutions or government, but instead become both domains of and infrastructures for *governance* (Guthman, 2007, p. 466). In appealing directly to end consumers, the logic of ethical certification makes supply network conditions everybody's responsibility (or at least people with the relative economic power to make reflexive consumption choices). This devolution of responsibility from institutions to individuals (or what Judith Butler (2010) calls "responsibalization") is not unique to ethical certification, but has been visible in many aspects of our economic lives under neoliberal capitalism. In production network relations, the effect of responsibalisation is similar to that in other sites of struggle for social and economic justice. Positioning the individual consumer as the agent with the power to create a more ethical system of production and trade devolves responsibility for structural and collective problems (e.g. postcolonial inequality and exploitation between countries). In so doing, it serves to increasingly obscure those structures.

Deepening Inequalities at Production Level?

While ethical certification schemes have continued to expand over the past three decades, many have pointed out that the key instruments of standards-setting and verification necessarily impose boundaries of inclusion and exclusion in ethical value networks (Guthman, 2007; Mutersbaugh, 2005). Despite Fair Trade's [the general movement – 'Fairtrade' is the particular labelling scheme; fair trade is the generic concept – see footnote 1 in Chapter 11] underpinning objective of empowerment for those most marginalised in global trade, observers have pointed out that, in some cases, the cost of certification, and the organisational capacity required to maintain it, effectively bars the poorest producers and most vulnerable workers from participating (Goodman, 2004). Further to this, certification is alleged to increase the gap between the included and excluded – rewarding those who already possess an advantage, while reducing options for the poorest producers.

FLO-Cert certification requires a significant amount of both financial and social capital to attain. Currently, a smallholder producer organisation of average size would pay an initial certification fee of approximately €5100, and a further €3900 annually.[2] In other realms of certification, such as some organic schemes, producers have also been required to pay the costs of travel and accommodation for international auditors (Barrett et al., 2002). The choice of certification body is often stipulated by trade partners such as European importers or retailers, leaving producers unable to utilise local auditors, who are likely to be cheaper. Moreover, organic certification requires a three-year period of transition and reduced yields, an impossible expense for many. Access to the resources necessary to produce goods of higher quality has also been shown to be an important determinant of access to Fairtrade networks. In the case of smallholder coffee, Valkila and Nygren (2009) found that farmers who lacked the resources to improve their coffee's quality were unable to participate in Fairtrade networks. My own research with a coffee cooperative in Timor-Leste found the same correlations between limited resources, lower quality, and exclusion from Fairtrade (Howson, 2015).

In addition to capital, entry into ethical certification generally requires technical knowledge and institutional capacity (Raynolds et al., 2007). As Goodman (2004) highlighted, "Complying with production and quality standards denotes a sophisticated institutional structure that may or may not be attainable or maintainable for many cooperatives or small farmers" (p. 909). As fair trade grows in scope and popularity, the technical and volume requirements of buyers increase, favouring larger and more commercialised suppliers. This trend has been documented in several studies, including of coffee cooperatives in Mexico (Pérez-Grovas & Renard, 2007), quinoa producers in Bolivia (Cáceres et al., 2007), tea and coffee producers in South India (Neilson & Pritchard, 2010), and coffee producers in Nicaragua (Valkila & Nygren, 2009). Again, this commercialising trend facilitates a shift in focus towards ethically certifying plantation agriculture, which displaces smallholdings (Raynolds, 2014).

Neilson and Pritchard's (2010) research in South India is one of few studies that has taken, in their words, a 'horizontal approach' to assessing the impacts of certification on whole regional production systems. They explicitly investigate the effects of certification for development and empowerment of wider farming communities. Has the rising tide of ethical certification lifted all boats, or a few? While the authors highlight the need for more empirically-grounded research on this question, their observations suggest that certification may serve to exacerbate inequalities within producing regions. Participation in ethical trade may shift emphasis away from locally-driven development.

The authors distinguish between fair trade and ethical trade in this context, noting that fair trade includes the provision of price premiums to producers and workers, whist ethical trade introduces and monitors compliance with minimum standards, often as part of a mandatory "de facto" upstream regulatory structure, while offering no financial benefits for participation (Neilson & Pritchard, 2010, p. 1841). As Neilson and Pritchard found, the former is sought by a small subset of higher-quality producers to further differentiate their brands in high-value market niches, whereas the latter is imposed on the majority of primary commodity producers fetching the basic market price, and simply represents an added cost. This issue is also emphasised by Klooster (2005) with regard to environmental forest certification. In South Indian tea and coffee production, Fairtrade appears to be exclusively attainable for commercial producers with economies of scale: "It is clear that, in India at least, the organisational requirements of obtaining Fairtrade certification are beyond the capacity of most smallholder producers without some kind of development assistance" (Neilson & Pritchard, 2010, p. 1846). This effectively creates spaces of exclusion, deepening regional inequalities.

Centralisation and De-contextualisation

Mirroring the hegemonic development discourse of neoliberalism itself, market-driven ethical development constitutes a universalising and essentialising view of development, which effectively disregards the specificities of local contexts and local perspectives. The increasing codification of Fairtrade and competing certifications, on the one hand, allows for consistency and standardisation, but on the other hand constitutes a one-size-fits-all approach to ethics and justice. Although a key element of ethical certification philosophy is the mission of re-embedding products in the conditions of their provenance, certifications such as Fairtrade are a globalising discourse which leave little room for the meaningful assertion of local values, epistemologies, needs, or different forms of economic organisation.

There is limited research on the sensitivity of international certification schemes to geographical context, however, some case studies have shortcomings in the top-down centralised approach of many certifications. In a comparative study of ethical labour certifications in the Kenyan cut flower industry, the South African fruit industry, and Zambian vegetable production, Tallontire et al. (2005) identified geographically specific issues that were not being addressed by international codes. They showed that these industries had particularly high levels of temporary, seasonal, and casual work, which was less likely to be protected by certifications. Further, they showed that women were over-represented in these precarious types of employment. The authors argued that codes driven by overseas consumers or retailers, which implemented universal criteria, had largely failed to benefit women workers in these industries, due to the particular nature of horticultural employment in Sub-Saharan Africa. The study asserts that "it is only by addressing the local gendered economy that working conditions are likely to improve through codes of practice. A top-down approach to code implementation will neither adequately address embedded gender inequality nor reach marginalised workers" (Tallontire et al., 2005, p. 569).

Despite the homogenising effects of globalisation, each production context retains its own social relations, physical geography, evolutionary pathways, and path dependencies. Ethical challenges and solutions naturally differ from place to place. However, local issues and local voices are increasingly subsumed into globalised discourses that codify and cement definitions of what is ethical. It is therefore important for research on the impacts of ethical certification to examine the geographical contingency of the outcomes of certification, and the extent to which local social and economic relations support or constrain its potential for development and empowerment.

CONCLUSION: CARRYING ETHICAL CERTIFICATION STUDIES FORWARD

Numerous commentators have pointed out the inherent paradox of certifications which attempt to use market mechanisms to respond to the inequities of global capitalism (see Bidwell et al., 2018; Modelo, 2014). While ethical certification may be read as an inherent critique of neoliberalism, in that it attempts to regulate global markets to produce more equitable and sustainable outcomes, it also relies wholly on consumer demand to do so. In this pursuit, ethical certification monetises and fetishises ethicality. A key question in the literature has been: does ethical trade constitute resistance to neoliberalism, or is it a particular manifestation of it? This chapter has addressed the main constraints on the ability of ethical certification to facilitate avenues out of commodity dependence and towards empowerment for commodity producers in low-income countries, based on existing empirical and theoretical work since the 1990s.

Certain themes are present throughout this analysis. First, the main-streaming of ethical certification has led to its increased domination by large corporate actors, who are influencing standards, and shifting emphasis from empowerment to control. Second, simultaneous processes of embedding and disembedding have occurred through the rise of ethical certification. While commodities may have become re-embedded in their territorial and social origins in the imaginations of consumers, through the increased marketing of place, ethics themselves have become disembedded from the cultural and economic contexts which they formally and informally regulate. The ethical conventions governing production have become codified and universalised through top-down standard-setting, losing an element of geographic sensitivity in this process. What do these trajectories of fetishisation and homogenisation of ethics mean for producers in the South, in both conventional and certified value networks? Although some sustainable development and value chain upgrading progress has been identified in selected case studies, overall com-mentators have painted a discouraging picture of the ability of ethical certifi-cation to contribute to empowerment at the local scale. The ongoing costs of certification, limited representation of producers in certification governance structures, and limited access to training and capacity-building have all cast doubt on a more equitable redistribution of power and profit in EVeNs.

In examining new relationships of governance and power in EVeNs, perhaps the most fundamental question to be asked of privately governed certifications of fairness, ethicality, and sustainability is: who decides what is fair, ethical, and sustainable? These claims are normative, non-specific and open to manip-ulation. If we acknowledge that, as Goodman (2004) pointed out, consumers can only possess limited or imperfect information about the products they are buying, and that claims to ethicality are communicated through symbols, images, and cultural meaning and rest primarily on trust, then we must accept that the ability of reflexive consumers to define what is ethical is not informed or objective, but is mediated by marketing and commercial interests. Can we rely on compliance with centrally formulated standards to ensure products have been produced ethically? Proliferating ethical certifications have differ-ent levels of ethical standards and, furthermore, as local impact studies reveal, systems of compliance have produced very different outcomes in different contexts. Should consumers conclude that there is a spectrum of fairness within fair trade? Or that, for example, one Fairtrade certified product may not be quite as fair as another?

A number of areas requiring further empirical inquiry have been alluded to. A lot of the thinking on the topic simply requires updating. Recent devel-opments have taken place within the wider ethical trade movement, and some issues require renewed scrutiny. This includes the impacts of the expansion of ethical certification (and particularly fair trade) into hired labour and plantation production. Researchers are beginning to examine this trend but it demands extensive assessment of both its potential to benefit a broader base of marginalised network participants, and its potential to further weaken the vision of the fair trade movement by facilitating economies of scale controlled by corporate oligopsonies, placing smallholders at a disadvantage. Ethical certification is also increasingly expanding into new products with market circumstances very different to the original tropical trio of coffee, cocoa, and bananas. Wine, for example, is a relative newcomer to social and environmental certification. It can be a highly embedded product with a broad quality differential, and may not be subject to the same precariousness as primary commodities such as coffee (Overton & Murray, 2013, 2016). Because wine in effect 'sells place', industrial clustering is a common feature of wine production (Murray & Overton, 2011; Overton & Murray, 2013, 2016). More research is called for in order to understand how such products fare in ethical markets – whether, for instance, there is sufficient consumer demand for ethically certified wine to secure the market advantages necessary for benefits to be passed on to producers and workers.

Another relatively new trend in EVeNs is a growing convergence in the scope of ethical certifications – an increasing consolidation of social, environmental, technical, and traceability standards into single certifications. Scant analysis has scrutinised the impacts of this at various network scales. Furthermore, while the scope of individual certifications is broadening, the number of separate certifications is proliferating, as more and more firms and industries develop their own ethical assurance schemes. The question of the extent to which this proliferation is leading to competition or co-operation amongst certifications is deserving of more scholarly attention.

Finally, few have taken a truly integrated view of the contribution of all ethical certifications operating within a given industry, or a given region. Although some scholars have identified this deficit, the majority of ethical trade and fair trade impact research comprises specific isolated case studies. A consolidated approach would acknowledge both the heterogeneity of certifications, and their commonalities; their common philosophy, methods, and discourse. This methodology includes, and goes beyond, Neilson and Pritchard's (2010) 'horizontal' analysis of the development outcomes of a particular certification for all producers in a region, both certified and non-certified, and asks how have all social, environmental and geographical certifications impacted ethical development in a case study industry or location, and what macro-scale function do they fulfil vis-à-vis global capitalist relations?

NOTES

1. The cumulative rate of inflation of the US dollar between 1988 and 2017 was calculated at 106.9%, using the online inflation calculator tool, at http://www.u sinflationcalculator.com/ (accessed 16 August 2017).
2. Calculated using the FLO-Cert 'Fairtrade Certification Fee Calculator' (FLO-Cert, 2018). The average size of a producer organisation was determined by dividing the number of certified small farmers in Africa and the Middle East (978,977), by the number of certified producer organisations (286) (data taken from Fairtrade International's annual report, Fair Trade International, 2016). Calculation based on an organisation that owns no 'processing installations' and uses three 'subcontracted entities'.

REFERENCES

Auld, G., Renckens, S., & Cashore, B. (2015). Transnational private governance between the logics of empowerment and control. *Regulation and Governance*, *9*(2), 108–124.

Barrett, H., Browne, A., Harris, P., & Cadoret, K. (2002). Organic certification and the UK market: organic imports from developing countries. *Food Policy*, *27*(4), 301–318.

Bidwell, S., Murray, W. E., & Overton, J. (2018). Ethical agro-food networks in global peripheries, Part I: The rise and recommodification of fair trade and organics. *Geography Compass*, *12*(4), online DOI: 10.1111/gec3.12366 11pp.

Bowen, S. (2010). Development from within? The potential for geographical indications in the Global South. *The Journal of World Intellectual Property*, *13*(2), 231–252.

Bowen, S. & Mutersbaugh, T. (2014). Local or localized? Exploring the contributions of Franco-Mediterranean agrifood theory to alternative food research. *Agriculture and Human Values*, 31, 201–213.

Butler, J. (2010). *When is life grievable?* Verso.

Cáceres, Z., Carimentrand, A., & Wilkinson, J. (2007). Fair trade and quinoa from the Southern Bolivian Altiplano. In L.T. Raynolds, D. Murray, & J. Wilkinson (Eds.), *Fair trade: The challenges of transforming globalization* (pp. 180–199). Routledge.

Cafaggi, F., & Pistor, K. (2015). Regulatory capabilities: A normative framework for assessing the distributional effects of regulation. *Regulation and Governance*, *9*(2), 95–107.

Child, C. (2015). Mainstreaming and its discontents: Fair trade, socially responsible investing, and industry trajectories. *Journal of Business Ethics*, *130*(3), 601–618.

Dalvai, R. (2017, 10 August). The metamorphosis of fair trade. WFTO. Retrieved from http://www.wfto.com/our-path-fair-trade/metamorphosis-fair-trade

Fair Trade International (2016). *Annual Report 2015–16*. Retrieved from: http://www.fairtrade.net/annual-reports.html, December 2016.

FLO-Cert (2018). Cost Calculator. Retrieved from: https://www.flocert.net/solutions/fairtrade-resources/cost-calculator/, May 2018.

Fridell, M., Hudson, I., & Hudson, M. (2008). With friends like these: The corporate response to fair trade coffee. *Review of Radical Political Economics*, *40*(1), 8–34.

Gereffi, G., Humphrey, J., & Sturgeon, T. (2005). The governance of global value chains. *Review of International Political Economy*, *12*(1), 78–104.

Goodman, D. (2004). Rural Europe redux? Reflections on alternative agri-food networks and paradigm change. *Sociologia Ruralis*, *44*, 3–16.

Griffiths, P. (2012). Ethical objections to fair trade. *Journal of Business Ethics*, *105*, 357–373.

Guthman, J. (2007). The Polanyian way? Voluntary food labels as neoliberal governance. *Antipode*, *39*(3), 456–478.

Heynen, N., & Robbins, P. (2005). The neoliberalization of nature: Governance, privatization, enclosure and valuation. *Capitalism Nature Socialism*, *16*(1), 5–8.

Howson, K. (2015). *Fair trade for whom: The contribution of Fair Trade to combatting trade inequities faced by East Timorese coffee producers*. Master's thesis, Victoria University of Wellington.

Hughes, A. (2005). Geographies of exchange and circulation: Alternative trading spaces. *Progress in Human Geography*, *29*(4), 496–504.

Hughes, A., Wrigley, N., & Buttle, M. (2008). Global production networks, ethical campaigning, and the embeddedness of responsible governance. *Journal of Economic Geography*, *8*(3), 345–367.

Jaffee, D. (2012). Weak coffee: Certification and co-optation in the fair trade movement. *Social Problems*, *59*(1), 94–116.

Jaffee, D., & Howard, P. (2010). Corporate co-optation of organic and fair trade standards. *Agriculture and Human Values*, *27*, 387–399.

Klooster, D. (2005). Environmental certification of forests: The evolution of environmental governance in a commodity network. *Journal of Rural Studies*, *21*(4), 403–417.

Lyon, S. (2006). Evaluating fair trade consumption: Politics, defetishization and producer participation. *International Journal of Consumer Studies*, *30*(5), 452–464.

McCarthy, J. (2006). Rural geography: Alternative rural economies – the search for alterity in forests, fisheries, food, and fair trade. *Progress in Human Geography*, *30*(6), 803–811.

Moberg, M., & Lyon, S. (2010). *Fair trade and social justice: Global ethnographies*. NYU Press.

Modelo, M. (2014). The paradox of fair trade. *Stanford Social Innovation Review*. http://ssir.org/articles/entry/the_paradox_of_fair_trade

Murray, W.E., & Overton, J. (2011). Defining regions: The making of places in the New Zealand wine industry. *Australian Geographer*, *42*(4), 419–433.

Mutersbaugh, T. (2005). Just-in-space: Certified rural products, labor of quality, and regulatory spaces. *Journal of Rural Studies*, *21*(4), 389–402.

Neilson, J., & Pritchard, B. (2010). Fairness and ethicality in their place: The regional dynamics of fair trade and ethical sourcing agendas in the plantation districts of South India. *Environment and Planning A*, *42*(8), 1833–1851.

Overton, J., & Murray, W.E. (2013). Class in a glass: Capital, neoliberalism and social space in the global wine industry. *Antipode*, *45*(3), 702–718.

Overton, J., & Murray, W.E. (2016). Fictive place. *Progress in Human Geography*, *40*(6), 794–809.

Pérez-Grovas, V., & Renard, M.-C. (2007). Fair trade coffee in Mexico: At the centre of the debates. In L.T. Raynolds, D.L. Murray, & J. Wilkinson (Eds.), *Fair trade: The challenges of transforming globalization* (pp. 138–156). Routledge.

Ponte, S. (2009). Governing through quality: Conventions and supply relations in the value chain for South African wine. *Sociologia Ruralis*, *49*(3), 236–257.

Ponte, S., & Ewert, J. (2009). Which way is 'up' in upgrading? Trajectories of change in the value chain for South African wine. *World Development*, *37*(10), 1637–1650.

Raynolds, L.T. (2000). Re-embedding global agriculture: The international organic and fair trade movements. *Agriculture and Human Values, 17*(3), 297–309.

Raynolds, L.T. (2012). Fair trade: Social regulation in global food markets. *Journal of Rural Studies, 28*, 276–287.

Raynolds, L.T. (2014). Fairtrade, certification, and labor: Global and local tensions in improving conditions for agricultural workers. *Agriculture and Human Values, 31*(3), 499–511.

Raynolds, L.T. (2017). Fairtrade labour certification: The contested incorporation of plantations and workers. *Third World Quarterly, 38*(7), 1473–1492.

Raynolds, L.T., Murray, A P.E.D., Murray, D., & Wilkinson, J. (2007). *Fair trade: The challenges of transforming globalization*. Routledge.

Renard, M.-C. (2005). Quality certification, regulation and power in fair trade. *Journal of Rural Studies, 21*(4), 419–431.

Shreck, A. (2002). Just bananas? Fair trade banana production in the Dominican Republic. *International Journal of Sociology of Agriculture and Food, 10*(2), 13–23.

Sidwell, M. (2008). *Unfair trade*. ASI (Research) Ltd.

Stiglitz, J.E. (2007). *Making globalization work*. Norton.

Stock, R. (2017, February 26). Is Cadbury's in-house 'Cocoa-Life' the same as Fairtrade? *Stuff*. Retrieved from http://www.stuff.co.nz/business/89720276/Is -Cadburys-in-house-Cocoa-Life-the-same-as-Fairtrade

Tallontire, A., Dolan, C., Smith, S., & Barrientos, S. (2005). Reaching the marginalised? Gender value chains and ethical trade in African horticulture. *Development in Practice, 15*(3-4), 559–571.

Valkila, J., & Nygren, A. (2009). Impacts of fair trade certification on coffee farmers, cooperatives, and laborers in Nicaragua. *Agriculture and Human Values, 27*(3), 321–333.

van der Wal, S., & Scheele, F. (2015). *Goodness guaranteed: Assessing the impact of sustainability certification on the labour conditions of farm workers*. SOMO.

PART II

Locality studies

6 Discursive power in ethical value networks: an analysis of the South African wine industry

Kelle Howson

INTRODUCTION

Because ethical certifications aim to foster areas of cooperation amongst divergent interests, they are sites of conflict, negotiation, and power imbalance (Mutersbaugh et al., 2005; Renard, 2003) The ethical value networks they establish attempt to balance the concerns of diverse actors, ranging from non-profit, to cooperative, and corporate enterprises, and as such involve myriad forms of interaction along a spectrum from partnership to conflict (Becchetti & Huybrechts, 2008). Actors jostle to determine who can access certification, who benefits from it, and who controls legitimacy. Many case studies of EVeNs have focused on tracing the impact of ethical certification on the distribution of value and profit in networks, to draw conclusions about the overall potential of certification to create more even outcomes in terms of the distribution of power and profit. However, few case studies have probed the discursive dimensions of ethical certification adoption in specific places, in order to understand how their construction and outcomes are historically and socially contingent. This chapter draws on qualitative fieldwork conducted with wine producers and other stakeholders in South Africa's Western Cape in 2016, and completed in 2018,[1] in order to elucidate the power discourses surrounding ethical certification in this context, and what they reveal about changing patterns of agency, wealth and power in the wake of South Africa's transition to democracy, and enduring racial inequality (see Figure 6.1 for the location of the wine producing regions).

This chapter explores the constructions of meaning, or narratives, which have emerged to explain the role of ethical certification in the South African wine industry. I seek to answer the questions of why South African wine producers have entered EVeNs, how they conceptualise the role of certification in their operations, and what outcomes they hope to generate. Unlike many other producing contexts in the Global South where ethical certification is pursued by smallholders in order to increase their collective bargaining power and improve their terms of trade, in the commercialised plantation context of the South African wine industry, the decision to adopt ethical certification is usually made by those with a significant amount of power, at least on a local scale. These actors have power not only in terms of employment and working conditions, but also in terms of the cultural construction of meaning, and strategic framing (Zald, 1996). This latter form of 'soft' power plays an important role in dictating industry relations and reproducing inequities.

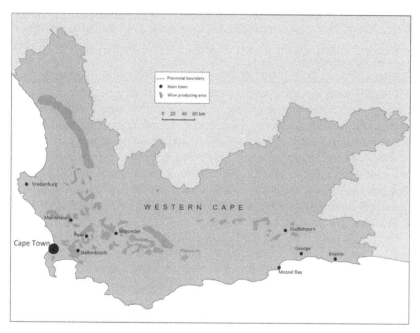

Figure 6.1   Wine producing regions of Western Cape, South Africa

BACKGROUND TO THE SOUTH AFRICAN WINE INDUSTRY

In 2019, the export value of the South African wine industry was ZAR8.5 billion, down 7% on the previous year due to unfavourable weather conditions (WOSA, 2020). A 2015 report provides a breakdown of the demographic distribution of wine earnings. Of the income created in 2015, 53% remained in the Western Cape, illustrating the economic importance of the wine industry to the region. A further illustration is the fact that the industry employs 167,494 people in the Western Cape, and 289,151 nationally (including in tourism). Of this number, 55.6% of jobs are unskilled, compared with 29.3% semi-skilled and 15% skilled (Conningarth Economists, 2015). Household income generated by the wine industry amounted to R23,579 million in 2015, of which R3994 million (approximately 17%) reached lower-income groups.

Previous scholarship on ethical certification in the South African wine industry has generated a series of critiques and predicted barriers to ethical certification's ability to facilitate meaningfully ethical production and emancipatory empowerment. Cheryl McEwan and David Bek in particular have criticised the potential for certification to depoliticise empowerment (McEwan & Bek, 2006) and "the meaning and nature of transformation" (McEwan & Bek, 2009, p. 256). Andries Du Toit has been critical of what he has viewed as imported 'social technologies' as a strategy for 'normalising and regularising' existing power relations (Du Toit, 2002). Kruger and colleagues (2007) have contended that ethical certification performs a useful dual function for producers, allowing them to both gain credibility with the new African National Congress (ANC) government in the early years of democracy, amid concerns about more radical state-led land redistribution, and also to gain legitimacy in international markets. Kruger et al.'s view sees ethical certification as a public relations and marketing strategy to allow producers to sanitise the reputation of South African wine, rather than a tool for the meaningful redress of social and economic injustice in the wine industry (2006). Other commentators, prominent among them Stefano Ponte (Ponte, 2009; Ponte & Ewert, 2007, 2009), have positioned the wine industry's embrace of ethical certification as a strategy for value chain upgrading to differentiate the South African brand in a crowded international marketplace, and to access a premium, value-added niche without the need for great investment in improved material quality or technological innovation.

Indeed, the transformation of land ownership and deracialisation in the wine industry lags behind other sectors of the South African economy. VinPro data revealed that, in 2017, 1.5% of wine-producing land is black-owned (Basson, 2017a). This number is vastly out of step with the demographic structure of the Cape Winelands, where only 12.9% are white. Land reform has fallen far short of targets laid out in post-apartheid policy. VinPro's 'ideal future state for 2025' envisages 20% black-owned land and water, a seemingly impossible goal based on current figures, barring the event of radical overhaul (Basson, 2017b).

In the South African wine industry, the issues of racialised wealth distribution, farm paternalism, alcohol dependence, and extreme inequality are all rooted in historical labour relations paradigms, enforced by long-established networks of power (Dooling, 2007; Du Toit, 1993; Ewert & Hamman, 1999). Scholars have described a South African 'wine industry complex', arguing that even after the transition to democracy, wine producers remain a tight-knit community, and that a network of political consensus operates which links the South African wine cluster (Bek et al., 2007, 2012; Ewert & Du Toit, 2005).

SIX NARRATIVES TO EXPLAIN THE ADOPTION OF CERTIFICATION IN SOUTH AFRICA

A majority of research participants said that their primary motivation for participating in ethical certification was market access and market positioning. While these fall under the same umbrella they are distinct: the former situates certification adoption as a minimum requirement for accessing shelf space while the latter refers to conscious value chain upgrading, a strategy undertaken by some producers to gain a more advantageous market position. While the former group tended to engage with certifications reluctantly and see them as an imposition, only participating as much as required, the latter group was more enthusiastic about certifications, and more likely to incorporate ethical associations into their own branding.

Several narratives have been identified, which participants align with when discussing the emergence of certification in the industry. These narratives are not mutually exclusive, and participants frequently employed multiple narratives in discussing their relationship with ethical certification. They are, however, distinct from each other and clearly identifiable across multiple interviews. The following narratives are considered: (1) Certification as a moral imperative and the 'right thing to do'; (2) certification as proof of existing good practice; (3) certification as a market imperative; (4) certification as persecution or punishment; (5) certification as a technocratic upgrading tool or 'social technology'; and (6) certification as a method of pacification of labour.

Every interviewee invoked at least one of the narratives, with a substantial degree of repetition. I do not take these narratives at face value, but see them as part of a conscious power discourse, as actors attempt to construct legitimising frames which play into political and economic strategies. Agatha Herman makes a similar point in her exploration of 'tactical ethics' in the South African wine industry – arguing that adaptive 'discursive tactics', including ethical discourse, are employed by actors in order to sustain formations of industry relations (Herman, 2012). Accordingly, the narratives identified are not merely reactions to novel processes but methods of interpreting and appropriating those processes to support pre-established perspectives and interests. As such, this chapter presents participants' perspectives in their own words but also interprets and reads between the lines with a critical lens to examine both superficial and strategic discourse.

The Right Thing to Do

In interviews, many producers said that they had adopted certification because they felt it was simply the right thing to do. This group expressed a moral imperative to contribute to the 'upliftment' of working communities and practice stewardship of the environment. Interviewees who aligned with this perspective used personal and emotive language. One producer said: "My decision to do Fairtrade comes from my heart and not from a business deal" (P18).[2] Generally, these producers were not forthcoming on what was unethical, or in need of transformation in the industry. However, producers who saw certification as moral often connected it with a sense of historical belonging to the land and a generational connection with their workers. Within this group, the majority represented long-established family businesses dating back generations. A certifier noted that "many of the farms are run by families, so many of them would say [ethical business] is part of our family values system" (C4). Although wine industry researchers have long seen inter-generational relationships between farmers and workers as part of an institutionalised system of consolidated power and disenfranchisement (see Du Toit, 1992, 1993; Ewert & Hamman, 1999), producers and other stakeholders said that landowning families' long-spanning relationships with their farmworkers gave them a deeper sense of social responsibility – some producers would also refer to workers as family.

While on the surface this narrative appears benevolent, the research of Andries Du Toit and others shows that it may in fact play into a discourse that casts workers as less than autonomous adults, and perpetuate a relationship of dominance and dependence (Du Toit, 1992, 1993). While much has changed on South African wine farms since the heyday of master–servant style paternalism, within this narrative there is an echo of paternalism, or what some have characterised as neo-paternalism (Ewert & Du Toit, 2005). Producers navigate a strategic conundrum in adopting ethical certification. If they choose to frame it as part of a progressive process of transformation, they position themselves as both the vehicles for and the obstacles to transformation. Although they are identifying as the agents of change, they are also demonstrating that they remain the ones with agency. When producers affirm that for them, certification is the 'right thing to do', they are potentially acknowledging past complicity in an unethical system. Therefore, this progressive narrative holds strategic advantages and disadvantages for producers – the end point of true progressivism may constitute the dismantling of the very structures that protect their social and commercial position.

Proof and Protection

One response to this tension discussed above was the assertion that South African wine producers had always practised ethical production, and that certification was simply a way of affirming and demonstrating this. For this group, certification offered a type of proof of what they had already been doing. "It's a nice tool to show to the world what we are actually doing, and have been doing all along" (P10). Producers were eager to show that they believed in the need for ethical transformation in the wine industry, while also distancing themselves from the parts of the industry that needed ethical transformation. This strategic narrative sits at the intersection between those two concerns, enabling producers to emphasise that their social and environmental practices are not the result of a recent certification process, but a tradition of ethical operation.

Another participant said, "long before I started Fairtrade I did a lot of things that Fairtrade want you to do. For instance, I built a clinic out of my money for the community, and not only my farm, for the whole community" (P18). On the surface this finding could suggest that it is the already 'ethical' operators who are more inclined to adopt ethical certification. One potential consequence could be that certifications are more likely to reach farms already implementing better practices, bypassing the most vulnerable workers and farming landscapes. This could contribute to widening the gap between good and bad farming and employment practices; benefiting communities with better working conditions whist further marginalising the rest. However, as the following sections will show, certifications are adopted for myriad reasons other than the outward declaration of a producer's pre-existing value system. That certification appeals to more self-interested or pragmatic adopters may in fact assist in mitigating its potential for uneven outcomes, and allow it to reach workers in less inherently progressive or ethical settings.

An article by industry promotions body Wines of South Africa (WOSA), on the Winelands blog in 2015 reminded producers that, "Besides the moral objective of doing the right thing, the importance of industry-wide, ethical certification for South-African wines is that it can protect the industry from unfair or poorly researched reports and media coverage" (WOSA, 2015). Many in the industry see certification as offering a form of protection from accusations of poor treatment of workers. Even though producers see themselves as socially and environmentally responsible, they worry that they may still fall victim to the attention of journalists and advocacy groups, who come with preconceived ideas and agendas. While it seems rather contradictory to assert both that you are committed to ethical operation, and you are afraid of being exposed as unethical, many producers truly believed that the risk of being accused was largely unrelated to whether you were truly ethical or not. Reports and exposés were seen as sensationalised: "Bad news always sells a story. Someone is always, always trying to, you know, dig up the dirt" (A3).

Indeed, in 2011, a report by Human Rights Watch entitled *Ripe with Abuse*, implicated wine farms in exploitative practices, including provision of substandard housing, arbitrary evictions of workers, pesticide exposure, lack of access to sanitation facilities, barriers to freedom of association and intimidation of union members, wage docking and ongoing dop practices,[3] and racial and gender discrimination (Human Rights Watch, 2011). This report, as a participant told me, was the impetus for the launch of the 'Wine Industry Ethical Trade Association' (WIETA) certification. However, the same person stated that the bulk of the report's findings came from fruit and table grape farms, and that the wine industry only represented 20% of farms surveyed. Nevertheless, because of the consumer profile of wine, the industry bore the brunt of the fallout. Thus, uptake of WIETA certification and the WIETA seal was, for some participants, an attempt to protect themselves from being targeted by such exposés, by proving their ethical credentials in advance: "People accuse you of things, and although it didn't happen to us, it would be nice then to stand back and say, 'Well, I'm WIETA accredited' and so forth" (P10).

One producer told me:

> You don't want a television series taken and some people on a farm on television say they got abused, they don't get salaries, and they have to do child labour, whatever, all of these things. So to protect the system, that's why they created this accreditation, just to make sure. (P11)

While I was conducting field research in 2016, the industry was confronting the impact of a documentary called *Bitter Grapes*, which was widely televised in Europe, and had found abuses including barriers to union membership, lack of access to drinking water and toilet facilities on farms, and pesticide exposure. Furthermore, the filmmakers alleged this to be taking place on selected WIETA and Fairtrade certified farms. The filmmakers encountered hostility from the industry. An email was circulated amongst farmers while the documentary was being made, which the journalists received and featured in the programme:

> HEADS UP: It has been brought under our attention that there are an international man and woman doing their rounds on the farms. ... They are asking unethical questions to workers and changing the angle to a negative. Be careful and avoid where possible. (In Heinemann, 2016)

Bowen Botha, Director of the large Robertson Cooperative, was featured in the documentary in a heated confrontation with the filmmaker, in which Botha accuses the filmmaker of having an agenda, refuses to shake his hand, and calls him a "disgusting piece of rubbish."[4]

Interviews also revealed that it was not only local farmers concerned about being implicated in exposés, but also international retailers increasingly requiring proof from suppliers of ethical practices, in response to the potential 'reputational risk' they faced from investigation of their supply chains. As one participant noted, "The supermarkets are really, really keen on making sure that the letter of the law has been complied with, with regard to the eco-labelling. It's a reputational risk issue" (E5).

Telling the Story: The Market Imperative

Promotion of ethical certification has been a key part of WOSA's marketing strategy for South African wine. WOSA maintains close relationships with, and input into, certification schemes, WIETA, Integrated Production of Wine (IPW), and Fairtrade, as these initiatives serve to distance the industry from negative apartheid-era associations, by leveraging the positive qualities of community and diversity. It is hoped by many in the industry that the adoption of ethical certifications across the cluster will differentiate South African wines in crowded marketplaces, and allow exports to reach higher value niches. Wine is particularly well-disposed to marketing on the basis of ethical origins. Its embeddedness in place and broad quality differential make it suited to the ethical consumption market, as much of its added value already lies in communicating information about its origin (Overton & Murray, 2016). As a stakeholder put it, "they are getting into international markets without lifting – well, just through certification" (C1). Fairtrade's own marketing to potential members has emphasised the contribution certification can make to sales and margins through improved branding. The Fairtrade Foundation launched a campaign in 2018 encouraging brands to "tell your Fairtrade story" (Fairtrade Foundation, 2018).

The idea of the certification 'story' was a common motif in field research. The perceived importance of a unified marketing message came through strongly, and participants felt that the industry needed to collectively commu-nicate a specific story about itself. Interviewees said "most of the time people just want the shortcut, they just want the happy story" (C2), and "you have to have a story behind your wine otherwise your wine is not going to sell" (C3). Many viewed ethical certifications as pre-packaged stories that they could purchase in order to bolster their branding. For these participants, certification performed the role of outsourced marketing, with the added advantage of benefiting from association with a collective and unified strategy across the South African wine cluster. WOSA's 'Wine for good social stories' marketing campaign gained traction on Twitter in 2017.

For some – especially those with capacity to satisfy the financial and organ-isational requirements of certification, and resources to devote to branding – aligning with ethical certification results in brand differentiation, access to higher value markets, and increased margins. However, as the following section discusses, some producers feel forced to participate in EVeNs, which fosters resentment towards certification and towards projects of empower-ment, development, and transformation.

Persecution and Resentment

Some producers said they had not adopted certification of their own volition but had been compelled to by market conditions and by buyers, including estates, cellars and supermarkets. The multitude of codes that producers need to comply with in order to sell wine internationally include both basic produc-tion and quality monitoring, such as ISO and HACCP, and increasingly social and environmental codes which are specified as buying conditions on tenders, or simply necessary to establish relationships with buyers. Interview partic-ipants spoke of feeling forced to adopt supposedly voluntary certifications – "it's just become a requirement for doing business by supermarkets rather than a selling point" (P15).

Susan Freidberg (2003) argued that, in the context of the Zambian cut-flower industry, the 'ethical turn' of British supermarkets resembles aspects of an earlier colonial relationship which attempted to 'civilize' Africa by bringing new technologies and systems of hygiene, social organization, and "norms of taste and behavior" (p. 34). While the majority of South African wine produc-ers have European heritage, the historical antagonism between Afrikaners and British, among other factors, may lead South African wine producers to feel subject to a neo-colonial civilising mission, which attempts to homogenise and sanitise production spaces in line with European tastes and standards. As a participant expressed it; "because Fairtrade originated in the North it is the supply pressure coming down. It's just again the market making a demand on the developing, the sourcing country or the producer country" (C1).

These negative views largely congealed around two narratives: first that conditions were imposed unfairly on South African producers because the South African wine industry is an international pariah; and second that the administrative and financial costs of maintaining certifications were unduly burdening producers, and even making it more difficult to invest in empower-ment and social initiatives at farm level. This group saw ethical certification as another form of 'policing', on top of increased labour regulation. A certifier described the exasperated attitudes they often encountered from producers,

> Just another thing you're expecting me to do, just another thing you are coming to police me on. I am absolutely persona non grata, I need to jump through hoops to appease government, to appease my workers, to appease the markets. (C1)

Some producers perceived, to put it simply, that they were still being punished for apartheid by government, consumers and buyers, despite what they felt had been significant political, industry-level, and sometimes personal efforts to address the inequities in the industry. This perpetuated a sense that outsiders who point out ongoing structural inequalities and disadvantages connected to colonialism and apartheid are being unfair. A sense of persecution came through strongly in interviews: "I feel like we've gone beyond having to suffer through collective punishment as a country" (P19).

Other participants, however, acknowledged that problems existed, but directed responsibility for this elsewhere, pointing out perceived shortcomings in government oversight of the wine industry, which have created the need for private regulation in the form of ethical certification. Some also felt there was a conscious lack of government support for agriculture and for transformation initiatives. Some interviewees claimed that the wine industry was subject to stricter requirements than other agricultural sectors in South Africa. They noted that consumers are less likely to be concerned with the conditions under which their fruit was produced for example, because they are less aware of where it comes from. Much of the resentment resulting from the imposition of certifications was connected to the idea that outsiders, such as consumers, advocacy groups and buyers, didn't understand the world of the wine farm, and didn't understand the pressures faced by producers. A local agent lamented, "Those lovely customers sitting on that side, are very happy to sit in their lovely houses drinking their fancy wine every day and expect it at a really good price and not be prepared to pay any more for it" (A3). A wine industry expert spoken to had observed a recent reversion to farm insularity in response to both labour unrest and heightened ethical scrutiny of farm practices: "So on the farms you've got mostly coloured, some Africans, but virtually everyone speaks Afrikaans, so these are the insiders, these are 'our people'. The outsiders are outsiders" (E3).

Many participants ascribed to a narrative of post-apartheid persecution, conceiving of certification as punishment. For some, ethical certification constituted not a locally-driven vehicle for sustainable development, but the policing of wine producers by outsiders. These producers felt exasperated, powerless, and victimised as a result. The resentment that producers expressed towards ethical certification did not only stem from the idea that they were being treated punitively because of the history of the industry but was also derived from the administrative and financial burdens that certification entailed. This resentment directly informed a lack of commitment to the objectives of certification on the part of producers, and reported attempts to circumvent or dilute ethical standards.

A small number of producers expressed the view that it was better to adopt ethical certification on their own terms than to have it externally imposed. These participants feel that at least schemes like WIETA and IPW have been designed with the input of South African producers, governed by the industry, and overseen and audited by people who have direct knowledge of the local context and who speak Afrikaans, as opposed to international auditors. A producer said, "Not always the [Fairtrade] auditors are South Africans, so, again, if you're not South African or you're not living in South Africa for a long time you can't exactly give suggestions to us" (P14). This perspective assumes that increased monitoring will inevitably happen, and that designing local responses to this is better than having it imposed and being passive in that process. This way, even if certain certifications become supply requirements, they are still sensitive to the local context, and understanding of local needs and limitations.

Social Technologies

Although a large number of interviewees saw ethical certification as having a wholly negative or burdensome impact on wine businesses, others saw it as being useful in ways not immediately obvious. Some participants emphasised the practical tools and services certifications offer in terms of management and administration: "[WIETA] helps me to give structure to the paperwork, to give structure to the rules, to give structure to the relationship. They know exactly what they have to have" (P14). Stefano Ponte (2009) argues that an integral part of the South African wine industry's post-apartheid modernising mission involved improving capabilities at production level through technological innovation. Producers embarked on knowledge-oriented upgrading activities; and the implementation of scientific management systems and innovative technologies to improve production efficiency and consistency. These include such things as "cultivar-terroir adaptation, vigor and yield control, and environmentally-friendly production" (Ponte & Ewert, 2009, p. 19).

A key theme is the application of science and expertise to foster improved productivity and margins, and certifications play a crucial role in disseminating implementation and measurement frameworks. Cusmano et al. (2010) also highlight the technological and knowledge-based procedures which formed a large part of the South African wine industry's 'catching-up trajectory'. However, they emphasise the application of 'social technologies' as well as physical technologies. A concept adapted from Nelson and Sampat (2001), social technologies are patterned systems of interaction and knowledge transfer "where the effective coordination of interaction is key to accomplishment" (p. 40).

It is interesting to conceptualise the emergence of standardised and codified systems of social and environmental certification as forming part of the process of building new technological and knowledge-based capabilities in response to the changing dynamics of market demand. In doing so it becomes evident that the development of ethical certifications has formed part of a push towards product standardisation and marketing innovation. Du Toit refers to this framework as a 'globalising technology of ethics' (Du Toit, 2002, p. 363). This idea was expressed by research participants, including certification representatives, who asserted that members were attracted by the technical support offered by certification:

> [We asked our members] 'what is it that keeps you sticking with us?' And some of them said that it's the extension services, which is basically the technical knowledge that our team provides to them, [...] and also the technical assistance in terms of setting up a management plan and a map for their farm. (C5)

One participant drew a parallel between systems instituted in the apartheid era, and the current traceability and sustainability certification IPW, arguing that the high level of oversight in a period when production was controlled by the state had set a precedent for systematised and measurable practices which set the industry apart from other wine producing countries:

> I mean look, largely, there are very few benefits of apartheid. But one of the benefits of apartheid is the fact we lived in a semi-police state with a lot of bureaucracy, and this system was created out of bureaucracy because the authorities wanted to control the production of wine ... And the whole process starts following it all the way through, so the system is quite thorough ... So in this day and age where traceability becomes a real point of difference, South Africa I think should really be playing to this competitive advantage more. (A1)

Some saw the role of certifications as being about streamlining operations, both physical and social, based on scientific and technical expertise. This view privileges systems and efficiency above other ideals of 'good' business, and, for some, all aspects of business – including employees – are simply systems to be improved through technological innovation. In this narrative, certification exists "...to make sure your tractors and trailers and farm workers and pesticides can all be utilised correctly, so that you don't have any disturbances to your work" (E5). Many participants saw ethical certification as useful, because it made their businesses run better. Here we see social and environmental ethics and empowerment 'by the numbers', presented as a component part of the realisation of maximised efficiency. They are subsumed into a technological infrastructure of knowledge development and dissemination which discursively removes a key process of political contestation. Reducing ethics to a science hides the underlying power formations that determine who has the agency and ability to construct meaning within ethical discourses. Ethical production as a managerial strategy depoliticises sites of struggle – around race, labour and the use of land – with the non-threatening and bland corporate language of auditing and accounting.

Pacification

Another justification for ethical certification adoption was neither altruistic nor economically aspirational, but pragmatic. This group saw certification as addressing immediate practical issues; foremost of which was the threat of crime and social unrest. They believed that by demonstrating their commitment to transformation and ethical practice through certification, farmers were indirectly protecting themselves from the anger of impoverished rural communities who are "… unhappy because they've got to live in a shanty. They're unhappy because they're practically jobless, poor service provision – and the poor farmer – he ends up facing their unhappiness" (P4). One pioneering Fairtrade adopter spoke of the certification as a "useful social release valve" (P15), meaning it provided an outlet for the frustrations of farm-working communities to be safely defused. This producer said Fairtrade for them represented a reciprocal arrangement where the workers received benefits from Fairtrade and in return the farmer was more secure: "It's a little bit of reciprocal altruism. You make something better for other people and in the process that maybe makes your life or your safety or your future or your children's future slightly better" (P15).

The issue of violence against rural landowners has captured a lot of public and media attention in South Africa in recent years. While much of the data is unreliable (BBC, 2017), South African farmers are said to be the victims of a disproportionate number of violent crimes. Homicide committed against white farmers and their families is a particular flashpoint for political-racial tension. Right-wing groups such as AfriForum have stoked racially-charged anxieties with the claim a genocide is taking place against white farmers (BBC, 2017). While claims of genocide have been widely debunked, the details of farm attacks have been chilling, sparking protests and demonstrations.

It is likely that much of the violence committed on farms stems from the immense issue of rural poverty and constitutes opportunistic material crime. However, the murkiness and complex politics of the issue itself does not negate the fact that farmers are afraid for their safety and that of their families:

"Especially with crime nowadays you must have read about all these farm attacks and how many people have been killed and whatever. [...] People must understand [the need for] safety and security" (P4). Protection and security discourse has risen to prominence in farming communities, with security measures taking myriad forms besides barbed wire and armed guards. A 20-point checklist for farm security dispensed by *Farmers Weekly* in 2017 included, at Number 14: "Treat workers fairly. History confirms that the majority of farm incidents are linked to labour disputes" (Uys, 2017).

It is not only farm attacks that have stoked farmers' anxieties but the issues of labour unrest and union activity. Several participants talked of producers feeling threatened by unions, fears which have been contributed to greatly by the unrest surrounding the wine-growing centre of De Doorns in 2012 and 2013, which saw violent confrontations between workers and police, leading to the deaths of three workers.

> They are afraid that if they allow unions, tomorrow their tractors will be burned down, their sheds will be burned down. Because sometimes as you know a lot of these demands are totally unreasonable and so, yeah, there are farmers that do fear them. (P4)

Some noted that Fairtrade certification informally negated the need for unions: "It has been acknowledged that you rarely find labour unrest in areas that have Fairtrade certification" (C1), "I think there's an awful threat from the unions, whereas I think there are other ways to achieve a goal" (CS4). Fairtrade and WIETA both facilitate a structured environment for dialogue between employers and employees, allowing for relationship-building, even if on limited terms which are controlled mostly by employers. This allows farmers to demonstrate care and concern for the needs of working communities; in a forum in which expectations are laid out from the outset, farmers can be sure of the extent of their commitments, and negotiation and tension are replaced by the implementation of pre-ordained standards and rules.

CONCLUSION: WHO SAYS WHAT IS ETHICAL?

While motivations for the adoption of ethical certification in the South African wine industry were varied, they contained a number of common themes which are relevant to analysis of the ability of EVeNs to facilitate empowerment and ethical transformation. The motivations identified in this chapter comprise narrative responses to global and local political and market conditions. These narratives reveal patterns of agency, demonstrating how agency resides at different points within networks. Some certification adopters identified themselves as the ones with agency and opted to use their position to benefit disadvantaged parties. However, the way this moral imperative was expressed through the narrative of taking responsibility for one's workers still views workers through a paternalistic lens, imagining them as passive beneficiaries of the decision to certify, rather than as participants in the certification process. Other motivations for adoption were outwards-looking, responding to network conditions, and viewing certification as protection from targeting by activists and journalists, or as a strategy for achieving a better market position by capitalising on 'good stories' about wine origins. Although some industry actors resented the need to disseminate good stories, in response to the perceived unjustified bad reputation of the South African wine industry, it is in fact this bad reputation, and fraught history, that has created space for the leveraging of good stories, a marketing strategy which might not be so potent for producers from other countries. However, the pace at which certifications are becoming a minimum requirement as opposed to an opportunity for differentiation suggests that such strategies might no longer be sufficient to carry the industry forward.

Moreover, the concept of certifications as proof and protection sees certification not as transformative, but performative. It is less focused on fostering ethical transformation, and more on outwardly demonstrating commitment to a series of network-governing conventions, and thereby gaining legitimacy in networks. This raises questions as to the progressive potential of ethical certifications governed and implemented as a means to protect against scrutiny – what level of ethical commitment and compliance is required to achieve the basic objective of 'covering [one's] derrière' (as one producer put it), and is this sufficient to address underlying ethical issues?

South Africa's entrenched racial politics is visible within ethical certification discourse. A narrative of white persecution came through in interviews. Filtered through embedded cultural and political framings particular to the post-apartheid South African context, certification was seen by some more as punishment than opportunity. Many wine farmers feel marginalised and persecuted themselves, and while some claim that government policy could be more responsive to this issue, it is a perspective that allows little room in wine industry discourse for consideration of the ongoing ways in which farm-working communities are marginalised and structurally disadvantaged. In some cases it leads producers to claim that farm-working communities are marginalised because farmers are marginalised, and that the government needs to facilitate farmers to facilitate worker 'upliftment'.

Following in-depth analysis of the motivations of certification-adopting agents in the South African wine industry it is clear that the discourse of ethical certification is relational, and able to be co-opted by various strategic narratives. In this case, as in other case studies of ethical certification it appears that ethical labels, which emerged from an attempt to defetishise globalised commodities have fallen subject to similar fetishisation processes (Freidberg, 2003; Fridell, 2007; Guthman, 2007). Removed from their original missions they become objects, brands and products in their own right. Most participants in this research related to certifications not as vehicles for trade justice or sustainable development but as tools, available for purchase, to assist in reaching other goals. This finding reinforces the necessity of continued scrutiny of the robustness of ethical certifications themselves – their ability to remain attractive to potential adopters while prioritising their primary objectives regardless of the other network interests at play.

Another tension revealed in this analysis is that of the inherent politics of the meaning of ethics, which is geographically contingent and constructed. Analysis of adoption narratives in EVeNs shows that contestation and political struggle are increasingly replaced with depoliticised managerial rhetoric, quantifiable standards, and de-contextualised global solutions to local problems. Structural transformation is not a political negotiation, but a business problem to be managed. This process was visible in the framing of production ethics as engineered and quantifiable systems, implemented to improve business performance, as well as the conscious use of certifications as bulwarks against more radical, messy, or scary forms of social progress. This neoliberalistion and depoliticisation of sites of post-apartheid class and racial struggle benefits established interests, who can enact minimal changes whilst co-opting the power to construct meanings of 'ethics'. Even while the post-apartheid struggle is sanitised and de-contextualised in the South African wine industry, deep geographically-contingent power relations are at play, utilising the discourse and mechanisms of ethical certification to maintain familiar patterns of agency, neo-paternalist relations, and access to resources, while dynamically responding to the evolving demands and constraints of market conditions. Certification discourse is shown to be adaptive and strategic, serving the interests of those in the best position to guide and influence it.

NOTES

1. Long-form, semi-structured interviews were conducted with 44 stakeholders, including 19 producers, six certification representatives, four wine agents, two civil society actors, two industry body representatives, two union representatives, and one government representative.
2. To ensure confidentiality, interviewees have been assigned codes based on their category as outlined above, and the order in which interviews took place.
3. A long-standing institution established after the Cape's abolition of slavery in the 1830s, the 'dop' system saw workers paid part of the remuneration in alcohol, dispensed in small measures (or 'dops') throughout the workday (see London, 1999; Williams, 2016).
4. The Robertson Cooperative was the site of industrial action in 2016 and 2017, with the release of *Bitter Grapes* falling within the period of the action.

REFERENCES

Basson, R. (2017a, 19 January). Unlocking value WISEly. Paper presented at the Nedbank Vinpro Information Day, Cape Town.

Basson, R. (2017b, 19 January). State of the SA wine industry. Paper presented at the Nedbank Vinpro Information Day, Cape Town.

BBC (2017, 3 November). Are protesters right on South Africa farm murder rate? *BBC News*. Retrieved from http://www.bbc.com/news/world-africa-41807642

Becchetti, L., & Huybrechts, B. (2008). The dynamics of fair trade as a mixed-form market. *Journal of Business Ethics*, *81*(4), 733–750.

Bek, D., McEwan, C., & Bek, K. (2007). Ethical trading and socioeconomic transformation: critical reflections on the South African wine industry. *Environment and Planning A*, *39*(2), 301–319.

Bek, D., McEwan, C., & Binns, T. (2012). The South African wine industry: Meeting the challenges of structural and ethical transformation. In P.H. Dougherty (Ed.), *The geography of wine* (pp. 137–157). Springer.

Conningarth Economists. (2015). *Macro-economic impact of the wine industry on the South African economy*. Retrieved from http://www.sawis.co.za/info/download/ Macro-economic_impact_study_-_Final_Report_Version_4_30Jan2015.pdf

Cusmano, L., Morrison, A., & Rabellotti, R. (2010). Catching up trajectories in the wine sector: A comparative study of Chile, Italy, and South Africa. *World Development*, *38*(11), 1588–1602.

Dooling, W. (2007). *Slavery, emancipation and colonial rule in South Africa*. University of KwaZulu-Natal Press.

Du Toit, A. (1992). *The farm as family: Paternalism, management and modernisation on Western Cape wine and fruit farms*. Stellenbosch Centre for Rural Legal Studies.

Du Toit, A. (1993). The micro-politics of paternalism: The discourses of management and resistance on South African fruit and wine farms. *Journal of Southern African Studies*, *19*(2), 314–336.

Du Toit, A. (2002). Globalizing ethics: Social technologies of private regulation and the South African wine industry. *Journal of Agrarian Change*, *2*(3), 356–380.

Ewert, J., & Du Toit, A. (2005). A deepening divide in the countryside: Restructuring and rural livelihoods in the South African wine industry. *Journal of Southern African Studies*, *31*(2), 315–332.

Ewert, J., & Hamman, J. (1999). Why paternalism survives: Globalization, democratization and labour on South African wine farms. *Sociologia Ruralis*, *39*(2), 202–221.

Fairtrade Foundation (2018). Tell your Fairtrade story. Screenshot. Retrieved 17 January 2018, from http://www.fairtrade.org.uk/For-Business/Using-Fairtrade -within-my-brand#

Freidberg, S. (2003). Cleaning up down South: Supermarkets, ethical trade and African horticulture. *Social and Cultural Geography*, *4*(1), 27–43.

Fridell, G. (2007). Fair-trade coffee and commodity fetishism: The limits of market-driven social justice. *Historical Materialism*, *15*(4), 79–104.

Guthman, J, (2007). The Polanyian way? Voluntary food labels as neoliberal governance. *Antipode*, 39(3), 456–478.

Heinemann, T. (2016). *Bitter grapes: Slavery in the vineyards*. Heinemann Media. DR International Sales.

Herman, A. (2012). Tactical ethics: How the discourses of fairtrade and black economic empowerment change and interact in wine networks from South Africa to the UK. *Geoforum*, *43*(6), 1121–1130.

Human Rights Watch (2011). *Ripe with abuse: Human rights conditions in South Africa's fruit and wine industries*. Human Rights Watch.

Kruger, S., Du Toit, A., & Ponte, S. (2006). De-racialising exploitation: 'Black Economic Empowerment' in the South African wine sector. *DIIS Working Paper*, *34*.

Kruger, S., Du Toit, A., Raynolds, L.T., Murray, D.L., & Wilkinson, J. (2007). *Reconstructing fairness: Fair trade conventions and worker empowerment in South African horticulture*. Routledge.

London, L. (1999). Addressing the legacy of the dop system: Tackling alcohol abuse among South African farm workers. *Urban Health and Development Bulletin*, *2*(1).

McEwan, C., & Bek, D. (2006). (Re)politicizing empowerment: Lessons from the South African wine industry. *Geoforum*, *37*(6), 1021–1034.

McEwan, C., & Bek, D. (2009). The political economy of alternative trade: Social and environmental certification in the South African wine industry. *Journal of Rural Studies*, 25(3), 255–266.

Mutersbaugh, T., Klooster, D., Renard, M.-C., & Taylor, P. (2005). Certifying rural spaces: Quality-certified products and rural governance. *Journal of Rural Studies*, *21*(4), 381–388.

Nelson, R.R., & Sampat, B.N. (2001). Making sense of institutions as a factor shaping economic performance. *Revista de Economía Institucional*, *3*(5), 17–51.

Overton, J., & Murray W. E. (2016). Fictive place. *Progress in Human Geography*, *40*(6), 794–809.

Ponte, S. (2009). Governing through quality: Conventions and supply relations in the value chain for South African wine. *Sociologia Ruralis*, *49*(3), 236–257.

Ponte, S., & Ewert, J. (2007). South African wine: An industry in ferment. *Tralac Working Paper*, *8*.

Ponte, S., & Ewert, J. (2009). Which way is "up" in upgrading? Trajectories of change in the value chain for South African wine. *World Development*, *37*(10), 1637–1650.

Renard, M.-C. (2003). Fair trade: Quality, market and conventions. *Journal of Rural Studies*, *19*(1), 87–96.

Uys, G. (2017). Farm security: Crucial tips to improve safety. *Farmer's Weekly*. https://www.farmersweekly.co.za/farm-basics/how-to-business/farm-security-crucial-tips-improve-safety/

Williams, G. (2016). Slaves, workers, and wine: The 'dop system' in the history of the Cape wine industry, 1658–1894. *Journal of Southern African Studies*, *42*(5), 893–909.

WOSA (2015). Certification matters. Retrieved from http://www.wineland.co.za/certification-matters/

WOSA (2017, 7 July). Tweet. Retrieved from https://twitter.com/WOSA_ZA/status/883266406313230337

WOSA (2020). South Africa wine statistics. https://www.wosa.co.za/The-Industry/Statistics/SA-Wine-Industry-Statistics/

Zald, M. N. (1996). *Culture, ideology, and strategic framing*. Cambridge University Press.

7 The rise of geographical indications in Latin America: the case of pisco

Peter B.F. Williams

INTRODUCTION

Geographic Indications (GIs) are becoming increasing prevalent beyond Europe, including across Latin America, as they mark a product's quality while seeking to protect 'locality'. This chapter analyses the application of GIs in a contentious case – that of pisco – which is claimed by both Peru and Chile as an authentic product. While acknowledging Chile's origin claim, this chapter explores the protected designation of origin (DO) mark on pisco – a distilled grape spirit produced under specific regulations in Peru – as a case study. To begin, the chapter briefly outlines the global expansion of GIs. Subsequently, the pisco origin debate and the development of the pisco DO mark in Peru are discussed. The chapter will then focus on the Peruvian case study, using findings from detailed fieldwork, to demonstrate some of the key opportunities, limitations and shortcomings of the pisco DO value network. Finally, the chapter offers some conclusions, demonstrating the importance of local economic, social and institutional contexts where a GI is embedded, which determine how a GI is likely to 'play out'.

This chapter applies research findings from fieldwork completed in Peru between July 2016 and January 2017 as part of doctoral research completed at Victoria University of Wellington, New Zealand (Williams, 2019). Forty-one semi-structured interviews were conducted in Peru during this fieldwork period with a range of participants including small, medium and large-scale pisco and pisco grape producers, local experts and regulatory groups. Interviews were completed in the Peruvian capital, Lima, as well as in the Ica Valley – Peru's most important pisco producing area (see Figure 7.2). Semi-structured qualitative interviews, using sets of open questions, were deemed the most suitable approach for interviews, as these provided the participants with the opportunity to express their experiences and viewpoints while also retaining enough structure to identify broader findings.

THE RISE OF GEOGRAPHICAL INDICATIONS IN THE GLOBAL SOUTH

While globalised agriculture has been increasingly linked to concerns over food safety, environmental destruction and rural poverty, models of agriculture which specify locality have conversely been associated with quality and trustworthy production (Murdoch et al., 2000). This localisation of food has fuelled the economic and cultural significance of GI products by providing consumers with reassurance by demonstrating where a product comes from and how it has been produced – thereby inserting 'place' back into production (Bowen & Zapata, 2009). Wider literature has demonstrated that if managed effectively, GIs can foster localised production by providing a means to protect and promote distinctive natural and social attributes, which have evolved through a place's history while also linking local producers and communities with global markets (Bowen, 2010a; Larson, 2007). In these ways, GIs can be considered 'ethical' as they can support broad community development in rural areas.

GI literature often highlights the successes of origin-based production in European contexts. In these contexts, GIs have been associated with promotion of community development and preservation of rural ways of life (Bramley et al., 2013). Unsurprisingly, countries in Latin America – and beyond – have been drawn to GI schemes as a means to increase the value of traditional production while protecting their industries from imitation and misuse through the protection offered by a GI mark (Sautier & van de Kop, 2006). The rise of the GIs outside of Europe has evolved from a two-way process. To begin, growing demand for GI protection for agricultural products from the Global South grew as a response to the successes of these schemes within Europe. Simultaneously, the European Union has supported the expansion of the GI model to non-European countries for strategic reasons (Bowen, 2010b). For example, the growth of GI schemes outside of Europe extends the markets for European GI products. It also allows for the 'clawing-back' of European products being produced in non-European countries (Josling, 2006). This two-way process has led to the expansion of GI products outside of Europe, including in Latin America. It is important to note that the term geographical indication (or GI) is used as a general concept of origin-based protection rather than focusing on the precise form of protection (WIPO, 2013). In this chapter, the term GI is used to include the various origin protection schemes that exist. In particular, this chapter concentrates on the Protected Designation of Origin for pisco, a product claimed by both Peru and Chile. A protected designation of origin or DO represents the strictest form of protection offered by the different GI schemes,[1] and DOs are reserved for unique and well-known products with significant cultural, economic and environmental relevance (Overton & Murray, 2017; Parasecoli & Tasaki, 2011).

ORIGIN DEBATE AND THE DEVELOPMENT OF THE PISCO DO IN PERU

As mentioned, pisco represents a contentious case as both Peru and Chile produce distilled grape spirits – albeit following different production methods – under the same name. This has led to a long-lasting debate over the geographical origin of pisco between their countries, and both Peru and Chile have implemented DO pisco marks for these products. In keeping with the scope of fieldwork findings, this chapter focuses on the Peruvian DO for pisco. The pisco case study does however provide important insights into the wider GIs debates over product origin.[2] Pisco's origins in both Peru and Chile are deeply entrenched in the Spanish colonisation of the Americas during the 16th century. Grapes were transported from Europe during the 1540s and 1550s to the Spanish American colonies, including to the Viceroyalty of Peru (which encompassed parts of modern Peru and Chile). Wine production expanded throughout the Spanish colonies, and by the 1560s Spanish American wine production exceeded local demand and colonial wine exports began to compete with Spain's domestic wine sector. In response, Spanish King Felipe II prohibited the expansion of the Spanish American wine in 1569. Wine producers in the Spanish American colonies were forced to look for alternative markets and, as a result, significant wine stocks across the Viceroyalty of Peru were distilled and used for pisco production (Cortes Olivares, 2005; Huertas Vallejos, 2004).

In the case of pisco from Peru, the name originates from the Pisco Port in Southern Peru, as the spirit was originally transported from this port from the 16th century (Huertas Vallejos, 2004; Vázquez-Rowe et al., 2017). The name pisco stems from the word for bird; *pishko*, in the indigenous language Quechua. The Pisco Port and Pisco Valley received their names from the large seabird populations that inhabit the area. The native populations in the area were also named *pishko* after these birds, while clay pots used by this group to hold liquids, were also named *pishkos* (see Figure 7.1). The name *pishko*, therefore, referred to the geographical area, the port, the people and clay pots. Resulting from the extensive shipments and growing reputation of the grape spirit transported from the Pisco Port, the product began to be known as 'pisco' during the mid-1700s (Dargent Chamot, 2014; Huertas Vallejos, 2012). In Chile, the town 'La Unión' in Northern Chile was renamed 'Pisco Elqui' in 1936, to support the country's efforts to create a Chilean DO for pisco. Although it is not in the scope of this chapter to discuss the Chilean pisco DO in detail, it is important to note that – as in the case of the Peruvian claim over pisco's origin – there is also historical evidence which supports the Chilean claims to the product's origin (Lacoste, 2016). For example, historical evidence demonstrates that the name pisco was also used to refer to grape spirits produced in Northern Chile in the mid-1700s (Lacoste, 2016). Despite Chile's historical claims to pisco, the renaming of 'La Unión' to 'Pisco Elqui' is a controversial point between Chile and Peru. Pisco would eventually become emblematic products for Peru and Chile and part of the national identities of both countries, while the origin of pisco would eventually cause a significant and unresolved GI debate between both countries (Gutiérrez, 2011; Huertas Vallejos, 2012; Mitchell & Terry, 2011). Further to the pisco origin debate between Peru and Chile, there have been issues with other groups in countries as diverse as Argentina, the USA and Australia, among others, which have illegally marketed products with names based on pisco-making traditions.

Source: Peter Williams
Note: Pishkos (clay pots) have been used in Peru since pre-Hispanic times to store and transport liquids. Since Spanish colonisation, variations of these clay pots have been traditionally used for storing and transporting wine and pisco in Peru.

Figure 7.1   Pishkos

In Peru, the pisco DO mark can only be applied when the product is made exclusively from the distillation of fresh grape musts from eight varieties of 'pisco grapes' recently fermented, using methods which maintain principles of tradition and quality, and produced along the coast in the regions of Lima, Ica, Arequipa, Moquegua and in the valleys of Locumba, Sama and Caplina in Tanca (Comisión Nacional del Pisco, n.d.). The designated pisco producing areas under Peru's pisco DO regulations are shown in Figure 7.2. Figure 7.3 shows examples of pisco production in the Ica Valley.

Figure 7.2   Designated pisco producing regions of Peru

Although pisco as a product has evolved over centuries, the Peruvian DO mark for pisco – which is owned by the Peruvian state – is relatively young. The imperative to adopt a DO for pisco had an international dimension, as Peru's attempts to protect pisco under international intellectual property laws have been largely motivated by the challenge to the Peruvian origin of pisco from Chile. This origin debate has heightened especially since the 1990s, resulting from the global expansion of GIs and the implications this has had on international trade (Gutiérrez, 2003; Lacoste et al., 2013). This DO debate is closely linked with important historical factors, such as nationalism, disagreements and conflicts between Peru and Chile (Mitchell & Terry, 2011).

Source: Peter Williams

Figure 7.3   Traditional pisco distillation in Ica, Peru

It is commonly perceived that the efforts to create and implement the Peruvian DO for pisco were largely abandoned until the aforementioned Peru–Chile debate over pisco's origin intensified in the 1990s. However, a review of the relevant laws and establishment of pisco-related institutions demonstrates that attempts to legally protect the Peruvian origin of pisco and quality of the product began as early as the late-19th century. These efforts sought to protect the intellectual property of the producers and local communities, as well as the traditional methods of production and the product's quality (Guerrero, 2004; Gutiérrez, 2003). Table 7.1 summarises the important laws and institutions associated with the evolution of Peruvian DO for pisco. Important efforts to improve and protect the Peruvian DO for pisco at the national and international levels have been implemented (see Table 7.1). This has been particularly

Table 7.1   Legal and institutional evolution of DO for Pisco in Peru

Year	Law, Treaty or Organisation	Description
1896	Riva Agüero – Wagner Treaty	Peru and France mutually committed to protecting the respective signs and designations of each country.
1925	Law 5102	Ended taxes on wine and grape alcohols produced in Southern Peru.
1940	Magisterial Reform 5.40	Prohibited the expansion of cane sugar alcohols in Southern Peru.
1988	Legal Regime for National Cultural Heritage of Peru	Pisco declared as national cultural heritage of Peru.
1990	Directorial Resolution 07087	Pisco declared as Peruvian designation of origin.
1994	Law 26426	Executive Power to protect the recognition of the Peruvian DO for pisco under all available avenues of international law.
2000	CITEvid established in 2000	Centre of Innovation and Technology for Viticulture (CITEvid) created to support improvements in the viticultural chain and pisco sector.
2002	National Institute for the Defence of the Competition and the Protection of Intellectual Property (INDECOPI) implements Technical Norm 211.001.2002	Technical Norm 211.001.2002 for pisco production and pisco DO implemented (updated in 2006 with Technical Norm 211.001.2006; more specification about types of pisco, grape varieties and elaboration processes added to the technical norm).
2003	The National Pisco Commission (CONAPISCO) created.	CONAPISCO established as platform for public–private coordination, bringing together institutions, associations and producers involved in pisco sector.
2005	Lisbon Agreement for the Protection of Appellations of Origin	Peru presented its accession instrument to the Lisbon Agreement, this came into force on 16 May 2005.
2005	World Intellectual Property Organization	On 14 July 2005, the World Intellectual Property Organization issued the international registration certificate for the designation of origin No. 865 pisco, corresponding to Peru.
2011	Regulatory Council for Pisco DO, a non-profit association created and recognised by Peruvian State	The Regulatory Council for Pisco DO represents the beneficiaries of the pisco DO. Its main objective is to administer the pisco DO and care for and protect the quality of pisco.
2016	Law 30460	Peruvian Congress approved Law 30460 declaring the promotion and dissemination of Peruvian wine and pisco as a national interest.

Sources: Adapted by the author using information from; Comisión Nacional del Pisco (n.d.), Gutiérrez (2003, 2011) evident since the early 1990s, through a range of laws and the establishment of related public and private institutions associated with the pisco DO in Peru.

THE PISCO DO IN PERU: KEY POSITIVE OUTCOMES AND OPPORTUNITIES

The implementation of the pisco DO mark has supported a reactivation of the pisco sector in Peru since the early 2000s. For the first time since the challenges posed by the agrarian reforms during the 1970s and the later social and economic crises during the 1980s and 1990s, Peruvian wine and pisco producers began to reinvest in viticultural production in the late 1990s and early 2000s. Importantly, the Peruvian state started to refocus on the viticultural sector during this period, particularly through the development of the DO for pisco following neostructural ideas (Dargent Chamot, 2014; Huertas Vallejos, 2004). As shown in Figures 7.4 and 7.5, national pisco production and exports have grown significantly since 2010, highlighting some of the key opportunities associated with the pisco DO. In particular, pisco production has expanded rapidly in recent years, growing from 1.6 million litres in 2000 to 10.9 million litres in 2017 (see Figure 7.5). With the inclusion of the significant informal segment of production, overall pisco and grape spirit production could be as high as 22 million litres in 2017 (Vázquez-Rowe et al., 2017). Nonetheless, this informal segment is a controversial topic and without the authorisation to use the pisco DO, the alcoholic products from the informal sector cannot be legally considered as pisco. These products are, however, commonly called pisco in the local markets despite not having the authorisation to use this name, highlighting a key challenge for the pisco DO (Pflucker, 2015). Growing national consumption of pisco has also occurred in Peru. For instance, between 2008 and 2018, the annual national consumption of pisco in Peru doubled from 955 thousand litres to 1.9 million litres (Ministerio de la Producción, 2019). This has mainly been associated with quality improvements and greater levels of state and private promotion generally related with the DO mark (Vázquez-Rowe et al., 2017).

The pisco sector in Peru, while still dominated by internal demand, has become increasingly oriented towards international export markets and higher-end niche liquor markets. For example, pisco exports as a percentage of overall sales grew from 6.5% in 2006 to 15% in 2014 (Pflucker, 2015). Additionally, the unit price of exported pisco has grown. For instance, between 2000 and 2015, the pisco unit export price grew from US\$4.4 to US\$7.8 per litre (Comisión Nacional del Pisco, n.d.). Total pisco export value grew from US\$141,000 in 2000 to reach US\$8.6 million in 2016, before dropping to US\$6.8 million in 2017 (see Figure 7.5). This important decline in pisco exports between 2016 and 2017 is mainly explained by the drop of pisco exports entering the Chilean market, following the reactivation of the debate over the pisco DO between Peru and Chile in early 2017[3] (Koo, 2017).

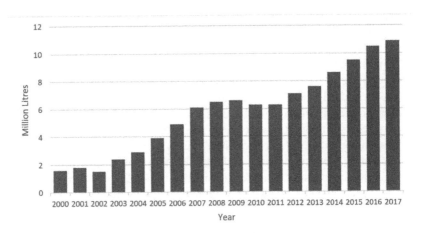

Source: Elaborated by the author with data from Comisión Nacional del Pisco (n.d.)

Figure 7.4   Pisco production in Peru, 2000–2017

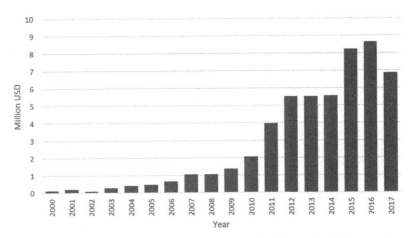

Source: Elaborated by the author with data from Comisión de Promoción del Perú para la Exportación y el Turismo (2018)

Figure 7.5   Pisco exports from Peru by value, 2000–2017

The development of the pisco DO and origin dispute between Peru and Chile stimulated the creation of a number of Peruvian public and private organisations which have defended Peru's origin claims and promoted the production and consumption of pisco since the early 2000s. For example, the public–private National Pisco Commission (CONAPISCO) was created in 2003 to support the industry's growth. Additionally, the creation of the state-owned Centre of Innovation and Technology for Viticulture (CITEvid) in 2000 was especially supportive of the industry's growth (Kuramoto, 2011). CITEvid has been an instrumental organisation in resolving many of the issues facing viticulture in Peru during the 1990s.

The majority of fieldwork interviews with pisco producers and local experts in Peru demonstrated that the key opportunities of implementing the pisco DO were mainly driven by commercial motivations, and a desire to promote pisco while protecting its unique qualities internationally. A particular motivation for the formation of a DO was to link the product's special qualities to its origin and mode of production. In the case of pisco, the formation of the DO has been based on the uniqueness of the product, the high quality it possesses, and the link to the human and natural factors that have developed pisco. Guillermo Vera, a historian and member of the Peruvian Academy of Pisco, explained these unique qualities thus:

> Nothing can be added to pisco, production does not include the use of wooden barrels which would change the flavours ... the DO has been applied to protect this unique product and distinguish it from other spirits. This product has the elements unique to Peru ... the local climates and the specific cultures that have developed that do not reflect viticulture internationally. (Interview, August 2016)

Likewise, the pisco DO was also implemented to attract consumers, especially from the Global North. This can be seen as a form of upgrading whereby the producers using the DO on their product are able to improve their position in national and international markets and add value to their product (Bolwig et al., 2010; Ponte & Ewert, 2009). As explained by José Carlos Falconí from CITEagroindustrial in Ica (a state-owned agricultural innovation and techno-logical centre):

> When a consumer sees that a product is controlled with a DO, they know that it is something unique and exclusive. The DO is particularly important for consumers in other markets such as in Europe and the North American, these groups understand that the DO is a sign of quality. (Interview, November 2016)

The majority of interviewees explained a key opportunity of the pisco DO being established was the protection this offers to both the consumers and the producers by separating the formal and informal sectors. The informal sector refers to groups that produce spirits and use the name pisco without receiving authorisation from the Peruvian government to do so. In these cases, the infor-

mal groups are not bound by the same regulations as the formal pisco producers who receive authorisation to use the DO. Separating the formal producers
from the informal ones has been shown to be an important motivation for the
development of the pisco DO in Peru. This was explained by Carlos Romero,
a medium-scale producer:

> The DO is a guarantee for the public and protection for the producer. For someone
> who wants to consume an authentic drink ... a DO means that the state guarantees
> that the production is genuine. And for a producer, they have the security that
> their product won't be imitated ... this means that low-quality imitation products
> cannot be sold in the pisco market. It is a protection against this unfair competition.
> (Interview, October 2016)

The DO has therefore also been established to improve the conditions of the
pisco producers in different markets by protecting the intellectual property
they have developed over centuries. A number of research participants,
including producers and other experts, demonstrated that the DO had increased
the value of pisco and assisted with other improvements in the sector. These
improvements included contributing to improvements in production methods
and attitudes towards pisco. Globally, GI marks such as DOs have been promoted as opportunities for broad local community development, particularly
in rural areas (Bowen, 2010b; Gerz & Dupont, 2006; Sautier & van de Kop,
2006). While local producers and communities identified as key stakeholders
for the pisco DO, it is critical to mention that the motives of supporting community development were not as explicit in this case when compared with
other examples of EVeNs. This said, most participants in Peru acknowledged
that the pisco network has had positive outcomes for the local communities
in the pisco producing region of Peru and described how it has promoted and
protected the culture of these areas. The development of the pisco DO, and
the associated expansion of the sector, has created notable direct economic
and employment outcomes, as well as indirect benefits associated with pisco
tourism in the local communities in pisco-producing areas. For example, Karl
Mendoza, an agricultural engineer and researcher explained how the pisco DO
was formed to include these concepts of local community development: "Pisco
has contributed to the development of the viticultural sector in depressed
localities in Peru ... The Peruvian state has established laws so that pisco
contributes to the social and economic development of the communities in the
production areas" (interview, October 2016).

These ideas were supported by Manuel Morón, Director at CITE agroIndustrial,
"There are direct and indirect benefits ... like the Pisco Trail, and important
events and festivals based around pisco ... this brings people and tourism,
which has many benefits for the community" (Interview, October 2016).
However, according to traditional medium-scale pisco producer Matías Grados

the impact in the community depends heavily on the type of producer. 'The smaller producers have a more positive impact in the community, what they earn they spend here, but the large producers do not live here and their money leaves the area' (interview, November 2016).

A central motivation for implementing the DO pisco network was also recognition of pisco's cultural importance and the product's role in Peru's national identity, patrimony and heritage. Likewise, the pisco DO has been partly motivated as an opportunity to protect the traditional methods and the cultural connections with pisco, which represent an important part of the DO. The majority of participants in Peru mentioned how the DO has functioned as an important guide for producers to ensure that their operations contribute to the traditions of the sector and of the local area. The drive to protect pisco's origin in Peru has mainly come from the aforementioned DO challenge from Chile. This importance of defending the Peruvian origin of pisco is explained by pisco producer Victor Santhome, from *Bellavista Bodega*:

> The pisco DO is something of pride for Peru … but, unfortunately, we have problems with Chile which claims that pisco has a Chilean origin. For me, it is extremely important that we focus on the high quality of our pisco … we also have historical and geographical factors which support the Peruvian origin of pisco … (Interview, October 2016)

THE PISCO DO IN PERU: CHALLENGES AND CONCENTRATION

Despite the key opportunities discussed, the practical implementation of the pisco DO in Peru has encountered a number of key limitations and shortcomings. Although the DO should delimit production and support local producers, pisco is an increasingly competitive value network dominated by a handful of industrial-scale[4], often extra-local pisco-producing firms. These companies control most of the processing and commercialisation stages of the pisco network and have strong links with national retail sales and exports. Local smaller-scale producers, conversely, are mainly concentrated in the conception stage in the grape production and in artisanal-scale pisco production, usually selling in local markets or in bulk to larger pisco companies for re-sale. Many of these smaller-scale producers remain in the informal market due to the financial and administrative barriers they face in receiving the DO. During fieldwork, diverse groups repeatedly mentioned the important barriers faced by smaller-scale producers in receiving the authorisation to use the pisco DO mark and explained how, as a result, these producers have been excluded from the DO networks. Almost all small-scale pisco producers interviewed explained that they felt unsupported and excluded from the authorisation process to use the pisco DO. For instance, small-scale pisco producer Dennis Grimaldo described the challenges of receiving the authorisation to use the DO and the lack of support for small-scale producers:

> We haven't received any support to receive the DO, everything must be done by ourselves. The certifiers hardly ever come out to the countryside ... The DO should be easier to use, they require us to have this mark but there are still many producers that don't have the resources to be involved. (Interview, November 2016)

The DO has failed to control the expansion of newer extra-local pisco producers from entering the pisco DO network. These newer extra-local actors have entered the network in recent years in search of opportunities for profits, resulting in the appropriation of the ethical value associated with the pisco DO. Manuel Bernales, a traditional pisco producer, described the challenges created by extra-local actors for the traditional producers:

> The competition in Peru is now very strong, not just from other bodegas but also from the '*piqueros*'. The *piqueros* are groups that come from outside of Ica and use third parties to make piscos ... it is very difficult to sell pisco in Peru as there are these new actors in the sector ... that have entered with a lot of force. (Interview, October 2016)

Similarly, Jorge Llanos from the Instituto del Vino y del Pisco at the Universidad de San Martín de Porres, explained that the expansion of extra-local actors in the pisco network means that most of the profits created through pisco in Ica do not stay in the area: 'the sector and markets for pisco have changed a lot [...] now, the profits made in Ica don't stay there, they go to Lima and are concentrated by middlemen, not the producers' (interview, December 2016). This has diminished the value captured by the small-scale and traditional grape and pisco producers as the value created in the network tended to be unevenly distributed amongst the other actors. Although DOs can privilege small-scale producers by granting economic incentives for these groups to maintain traditional agricultural practices and link them to wider markets, the majority of interviews demonstrated that this has not occurred in the pisco DO case study. Instead, the implementation of the pisco DO has favoured larger-scale and extra-local actors who do not suffer from the same financial and administrative challenges in receiving the pisco DO authorisation. This has displaced smaller-scale producers who had traditionally produced pisco. This has seriously limited the pisco DO mark's ability to create local development and assist small-scale producers. As in other parts of Latin America, the implementation of the DO has been difficult partly due to the Peruvian institutions, which are generally less effective than those in Europe where DOs originate. Further improvements to the national institutions in Peru are required to better protect the intellectual property, safeguard against fraud, and manage the genetic, biological and natural resources associated with the pisco DO. Without institutional strengthening and protection, the domination of pisco by extra-local actors is likely to continue in Peru.

In a similar vein, it was frequently stated during fieldwork that the pisco DO has prioritised the sector's growth over the protection of local pisco culture. For instance, it was perceived that the increasingly industrial nature of the network was prioritised over supporting the preservation of local cultures and traditions associated with pisco. Despite the DO, local grape producers have been excluded from the governance of the DO in the pisco network. As explained by pisco producer and researcher José Moquillaza, this is because an inter-professional regulatory organisation has not yet been developed:

> The supervision takes place at the Regulatory Council which is made up of private organisations. However, its vision is overly industrial and the grape producers are not represented. The council is not truly inter-professional like in other countries with DOs … As the council is not inter-professional, the different actors in pisco compete, argue and fail to work together, while only the second half of the value chain is included. (Interview, July 2016)

Furthermore, although the pisco network created employment, this employment was largely seasonal, which also caused hardship in the local towns. David Espinoza an official pisco connoisseur described how the DO and the network have not been fully taken advantage of to support community development:

> The producers are not well informed and do not understand the importance that the DO has on their product and the development of their communities … the connected benefits of the DO … should not only benefit the producers but also those that live in areas. (Interview, August 2016)

Despite the ethical claims that concentrated on the employment and economic benefits created by the pisco DO, various participants discussed the temporary nature of these benefits and described the hardship caused. For instance, agricultural engineer Karl Mendoza described some of the challenges and precarity of the employment created by the pisco sector: "The sector also has negative impacts. For example, the employment the sector offers is only seasonal, and there are moments that the population doesn't have work" (interview, October 2016). This was seen by different participants to cause hardship rather than support in the local community. This failing of the pisco network to support the wider community was explained by Homero Herrera, partner and adviser at a small-scale pisco producer cooperative: "The large bodegas only hire staff for short time periods, which creates hardship for these people as they do not have stable employment" (interview, September 2016).

The challenges outlined above support the assertion made by existing research which revealed that the capacity of a DO to encourage development and support local producers depends on the DO regulation and the local social, institutional and economic contexts where a DO is embedded (Bowen, 2010a; Mancini, 2013). Despite playing a critical role in the sector, grape producers remain largely excluded from the value created in the pisco network without genuine representation in the governance of the pisco DO. Although they are an important part of the DO value network, they have been integrated into this network as captive suppliers. These captive suppliers remain largely disconnected from important markets and receive a limited amount of the value created in the network. In some cases, vertical integration by the industrial-scale pisco producers has led to hierarchical governance by removing the grape producers from the network (Gereffi & Lee, 2012).

In Peru, the exclusion of small-scale producers from the regulatory bodies of pisco was identified by the majority of research participants as an important failing. As a result, the larger producers have been able to dominate decisions made regarding the regulation of the pisco DO and the value created in this network. Similarly, a significant number of interviewees highlighted that the pisco DO did not always create the broad community benefits often promoted. For instance, although the network created direct and indirect employment and economic opportunities, these opportunities were largely precarious and seasonal, which also caused periods of hardship in the local towns. For example, in areas dependent on pisco production, incomes significantly decrease when labour is not required in the pisco-related activities.

Finally, a majority of research participants discussed the failings of the DO regulatory institutions, such as the Pisco DO Regulatory Council (CR-DOPISCO), to establish the supervision and control required to protect the authenticity and high-quality of pisco. At the time of fieldwork, the CR-DOPISCO was not functioning effectively and, as a result, there was not enough supervision and enforcement of the pisco regulatory norms. For instance, David Espinoza, an official pisco connoisseur, described this problem as follows:

> The problem with the pisco DO is that we don't have a well-structured Regulatory Council ... people trust that our product is effectively regulated through the DO but this is not that case. ... the Regulatory Council has not worked as it should ... we don't have control in the sector and we can't say that the DO has been successful in establishing this control. (Interview, August 2016)

Due to budget deficiencies, the CR-DOPISCO has largely failed to fulfil its functions. President of the CR for the Pisco DO (at the time of fieldwork) Jaime Marimon described these challenges:

> Our role at the Regulatory Council is to verify the quality of pisco and to make sure every bottle with the name pisco on it is actually pisco … we have not been able to do a lot as we don't have any way to gain funding to complete our functions. (Interview, December 2016)

Partly resulting from the failings to establish effective supervision and control, there has been persistent uncertified production of pisco in the informal sector. This informal sector continues to damage the reputation of the legitimate production and, left unregulated, could ruin the authenticity and quality of pisco. Therefore, without an effective regulatory body, the pisco DO had at least partly failed to ensure one of the core objectives of a GI, to provide consumers with accurate information to allow them to select quality products while being protected from misleading information. In the pisco DO case study, the supervision, control and enforcement of the regulations have failed to ensure that all of the products currently sold as pisco have fulfilled all of the necessary requirements under the DO.

CONCLUSIONS

In the context of the increasing 'placelessness' of globalised agriculture, GIs can provide consumers with reassurance over food safety, authenticity and quality by demonstrating where a product comes from and how it has been produced. European examples have also revealed that GIs can be applied to promote community development and preservation of rural ways of life while linking local producers to global markets. Countries in Latin America have been drawn to GI schemes as avenues to protect traditional and unique products while promoting economic opportunities and broad community development. However, as highlighted by the pisco case study, GIs can also cause debate and contestation when two or more countries make exclusive claims over a product's origin.

Overall, through the pisco DO case study, this chapter has outlined the key opportunities GI schemes can create by supporting the development and reactivation of a sector. As in European cases, the Peruvian case study also demonstrated potential links to broad rural community development. However, as revealed, the motives of supporting community development were not as explicit in the case of Peruvian pisco when compared with other examples of ethical value networks. In this case, the DO was mainly developed to differentiate and promote pisco while protecting its unique qualities locally and internationally. However the pisco DO also sought to protect consumers and local producers and differentiate between the formal and informal sectors. Nonetheless, this chapter has highlighted some of the key challenges in implementing a GI mark in a Latin American context. Despite the emphasis on local producers, the pisco industry is a highly competitive network controlled by a small group of industrial-scale producers. The DO has been unable to control the influx of new extra-local pisco producers from entering the value DO network, causing the appropriation of the pisco DO's ethical value. Conversely, traditional (smaller-scale) pisco producers – practically unsupported – face serious barriers to receiving the DO. The chapter has also demonstrated that the enforcement of the pisco DO regulations has been problematic in Peru. Without an effective system of supervision and control, the persistent production of unregulated pisco continues to threaten the reputations of legitimate producers, which could ruin pisco's authenticity and quality.

Similar to other GI case studies in Latin America (Bowen & Zapata, 2009), the implementation of the pisco DO has therefore been uneven partly because of the lack of strong institutions in Peru. Primary producers have been largely excluded from the benefits of the pisco DO and the pisco grape producers have remained captive suppliers in the network with little representation in regulatory bodies. Finally, the chapter has demonstrated that the pisco DO – in its current application – is unable to create the broad community benefits often mentioned in wider GI literature. For instance, the direct and indirect employment and economic opportunities created are mainly seasonal and precarious. In sum, although the pisco DO has created a number of opportunities and positive outcomes in Peru, this case study also serves as a precautionary account for other GIs being developed. Without considering the uneven social, economic and institutional contexts where a GI is embedded, the positive real-world outcomes of these schemes are likely to be seriously hindered.

NOTES

1. The European Union issued regulation 2081 on GIs in 1992. This regulation was a significant step for GI recognition at the international level and provides a framework which outlines three categories for GI protection: Protected Designation of Origin (PDO) covers agricultural products and foodstuffs which are produced, processed and prepared in a given geographical area using recognized know-how. Protected Geographical Indication (PGI) covers agricultural products and foodstuffs closely linked to the geographical area. At least one of the stages of production, processing or preparation takes place in the area. Traditional Speciality Guaranteed (TSG) highlights traditional character, either in the composition or means of production (European Commission, 2015).
2. For greater detail on the Pisco origin debate see Mitchell & Terry (2011).
3. The inclusion in official statistics of pisco exports from Peru to Chile is a controversial topic as a product cannot be imported into Chile with under the name

pisco due to Chile's pisco DO. Therefore, a significant proportion of products recognized as pisco in the Peruvian official exportation statistics are actually sold as *aguardiente de uva* (grape spirit) in Chile.

4. In the pisco sector industrial or large-scale producers refers to those that produce more than 50,000 litres of pisco annually or own 51 hectares or more (INEI, 2012).

REFERENCES

Bolwig, S., Ponte, S., Du Toit, A., Riisgaard, L., & Halberg, N. (2010). Integrating poverty and environmental concerns into value-chain analysis: A conceptual framework. *Development Policy Review*, *28*(2), 173–194.

Bowen, S. (2010a). Embedding local places in global spaces: Geographical indications as a territorial development strategy'. *Rural Sociology*, *75*(2), 209–243.

Bowen, S. (2010b). Development from within? The potential for Geographical Indications in the Global South. *The Journal of World Intellectual Property*, *13*(2), 231–252.

Bowen, S., & Zapata, A.V. (2009). Geographical indications, terroir, and socioeconomic and ecological sustainability: The case of tequila. *Journal of Rural Studies*, 25(1), 108–119.

Bramley, C., Bienabe, E., & Kirsten, J. (2013). *Developing geographical indications in the South: The Southern African experience.* Springer Netherlands.

Cortes Olivares, H.F. (2005). El origen, producción y comercio del pisco chileno, 1546-1931. *Universum (Talca): Revista de Humanidades y Ciencias Sociales*, *20*(2), 42–81.

Comisión de Promoción del Perú para la Exportación y el Turismo. (2018). *Exportaciones de pisco y similares*. Lima: Comisión de Promoción del Perú para la Exportación y el Turismo (PromPerú).

Comisión Nacional del Pisco (n.d.). Estadísticas. Retrieved 18 May 2018, from http://www.conapisco.org.pe/estadisticas.html

Dargent Chamot, E. (2014). *Vino y pisco en la Historia del Perú*. Fondo Editorial Universidad San Martín de Porres.

European Commission (2015). Quality policy: Geographical indications and traditional specialities. Retrieved 1 December 2015, from http://ec.europa.eu/agriculture/quality/schemes/index_en.htm

Gereffi, G., & Lee, J. (2012). Why the world suddenly cares about global supply chains. *Journal of Supply Chain Management*, *48*(3), 24–32.

Gerz, A., & Dupont, F. (2006). Comté cheese in France: Impact of a geographical indication on rural development. In P. van de Kop, S. Denis & G. Astrid (Eds.), *Origin-based products: Lessons for pro-poor market development* (pp. 75–86). KIT Publishers.

Guerrero, C.C. (2004). La protección jurídica de las denominaciones de origen peruanas. *Docentia et Investigatio*, *6*(1), 139–151.

Gutiérrez, G. (2003). El pisco, denominación de origen peruana. *Agenda Internacional*, *10*(19), 245–298.

Gutiérrez, G. (2011). El desarrollo de la denominación de origen peruana pisco. Paper presented at the Simposio Mundial sobre Indicaciones Geográficas, Lima, Perú.

Huertas Vallejos, L. (2004). Historia de la producción de vinos y piscos en el Perú. *Universum (Talca)*, *19*, 44–61.

Huertas Vallejos, L. (2012). *Cronología de la producción del vino y del pisco: Perú, 1548-2010*. Universidad Ricardo Palma.

INEI (2012). Resultados definitivos. iv censo nacional agropecuario. Instituto Nacional de Estadística e Informática (INEI).

Instituto del Vino y del Pisco IDVIP. Promulgan ley que declara de interés nacional la promoción y difusión del vino peruano y del Pisco. Retrieved 18 October 2020 from http://idvip.edu.pe/promulgan-ley-que-declara-de-interes-nacional-la-promocion-y -difusion-del-vino-peruano-y-del-pisco/

Josling, T. (2006). The war on *terroir*: Geographical indications as a transatlantic trade conflict. *Journal of Agricultural Economics*, *57*(3), 337–363.

Koo, W. (2017). Pisco Perú exportación 2017 – Octubre. Retrieved 4 April 2018, from https://www.agrodataperu.com/2017/11/pisco-peru-exportacion-2017-octubre.html

Kuramoto, J.R. (2011). *Innovation, R&D and productivity: Case studies from Peru*: Inter-American Development Bank Department of Research and Chief Economist.

Lacoste, P. (2016). *El pisco nació en Chile. Génesis de la primera denominación de origen de América*. Ril Editores.

Lacoste, P., Jimenez, D., Castro, A., Rendon, B., & Soto, N. (2013). A bi-national appellation of origin: Pisco in Chile and Peru. *Chilean Journal of Agricultural Research*, *73*, 424–429.

Larson, J. (2007). *Relevance of geographical indications and designations of origin for the sustainable use of genetic resources*. Global Facilitation Unit for Underutilized Species.

Mancini, M.C. (2013). Geographical indications in Latin America value chains: A 'branding from below' strategy or a mechanism excluding the poorest? *Journal of Rural Studies*, *32*, 295–306.

Ministerio de la Producción (Peru) (2019). PRODUCE: Producción formal de pisco alcanzaría récord en el 2019. Press release. Retrieved 18 October 2020, from www .gob.pe/institucion/produce/noticias/46127-produce-produccion-formal-de-pisco -alcanzaria-record-en-el-2019

Mitchell, J.T., & Terry, W.T. (2011). Contesting pisco: Chile, Peru, and the politics of trade. *The Geographical Review*, *101*(4), 518–535.

Murdoch, J., Marsden, T., & Banks, J. (2000). Quality, nature, and embeddedness: Some theoretical considerations in the context of the food sector. *Economic Geography*, *76*(2), 107–125.

Overton, J., & Murray, W.E. (2017). GI blues: Geographical Indications and wine in New Zealand. In W. van Caenegem & J. Cleary (Eds.), *The importance of place: Geographical indications as a tool for local and regional development* (pp. 197–220). Cham: Springer.

Parasecoli, F., & Tasaki, A. (2011). Shared meals and food fights: Geographical indications, rural development, and the environment. *Environment and Society*, *2*(1), 106–123.

Pflucker, M.G.V. (2015). *Los secretos del pisco*. Lima: Universidad de San Martín de Porres, Fondo Editorial.

Ponte, S., & Ewert, J. (2009). Which way is 'up' in upgrading? Trajectories of change in the value chain for South African wine. *World Development*, *37*(10), 1637–1650.

Sautier, D., & van de Kop, P. (2006). Origin-based marketing: A rural development tool? In P. van de Kop, S. Denis & G. Astrid (Eds.), *Origin-based products: Lessons for pro-poor market development* (pp. 17–20). KIT Publishers.

Vázquez-Rowe, I., Cáceres, A. L., Torres-García, J. R., Quispe, I., & Kahhat, R. (2017). Life cycle assessment of the production of pisco in Peru. *Journal of Cleaner Production, 142*, 4369–4383.

Williams, P.B.F. (2019). *Creating ethical markets or marketing ethics? A critical exploration of ethical value networks in Chilean and Peruvian viticulture and oenology.* PhD thesis, Victoria University of Wellington.

WIPO (2013). *Geographical indications: An introduction.* World Intellectual Property Organization (WIPO).

8. Development with identity: connecting place, culture and food in Andean Latin America

Simon Bidwell

INTRODUCTION

To date, much study of what this book conceptualizes as ethical value networks (EVeNs) falls within one of two broad categories. First, researchers have studied networks in the Global North that seek to reconnect producers and consumers through mutually beneficial commitments to social responsibility, environmental sustainability and local authenticity (Goodman et al., 2012; Tregear, 2011). Second, they have looked at networks involving the export of products from the Global South for consumption in the North, which aim to responsibly exercise Northern consumer power and partially address the imbalances and inequities of North–South trade (Bidwell et al., 2018a, 2018b).

This leaves significant space for exploring EVeNs *in* and *from* the Global South. This means studying local networks of production and consumption that do not necessarily involve export to the North. Rather than just using examples from the South to assess whether ethical schemes such as fair trade, organics or geographical indications 'work', it means taking a place-based approach to evaluating what the variety of ethical networks offer for local livelihoods. Further, while much Northern-centric research explores alternatives to the corporate-controlled 'mainstream' agri-food system, a view from the South implies considering the potential for EVeNs to offer a positive agenda for development, including for groups that have not historically participated in mainstream agri-food markets.

This chapter explores the construction of networks linking place, food and identity as an agenda for development in the Andean countries of Latin America, with a particular focus on Peru. In doing so, it traces the intersection between two tendencies. The first involves attempts within development practice to mobilize distinctive biocultural features of Andean places as sources of social cohesion, marketable authenticity and environmental resilience. The second relates to the new visibilities and values accorded to Andean foods and farming practices, driven by a combination of social movement, academic and market agendas. The chapter looks at how these tendencies have come together into projects to link food, identity and development in the Andes, and it assesses the potential for these projects to deliver on their promises.

This chapter first gives a brief overview of how and why Andean agri-food products and practices have been accorded new recognition and value over recent decades. It then summarizes the aspirations for economic, sociocultural and environmental benefits that have been associated with initiatives to revalue Andean agri-food heritage. It explores the challenges facing these initiatives, looking particularly at the limits set by ecological and social realities that both mainstream and more radical theoretical perspectives can ignore or oversimplify. Finally, it reflects on the lessons from other ethical food networks that might be applied in the Andes.

REVALUING THE ANDES: DEVELOPMENT WITH IDENTITY AND LOCAL AGRI-FOOD HERITAGE

Studies of ethical value networks commonly present their development as a reaction against the threats from neoliberal globalization to actors who had a stable place in what McMichael (2009) terms the 'Fordist' agri-food regime. Globalization simultaneously disturbed the relatively privileged position of Northern farmers within domestic food systems, and the diverse pacts and quotas that had partially stabilized South–North trade in tropical commodities such as coffee and bananas (Fridell, 2007). These new insecurities intensified long-simmering cultural anxieties about the social and ecological harms of the Fordist food system (Goodman et al., 2012; Ray, 1998).

By contrast, in Andean Latin America, new attention to food provenance has been associated with places, products and practices that were largely ignored or undervalued within the Fordist regime. Pre-Conquest, the diverse and ecologically embedded farming systems developed by Andean cultures generated a food surplus that underpinned the development of monumental civilizations such as the Incas (Krogel, 2011). However, apart from those products that were quickly globalized, such as maize and potatoes, Andean agri-food products and practices were largely marginalized in the post-Conquest period. By the 20th century, they had come to be considered emblematic of 'backwardness', to be overcome by modernity and progress. In the post-Second World War era, agricultural development promoted input-intensive monocultivation of 'improved' crops and breeds (Grey, 2011; Shepherd, 2010). These modernizing agendas sat alongside deeply internalized prejudice towards indigeneity, rurality, and, in Peru, where political-economic and cultural power is concentrated in coastal Lima, towards the entire Andean highlands as an (imagined) geographical space (de la Cadena, 2001; Weismantel, 2001).

This combination of externally driven development agendas and cultural prejudice has not disappeared. However, alongside these continuities, in recent decades the food products and farming cultures of the Andes have gained new visibilities and values. This has come about through interactions between global political, economic and cultural changes, local social movements, and evolutions in academic research, policymaking and development practice. The remainder of this section gives what, for reasons of space, is a very brief overview of these interactions (see Bidwell, 2020 for a fuller account).

First, the post-1980s period saw changing views on the role of local and indigenous cultures in development, as state-led strategies to modernize and assimilate came under attack from across the political spectrum. Radcliffe and Laurie (2006) sum up the newly perceived worth of cultural diversity within mainstream development as *culture as a product* (the value added by cultural authenticity, whether in agri-food, craft or tourism markets); and *culture as institution* (the assumed power of shared identity and traditional authority to underpin social capital).

Second, within the growing attention to the environmental impacts of development was a re-evaluation of the benefits and costs of the agricultural Green Revolution. Increased emphasis on issues of sustainability, resilience and nutrition led to a growing interest in agrobiodiversity, bringing more attention to formerly maligned Andean crops and varieties, and the local knowledge and traditional practices that sustained them (Brush et al., 1996; National Research Council, 1989; Tapia, 1990).

These changes opened space for grassroots movements in the Andes who argued that cultural and environmental values were not only central to wellbeing but were fundamentally interconnected. The Andean Technology Recovery Project (PRATEC) drew links between Andean ontology, epistemology and ethics (often referred to as *cosmovision*), traditional knowledge and practices, and the rich diversity of Andean agricultural products (Apfell-Marglin, 2002). The Cuzco-based NGO Association for Nature and Development (ANDES) articulated the concept of *collective biocultural heritage*, which presented cultural and biological diversity as not only interconnected but also inseparable from indigenous control of territory and resources (Argumedo & Stenner, 2008).

In parallel, Northern consumer interest in food provenance and nutrition stimulated growing global demand for organic products and 'superfoods', generating export value chains for Andean products such as quinoa, kiwicha (amaranth) and maca, and offering new opportunities and challenges for Andean *campesinos* (Cáceres et al., 2007). Here too, culture was seen as adding value. In an analysis of marketing narratives since the 1980s, Loyer and

Knight (2018) identify an increasing tendency to associate superfoods with indigenous food cultures as a "[primary] framework for validating a food's healthfulness" (2018, p. 460).

In Peru, all of these tendencies were incorporated into, and amplified by, the 'gastronomic boom', an explosion of national interest in, and international recognition of, Peruvian food (see Figure 8.1). The 'boom' got underway in the 1990s, as Lima-based chefs incorporated native ingredients to create *novo andino* cuisine. However, it gained momentum as a national project in the mid-2000s by incorporating wider social and ecological agendas, with chefs such as Gastón Acurio emphasizing the stewardship role of *campesino* farmers in providing the diverse ingredients integral to Peru's gastronomy (Garcia, 2013; Matta, 2013). The concept of *patrimonio agroalimentario* (agri-food heritage), which became established in public discourse during the 2000s, articulated a vision of food as connecting values of cultural identity, environmental sustainability, social unity and economic development (Bidwell, 2020; Fan, 2013; Matta, 2013).

Source: Simon Bidwell

Figure 8.1   Products, producers and places in stalls at the 2018 Mistura fair in Lima

The discussion in the remainder of this chapter draws on doctoral research which combined national-level research on the development of ethical value networks in Peru, with case studies of local initiatives to revalue agri-food heritage in two localities in the Colca Valley, in the southern Peruvian Andes (see Figure 8.2). The case studies were underpinned by community-level fieldwork including semi-structured interviews and participation observation over several periods between 2010 and 2017.

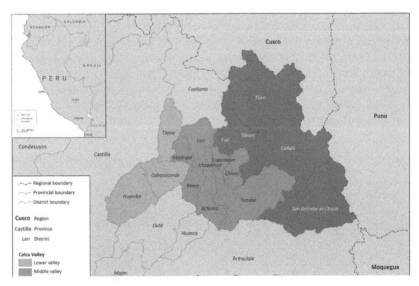

Figure 8.2   The Colca Valley, Peru

PROJECTS AND PROMISES OF FOOD, IDENTITY AND DEVELOPMENT

Unlike fair trade or organics, there is not a single ethical scheme involving Andean agri-food heritage whose scale and reach can be quantitatively tracked. Rather, the tendencies discussed in the previous section have generated a variety of projects, network connections and market niches in which Andean people, places and products have been accorded new visibilities and have gained new spaces for participation.

On one end of the spectrum are largely market-based initiatives, such as efforts to link native potato producers in the central Peruvian Andes with national processors and retailers (Devaux et al., 2018). On the other end are efforts to recover traditional cultural practices and strengthen non-market relations, such as initiatives to promote local food and seed exchange networks (Argumedo, 2013; Matta, 2019).

Most initiatives, however, have sought to achieve a combination of objectives both within and outside markets. Since the 1990s, development projects in the rural Andes have often had multiple aims including linking producers to national markets and export networks; supporting local processing, product transformation and tourism; promoting agroecological farming techniques, reintroducing diverse crop varieties for *in situ* conservation; recovering and revaluing local knowledge; and stimulating renewed local consumption of traditional products (Bidwell, 2020; Desco, 2014; Healy, 2001; Matta, 2019; Ofstehage, 2012; Saad, 2009; Turner, 2016).

Civil society-led initiatives have included the creation of *bioferias* (organic farmers markets operating in local and regional centres) and the involvement of farmers in Peru's national gastronomic fair Mistura through a 'chef-farmer alliance' (Palomino-Gonzales, 2016; Wu Guin & Alvarado de la Fuente, 2015). Government-led actions have included designating national days such as for Andean grains and native potatoes and the promotion of an 'Andean diet' in Peru; support for processed quinoa products in Bolivia; and the development of geographical indications for products such as maca, Cuzco giant maize, *pallares* (Lima beans) and *loche* (a regional squash) in Peru, and *quinua real* in Bolivia (Alianza de Aprendizaje Perú, 2011; Bidwell, 2020; Devaux et al., 2018).

Efforts to revalue Andean agri-food heritage have been particularly influenced by concepts and practices originating in Mediterranean Europe (France, Italy and Spain). This influence has come from international NGOs such as Slow Food, Rome-based development agencies such as the International Fund for Agriculture and Development (IFAD), European bilateral aid agencies, and the European connections of individual researchers, NGO workers and prominent chefs.

The diverse nature of these initiatives and their array of promises (sometimes varying depending on the audience or funder) make it useful to summarize and group their aspirations in the following three broad categories.

Equitable Socioeconomic Gains

Initiatives frequently promise to generate more income for people in marginalized rural areas by generating 'products with identity' (Ranaboldo, 2009) that command added value in markets for their authenticity, organic status or nutritional qualities. A (not always explicit) assumption is that indigenous and poorer groups will have a competitive advantage because of their tendency to maintain traditional, ecologically embedded products and practices (Bramley & Kirsten, 2007; IFAD and Slow Food, 2016). From the mid-2000s, efforts to revalue local products have also increasingly referenced objectives of food security and nutrition (Porras, 2015; Ranaboldo & Arosio, 2017).

Biocultural Sustainability

Other common objectives are to retain or recover agrobiodiversity, promote agroecological farming methods and retain or enhance local knowledge and traditional practices. Initiatives frequently envisage some kind of dynamic relationship between the socioeconomic and the biocultural objectives, with income and nutritional benefits expected to reward and thereby incentivize the conservation of diverse products and traditional practices (Bayer, 2017; Larson, 2007; Van de Kop et al., 2007; Vandecandelaere et al., 2010).

Territorial Identity and Social Cohesion

Most initiatives present collective action as both instrumentally necessary for achieving socioeconomic, cultural and environmental objectives, and as inherently desirable to achieve a sense of belonging and emotional wellbeing. Place, farming and food are commonly framed as a source of collective identity – whether this reflects European-influenced ideas of shared values and knowledge mediated by institutions (Fonte, 2008; Sanz Cañada & Muchnik, 2016), or indigenous philosophies of situated relationality between humans and non-humans (Argumedo & Swiderska, 2014; Grey, 2011).

An important point here is that a diverse range of actors have supported these initiatives. Arguably, ideological differences are less important in the Andes than in the North, where some discussions emphasize the 'bifurcation' between 'movement-oriented' and 'market-oriented' actors within organic and fair trade networks (Goodman et al., 2012). While there are philosophical differences between groups who favour market-led development and those with more transformational objectives, at a pragmatic level the projects they support often look quite similar. A good example is the Parque de la Papa (Potato Park) in the Cuzco region, which was founded to recover and conserve agrobiodiversity and promote indigenous rights, but has also established eco- and agro-tourism initiatives to generate income and a collective trademark to market local products (Argumedo, 2013; Asensio & Cavero Castillo, 2013).

CHALLENGES OF REVALUING ANDEAN AGRI-FOOD HERITAGE

What do the experiences to date of efforts to link food, identity and development in the Andes tell us about their prospects for generating positive economic, social and environmental impacts? Although this topic has not been studied with anything like the close attention accorded to some other ethical networks, the insights from a gradually accumulating body of research do allow some general reflections on successes and challenges. A common conclusion is that the impacts have been, on balance, positive, although often more limited, short-term and different in kind from those envisaged (Asensio & Avero Castillo, 2013; Bidwell, 2020; Healy, 2001; Kerssen, 2015; Matta, 2019; Turner, 2016). Rather than trying to summarize a very diverse group of experiences, the following sections discuss some general challenges to the assumed dynamics of ethical value networks focused on Andean agri-food heritage.

Productive and Ecological Challenges

Whether advocates of Andean agri-food heritage have more reformist or radical perspectives, or focus more on economic, social or ecological objectives, they tend to share certain representations. These depict Andean *campesinos* as dedicated small farmers with stable control of their land, cultural commitments to ecologically sustainable farming and a preference for traditional products and practices. While some truth underlies these representations, they can oversimplify or even essentialize the livelihoods and experiences of people in Andean rural areas.

On the one hand, traditional production systems are affected by ongoing social changes. Most people in the rural Andes now have diverse and mobile livelihoods, characterized by movement between rural and urban areas, an important role for non-agricultural employment, and a strong focus on ensuring access to education for their children (Bidwell, 2020; Leinaweaver, 2008; Paerregaard, 1997). Implications include reduced labour supply in rural areas, more land being cultivated under short-term rental and sharecropping arrangements, and general pressure to prioritize return on investment of money and time. This may translate into preferences for faster-growing, higher-yielding products and conventional farming practices.

On the other hand, demand for a reliable supply of products to ethical markets may upset the balance of Andean production systems. Kerssen (2015) shows how the quinoa boom on the southern Bolivian altiplano has shifted the traditional production zone for quinoa and disturbed its complementary relationship with alpaca and llama herding, while Turín et al. (2018) describe the ecological and social pressures in the Junín region of Peru resulting from increased global demand for maca. Conversely, my study (Bidwell, 2020) of the community of Tuti in the Colca Valley of Peru concludes that development projects aiming to increase organic quinoa exports were limited by local commitments to mixed farming, even before dwindling quinoa prices undermined these projects. Figure 8.3 illustrates the landscape of mixed farming in Tuti, with cultivated pasture for cattle (foreground), quinoa (middle) and broad beans (background).

Source: Simon Bidwell

Figure 8.3   Mixed farming in Tuti, Colca Valley

The main point here is that schemes to revalue Andean agri-food heritage are usually only partly compatible with the aspirations and livelihood challenges of *campesinos*. Andean rural populations do not necessarily have a 'natural' competitive advantage which just needs to be mobilized through the appropriate market channels; but nor do they necessarily have long-term commitments to ecologically sensitive farming and conserving diversity.

Challenges of Social Organization

As with ecological and productive relationships, advocates for both reformist and radical perspectives have a tendency to oversimplify social relationships in the rural Andes. Both perspectives present Andean communities as having an inherent tendency towards social solidarity and collective action, drawing on representations developed by the *indigenista* movements of the 1930s and elaborated by post-Second World War Andean anthropology (see Ferreira & Isbell, 2016). These assumptions of natural collectivity appeal to both development agencies (who see it as a source of social capital) and post-development advocates (who see indigenous solidarity as resisting capitalist individualism).

Again, there is some truth in these representations. Andean communities do maintain traditional collective institutions, especially to manage resources such as water and shared infrastructure while collective work parties (*faenas*), reciprocal exchange of labour and resources (*ayni*) and other collaborative arrangements continue to varying degrees in many places. However, these forms of collective action sit alongside longstanding internal conflicts and inequalities and increasing population diversity from migration and mobility (de la Cadena, 1988; Mayer, 2002; Paerregaard, 2017).

Importantly, the collective social arrangements that do persist do not necessarily provide a basis for business-like associations envisaged by development projects, which involve pooled resources, shared risk, and long-term financial and commercial planning. Given fear of corruption and mismanagement (sometimes well-founded based on past experiences), local engagement with these associations is often more short-term and transactional than project initiators expect (Bidwell, 2020).

Where sustained collective action is undertaken by Andean communities or producer associations, this may involve long-term support from NGOs, such as in Cuzco's Potato Park (Asensio & Cavero Castillo, 2013); platforms established by governments, peasant unions or other political or civil society groups, such as the National Quinoa Producers Association (ANAPQUI) in Bolivia (Cáceres et al., 2007); or partnership arrangements linking producer groups to buyers and processors, whether as part of solidarity-based or conventional networks.

These arrangements all have specific histories, and their own strengths and weaknesses. The point is that the kind of collective action required to conserve and promote local agri-food heritage does not spontaneously emerge out of existing community institutions. Whether the goal is reaching new niche markets or defending diversity, initiatives need serious consideration about the kind of collective action they require, and the resources and the support needed to sustain them.

Market-related Challenges

A third assumption made by advocates is that the special qualities of Andean agri-food products will be recognized and rewarded by markets that value authenticity and sustainability. This is particularly true of Mediterranean-influenced agendas to develop geographical indications for typical products, and it is also seen in optimism about the opportunities for *campesinos* to benefit from the gastronomic boom. Similar optimism is seen in discussions relating to Africa and the Pacific (Bramley & Kirsten, 2007; Jones et al., 2017).

Challenges with markets have been well covered by the literature on international fair trade and organic networks, which discusses issues such as the capture of much ethical value by large and powerful actors within 'buyer-driven' networks, and a tendency for the best-organized and supported producer groups to capture a disproportionate share of the gains that are retained in the South (Bidwell et al., 2018a; Howson, 2019).

However, it is worth noting the specific challenges for Andean and other indigenous agri-food products to obtain competitive advantage in markets that supposedly crave authenticity and 'beyond organic' uniqueness. On the one hand, highly place-based specialness rarely translates in distant markets. Given the fundamentally 'fictive' quality of authenticity (see Overton & Murray, 2016), it tends to be defined by the processors and retailers who control the relationship with consumers. As Yeung and Kerr (2011) argue, the legal protections provided by geographical indications are of little use when a product's reputation and meaning is not understood by consumers. On the other hand, in local spaces where the unique quality and reputation of Andean products *are* recognized, this cultural value is often associated with basic staples and home consumption, so demand for certified versions is limited to small tourism and speciality niches (Bidwell, 2020; Ofstehage, 2012).

Here we see a mismatch between Northern paradigms of 'value-added', identity-based products, which are generally packaged, semi-luxury foods that travel easily, such as wine and cheese, processed meats and oils (Acampora & Fonte, 2007; Rangnekar, 2004); and the kind of food identities valued in the Andes, usually linked to household-based processing, cooking and consumption (Bidwell, 2020). While international overviews of identity-based products may include colourful examples related to indigenous food traditions (Van de Kop et al., 2007; Vandecandelaere et al., 2010), discussions of commercially viable initiatives in the South usually involve the same handful of processed goods: primarily coffee, chocolate and cheese.[1]

WAYS FORWARD FOR ANDEAN AGRI-FOOD HERITAGE

This discussion of challenges should not be interpreted as implying a rejection of efforts to revalue Andean agri-food heritage. The biggest shortfall of these initiatives is not necessarily their implementation failures or unintended consequences but the marginal position they occupy in national development strategies based on mineral extraction, and, within agriculture, a favoured position for large agribusiness – even in those countries with expressed commitments to food sovereignty (Gysel, 2016; McKay et al., 2014).

Instead, an overall reflection emerging from the challenges discussed in the previous section is the importance of understanding the particular realities of the Andes and how they differ from the contexts for other ethical networks such as producer–consumer reconnection in the North, and the ethical export of tropical commodities from the South.

Another reflection is to take seriously the lessons from these other ethical networks. The first lesson – drawn particularly from Northern experiences – is the importance of building local markets. Discussions of origin-based products (especially in English) have focused on formal certification systems such as geographical indications (GIs). However, GIs only place a final seal on deep-rooted traditions, values and know-how that connect primary production with local processing and consumption cultures (Fonte, 2008; Sanz Cañada & Muchnik, 2016; Vandecandelaere et al., 2010). European experiences suggest that, first, local consumption is fundamental to any deep and sustainable appreciation of local agri-food identities; and second, this is a contested, political process. In France, the association of *terroir* with taste has evolved from pejorative to positive connotations, with disparagement of 'peasant food' only gradually giving way to appreciation of local authenticity; while political action by farmers was central to the inclusion of place-based criteria in French *appellations d'origine* (Nowak, 2018; Trubek, 2008). Likewise, Morgan et al. (2006) show that Tuscany's journey from productive backwardness to renowned food haven was based on local consumption and tourism.

This is a reminder that, in the wake of Peru's 'gastronomic boom', there are opportunities to move from an elite-mediated 'discovery' of Andean ingredients, to presenting products on their own terms, as valued and consumed in the village, home and field. This might involve moving organic and farmers markets from limited and occasional showcases to more regular, decentralized and accessible food sources; and from selective incorporation of 'exotic' native ingredients in the culinary creations of Lima-based chefs, to further developing *campesino* gastronomy in provincial eateries and tourism settings.

This point argues against basing development strategies primarily on export to national and international markets, but it also challenges post-development efforts to recuperate networks of local consumption and exchange, raising the question of how to scale up and embed these in national societies that are unlikely to divert from their increasingly cash-based and urbanized pathways.

The second lesson is the importance of sustained organizational efforts to build and maintain ethical networks, and particularly the resources and legitimacy offered by the state. In Europe, national governments and, more recently, the European Union, have had key roles in defining territories, setting quality standards, creating decentralized governance bodies and subsidizing initiatives that combine market and non-market objectives. In the South, the producer cooperatives that have become involved in fair trade and organic networks often date back to national agrarian reforms and associated state support for collective processing and marketing (see Bacon, 2013; Fridell, 2007; Giovannucci et al., 2009; Luetchford, 2008 for examples from Mexico, Peru, Colombia, the Dominican Republic, Nicaragua and Costa Rica).

Recognizing the role of the state does not necessarily conflict with agendas to decentralize and democratize food systems and it acknowledges the major organizational and advocacy role civil society groups have had in fair trade and organic networks. However, it does suggest that efforts to revalue agri-food heritage in the South may be limited in their scope and impact unless they are able to connect with and gain support from public policy agendas.

CONCLUSIONS

This chapter has offered an overview of ethical value networks that connect place, identity and food in Andean Latin America, particularly Peru. It has presented these networks not just as alternatives to mainstream food systems but as part of place-based strategies for development. The chapter has explored the striking way that formerly maligned Andean products and practices have gained new value. It has discussed the aspirations associated with initiatives to revalue Andean agri-food heritage, reflected on some general challenges they face, and made some suggestions about how these might be confronted.

To conclude, the chapter proposes a framework for further research that takes an integrated approach to assessing the impact of ethical value networks on places and livelihoods in the South. While drawn from study of the Andes, these suggestions may also be relevant to other contexts where peasant or indigenous communities have distinctive agri-food cultures.

First, research should evaluate what socioeconomic impacts ethical networks have, and for whom. This implies attention to how economic gains are shared, not only spatially but also socially. It means studying the patterns of inclusion and exclusion that networks create and assessing the impacts for smaller and poorer producers, women, young people, inward migrants, wage workers and local consumers.

Second, research should consider the impacts on ecological sustainability and biocultural diversity, including critical consideration of how these concepts are defined, and by whom. With regard to cultural aspects, this means recognizing the socially constructed and power-laden nature of 'tradition' and 'authenticity' and acknowledging the legitimate debates about cultural continuity versus innovation. A place-based approach can also allow careful attention to the relationships – and possible tensions – between biocultural and socioeconomic objectives.

Finally, and arguably most crucially, research should critically explore the kinds of collective action involved in initiatives to revalue agri-food heritage. This means applying special scrutiny to discourses about 'community', and looking closely at the history, power relations and institutional mechanisms of collective projects. Given the role assigned to place as a source of identity and value, a geographical lens is particularly useful for deciphering relationships between the spatial and the social.

Such a holistic and place-based approach can connect debates and insights in rural development with those from agri-food geographies, thus giving a richer view of ethical value networks in the Global South.

NOTE

1. The development of origin-based coffees and the growing attention to cacao origins in the burgeoning global craft chocolate industry show that this model can be partially reproduced in the South, although with significantly less agency for primary producers than in European examples.

REFERENCES

Acampora, T. & Fonte, M. (2007). Productos típicos, estrategias de desarrollo rural y conocimiento local. *Revista Opera*, 7, 191–212.

Alianza de Aprendizaje Perú, Agro Rural, INDECOPI. (2011). *Estudio de caso denominación de origen del maíz blanco gigante Cusco*. Authors.

Apfell-Marglin, F. (2002). From fieldwork to mutual learning: Working with PRATEC, *Environmental Values*, 11(3), 345–367.

Argumedo, A. (2013). *Collective trademarks and biocultural heritage: Towards new indications of distinction for indigenous peoples in the Potato Park, Peru*. IIED.

Argumedo, A. & Stenner, T. (2008). Association ANDES: Conserving indigenous biocultural heritage in Peru. *Gatekeeper*, 137a. IIED.

Argumedo, A. & Swiderska, K. (2014). *Biocultural heritage territories*. IIED.

Asensio, R.H. & Cavero Castillo, M. (2013). *El Parque de la Papa de Cusco: Claves y dilemas para el escalamiento de innovaciones rurales en los Andes (1998-2011)*. IEP, IDRC-CRDI, FIDA.

Bacon, C. (2013). Quality revolutions, solidarity networks, and sustainability innovations: Following Fair Trade coffee from Nicaragua to California. *Journal of Political Ecology*, 20(1), 98–115.

Bayer, K. (2017). Un ciclo virtuoso. Retrieved from: https://www.slowfood.com/es/un-ciclo-virtuoso/

Bidwell, S, (2020). *Cultivating what is ours: Local agri-food heritage as a development strategy in the Peruvian Andes*. PhD thesis, Victoria University of Wellington.

Bidwell, S., Murray, W.E., & Overton, J. (2018a). Ethical agro-food networks in global peripheries, Part I: The rise and recommodification of fair trade and organics. *Geography Compass*, 12(4), online DOI: 10.1111/gec3.12366 11pp.

Bidwell, S., Murray, W. E., & Overton, J. (2018b). Ethical agro-food networks in global peripheries, Part II: Re-placing commodity dependence. *Geography Compass*, 12(4), online DOI: 10.1111/gec3.12365 11pp.

Bramley, C. & Kirsten, J.F. (2007). Exploring the economic rationale for protecting geographical indicators in agriculture. *Agrekon*, 46 (1), 47–71.

Brush, S.B. (1996). Reconsidering the Green Revolution: Diversity and stability in cradle areas of crop domestication. *Human Ecology*, 20(2), 145–167.

Cáceres, Z., Carimentrand, A., & Wilkinson, J. (2007). Fair trade and quinoa from the Southern Bolivian Altiplano. In L.T. Raynolds, D. Murray, & J. Wilkinson (Eds.), *Fair trade: The challenges of transforming globalization* (pp. 180–199). Routledge.

de la Cadena, M. (1988). *Comuneros en huancayo. Migración campesina a ciudades serranas.* Instituto de Estudios Peruanos.

de la Cadena, M. (2001). Reconstructing race: Racism, culture and mestizaje in Latin America. *NACLA Report on the Americas*, 34(6), 16–23.

Desco (2014). Mejoramiento de las capacidades técnico-productivas y empresariales de productores rurales para la articulación de sus productos a mercados justos y competitivos. Project proposal presented to Fundación Paz y Solidaridad, Navarra, Spain.

Devaux, A., Velasco, C. & Ordinola, M. (2018). Desde los Andes a Africa y Asia: Vinculando pequeños productores al mercado: Lecciones para el desarrollo de cadenas de valor inclusivas. In M. Ordinola & D. Horton (Eds.), *SEPIA XVII Mesa Temática. Experiencias Latinoamericanas de aplicación del enfoque de cadenas de valor inclusivas.* Centro Internacional de la Papa.

Fan, J.E. (2013). Can ideas about food inspire real social change? The case of Peruvian gastronomy. *Gastronomica: The Journal of Food and Culture*, 13(2), 29–40.

Ferreira, F. & Isbell, B.J. (Eds.), (2016). *A return to the village: Community ethnographies and the study of Andean culture in retrospective.* Institute of Latin American Studies, University of London.

Fonte, M. (2008). Knowledge, food and place: A way of producing, a way of knowing. *Sociologia Ruralis*, 48(3), 200–222.

Fridell, G. (2007). *Fair trade coffee: The prospects and pitfalls of market-driven social justice.* University of Toronto Press.

Garcia, M.E. (2013). The taste of conquest: Colonialism, cosmopolitics, and the dark side of Peru's gastronomic boom. *The Journal of Latin American and Caribbean Anthropology*, 18(3), 505–524.

Giovannucci, D., Josling, T., Kerr, W.A., O'Connor, B. & Yeung, M.T. (2009). *Guide to geographical indications: Linking products and their origins.* International Trade Centre.

Goodman, D., DuPuis, E.M. & Goodman, M.K. (2012). *Alternative food networks: Knowledge, practice, and politics.* Routledge.

Grey, S. (2011). *Decolonization as relocalization: Conceptual and strategic frameworks of the Parque de la Papa, Qosqo.* Master's thesis, University of Victoria, British Columbia.

Gysel, A. (2016). *Food sovereignty and the role of the state: The case of Bolivia.* Center for Development and Cooperation (NADEL).

Healy, K. (2001). *Llamas, weavings and organic chocolate: Multicultural grassroots development in the Andes and Amazon of Bolivia.* University of Notre Dame Press.

Howson, K. (2019). *Bottling the colonial unconscious: Ethical value networks and the commodification of fairness in the South African wine industry.* PhD thesis, Victoria University of Wellington.

International Fund for Agricultural Development (IFAD) and Slow Food (2016). IFAD and Slow Food: A strategic partnership for inclusive and sustainable rural transformation [factsheet]. Retrieved from: https://www.ifad.org/en/web/knowledge/publication/asset/39594081

Jones, C., Murray, W.E., & Overton, J. (2017). FIJI Water, water everywhere – Global brands and democratic and social injustice. *Asia Pacific Viewpoint*, 58(1), 112–123.

Kerssen, T.K. (2015). Food sovereignty and the quinoa boom: challenges to sustainable re-peasantisation in the southern Altiplano of Bolivia. *Third World Quarterly*, 36(3), 489–507.

Krogel, A. (2011). *Food, power and resistance in the Andes: Exploring Quechua verbal and visual narratives.* Lexington.

Larson, J. (2007). *Relevance of geographical indications and designations of origin for the sustainable use of genetic resources.* Global Facilitation Unit for Underutilized Species.

Leinaweaver, J. (2008). Improving oneself: Young people getting ahead in the Peruvian Andes. *Latin American Perspectives*, 35(4), 60–78.

Loyer, J. & Knight, C. (2018). Selling the 'Inca superfood': nutritional primitivism in superfoods books and maca marketing. *Food, Culture & Society*, 21(4), 449–467.

Luetchford, P. (2008). *Fair trade and a global commodity: Coffee in Costa Rica.* Pluto Press.

Matta, R. (2013). Valuing native eating: The modern roots of Peruvian food heritage, *Anthropology of Food*, S8 [Online: https://journals.openedition.org/aof/7361].

Matta, R. (2019). Heritage foodways as matrix for cultural resurgence: Evidence from rural Peru. *The Journal of Cultural Property*, 26, 49–74.

Mayer, E. (2002). *The articulated peasant.* Westview Press.

McKay, B.N., Nehring, R. & Walsh-Dilley, M. (2014). The 'state' of food sovereignty in Latin America: Political projects and alternative pathways in Venezuela, Ecuador and Bolivia. *Journal of Peasant Studies*, 41(6), 1175–1200.

McMichael, P. (2009). A food regime genealogy. *Journal of Peasant Studies*, 36, 139–169.

Morgan, K., Marsden, T. & Murdoch, J. (2006). *Worlds of food: Place, power, and provenance in the food chain.* Oxford University Press.

National Research Council (1989). *Lost crops of the Incas: Little-known plants of the Andes with promise for worldwide cultivation.* National Academy Press.

Nowak, Z. (2018). Terroir: A socially constructed subterranean landscape gone global. In J. Zeunert & T. Waterman (Eds.), *Routledge handbook of landscape and food* (pp. 543–551). Abingdon: Routledge.

Ofstehage, A. (2012). The construction of an alternative quinoa economy: Balancing solidarity, household needs, and profit in San Agustın, Bolivia. *Agriculture and Human Values*, 29(4), 441–454.

Overton, J. & Murray W.E. (2016). Fictive place. *Progress in Human Geography*, 40(6), 794–809.

Paerregaard, K. (1997). *Linking separate worlds: Urban migrants and rural lives in Peru.* Berg.

Paerregaard, K. (2017). Ayni unbounded: Cooperation, inequality, and migration in the Peruvian Andes. *The Journal of Latin American and Caribbean Anthropology*, 22(3), 459–474.

Palomino-Gonzales, M.M. (2016). Gourmetización del alimento andino y la estetización del agricultor como parte del boom gastronómico peruano. *Razón y Palabra*, 20(3), 573-586.

Porras, C. (2015). Innovación, identidad, inclusión social y sostenibilidad ambiental premiadas en el concurso Sabores y Delicias de Nuestro Ecuador. Retrieved from: http://www.diversidadbioculturalyterritorios.org/

Radcliffe, S.A. & Laurie, N. (2006). Culture and development: Taking culture seriously in development for Andean people. *Environment and Planning D: Society and Space*, 24, 231–248.

Ranaboldo, C. (2009). Recorridos de una mirada latinoamericana. In C. Ranaboldo & A. Schetjman (Eds.), *El valor del patrimonio cultural* (pp. 13–38). Lima: Instituto de Estudios Peruanos.

Ranaboldo, C. & Arosio, M. (2017). Patrimonio agroalimentario regional para la seguridad alimentaria y el desarrollo territorial colombiano. Retrieved from: http://www.fao.org/in-action/territorios-inteligentes/articulos/colaboraciones/detalle/en/c/883975/

Rangnekar D. (2004). *The socio-economics of geographical indications: A review of empirical evidence from Europe.* Issue Paper No. 8. ICTSD, UNCTAD.

Ray, C. (1998). Culture, intellectual property and territorial rural development. *Sociologia Ruralis*, 38, 3–20.

Saad, N. (2009). Agrobiodiversity conservation as 'symbolic conquest': The case of in situ potato conservation in Bolivia. *Canadian Journal of Latin American and Caribbean Studies*, 34(68), 89–109.

Sanz Cañada, J. & Muchnik, J. (2016). Geographies of origin and proximity: Approaches to local agri-food systems. *Culture & History Digital Journal*, 5(1), e002.

Shepherd, C.J. (2010). Mobilizing local knowledge and asserting culture: The cultural politics of in situ conservation of agricultural biodiversity. *Current Anthropology*, 51(5), 629–654.

Tapia, M. (1990). *Cultivos andinos subexplotados y su aporte a la alimentación.* FAO.

Tregear, A. (2011). Progressing knowledge in alternative and local food networks: Critical reflections and a research agenda. *Journal of Rural Studies*, 27, 419–430.

Trubek, A. (2008). *The taste of place: A cultural journey into terroir.* University of California Press.

Turín, C. Carbajal, M., Zorogastúa, P., Chamorro, A. & Quiroz, R. (2018). El boom de la maca: transformando paisajes y sociedades rurales de la zona central altoandina del Perú. In R. Fort Meyer, M. Varese Zimic & C. de los Rios Farfán (Eds.), *Perú: el problema agrario en debate – SEPIA XVII* (pp. 761824). Lima: SEPIA.

Turner, K.L. (2016). *Feeding local economies: Bolivia's edible biocultural heritage and rural territorial development.* PhD thesis, University of Manitoba.

Van de Kop, P., Sautier, D., & Gerz, A. (2007). *Origin-based products. Lessons for pro-poor market development.* Royal Tropical Institute & CIRAD.

Vandecandelaere, E., Arfini, F., Belletti, G. & Marescotti, A. (2010). *Linking people, places and products. A guide for promoting quality linked to geographical origin and sustainable geographical indications.* FAO.

Weismantel, M.J. (2001). *Cholas and pishtacos: Stories of race and sex in the Andes.* University of Chicago Press.

Wu Guin, S. & Alvarado de la Fuente, F. (2015). Cronología para la historia del movimiento de agricultura ecológica en el Perú. Unpublished working document, Centro IDEAS.

Yeung, M. T. & Kerr, W. A. (2011). Are geographical indications a wise strategy for developing country farmers? Greenfields, clawbacks and monopoly rents. *Journal of World Intellectual Property*, 14(5), 353–367.

9   Old wine in new bottles? Fair trade wine in Chile

Peter B.F. Williams

INTRODUCTION

Chile was the first country in Latin America to introduce fair trade wine, and evidence suggests that it has proven relatively successful. Drawing on findings from doctoral research fieldwork, this chapter begins by briefly discussing the rise of fair trade in Chile, before focusing on the growing use of fair trade certifications in Chilean viticulture and oenology. In particular, this chapter concentrates on the key opportunities and challenges of the expanding fair trade wine sector in Chile, with an emphasis on the perspectives and experiences of small-scale grape growers and wine producers. The chapter asks if fair trade certifications have been applied successfully to create a more ethical wine sector in Chile, or if fair trade wine merely represents old wine in new bottles.

This chapter draws from research findings from fieldwork completed in Chile between January 2017 and June 2017, as part of doctoral research completed at Victoria University of Wellington, New Zealand. Forty-one semi-structured interviews were conducted in Chile during this fieldwork period with a range of participants: including small, medium and large-scale wine and wine grape producers, local experts and fair trade certifier groups. Semi-structured interviews, using sets of open-ended questions, were deemed the most appropriate approach for interviews, as they provided the participants with the opportunity to discuss their experiences and perspectives while also retaining enough structure to identify common themes (Given, 2008). Interviews were completed in the Chilean capital Santiago, as well as the wine producing areas of the Curicó Valley in the Maule Region and the Colchagua Valley in the O'Higgins Region (see Figure 9.1). Throughout the fieldwork stages in Chile, the research expanded beyond Curicó and Colchagua to include a fair trade certified wine cooperative Cooperativa Vitivinicola Loncomilla located to the south of Curicó, in San Javier de Loncomilla. Fieldwork in Chile also included the producer union Coalición Nacional de Viñateros por una

Industria Sin Abusos whose directive is based in the Itata Valley in the Bío Bío Region in Southern Chile.

Figure 9.1   *Wine producing regions of Chile*

THE BEGINNINGS OF FAIR TRADE IN CHILE

Over the last 20 years, and especially during the last decade, there has been significant growth in certification schemes in Chile's viticultural sector targeted towards consumers concerned with ethical and sustainable production. This has included concerns about social inequalities and labour practices, demonstrated particularly through the growing use of fair trade certificates (Kleine, 2008). Fair trade certifications were first implemented in Chile in the 1990s. Three organisations, outside of the viticultural sector, led the initial implementation of fair trade products: la Cooperativa Campesina Apícola Valdivia, Comparte, and la Fundación Solidaridad. These three groups emerged in the difficult social and political context of rural Chile under the Pinochet dictatorship in the 1970s and 1980s. In this context, these groups emerged to support vulnerable small-scale producers to escape cycles of poverty and to promote fairer conditions and market access for these groups, eventually linking with international fair trade networks in the 1990s (Kleine, 2008; Malo & Mori, 2003; Wijnant et al., 2015). In 2018, there were 42 Chilean organisations and companies certified with one of the three fair trade certifications: World Fair Trade Organisation (WFTO), Fair Trade International (FLOCERT), and Fair for Life (Herman, 2019; Kleine, 2008; Wijnant et al., 2015; Williams, 2019). The domestic Chilean market for fair trade products, however, remains limited, and fair trade products are oriented towards markets in the Global North (Wijnant et al., 2015).

THE RISE OF FAIR TRADE IN THE CHILEAN WINE SECTOR

The highly concentrated export oriented wine sector in Chile provides the contextual background to the rise of fair trade there. From the mid-1990s until recently, Chilean wine production and exports have experienced sustained growth despite some dips, as shown in Figure 9.2. The number of vineyards, however, have declined over the last four decades. For example, in 1975, there were 22,000 vineyards, by 1997 there were only 11,000 despite the growing levels of wine exports and production. In 2007, the number of vineyards in Chile had only grown to just over 14,000 despite impressive and sustained sector growth over the ten-year period between 1997 and 2007. These trends highlight the concentration of Chilean wine production and exports (del Pozo, 2014; Morel-Astorga, 2002). Chile's remarkable viticultural growth, particularly over the last three decades (see Figure 9.2), has been supported by the upgrading of the sector and the influx of foreign and national investment (Overton et al., 2012). Over this period, the Chilean wine sector has developed from a traditional sector oriented towards a relatively stagnant national market into an intensive export-oriented industry, with over 60% of total wine production exported (Farinelli et al., 2017).

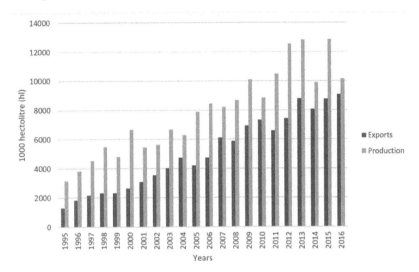

Source: Elaborated by the author using data from Organisation of Vine and Wine (2020)

Figure 9.2   Wine production and exports in Chile, 1995–2016

Since 1990, a few industrial-scale wine producers have dominated the Chilean wine industry: Concha y Toro, San Pedro, Santa Rita, Santa Carolina and Undurraga. In 1995, these five companies produced around 160 million litres of wine, over half of all of Chile's wine production that year (del Pozo, 2014). By 2010, the domination of a few companies further consolidated, and only three companies; Concha y Toro, San Pedro and Santa Rita controlled the large majority of total wine production and exports (del Pozo, 2014). These companies therefore have substantial influence in the industry and are able to set the prices of the grapes mainly produced by small and medium scale producers. Researcher Fabiola Argandoña from Universidad de Santiago de Chile described this situation as follows:

> Three Chilean companies now control 70–90% of the national wine production … unfortunately these monopolistic practices have not really been investigated. The small producers sell in a disadvantaged position in relation to the large companies which set the prices. (Interview, March 2017)

Chile's neoliberal policies that encouraged trade liberalisation and exports promoted the growth of these companies (Overton & Murray, 2011). Since 1990, small-scale domestic wine producers oriented towards low-end local markets have almost vanished altogether in the context of sectoral concentration (Morel-Astorga, 2002).

Vineyard ownership has also become increasingly concentrated since the 1990s. Between 1990 and 2010, the large-scale Chilean wine producers have expanded their vineyards, thus relying less on small-scale producers for the supply of grapes (Morel-Astorga, 2002). In this increasingly concentrated industry, Chile's small-scale grape producers have become progressively more vulnerable to market forces and unfair competition. Many of these small-scale producers have not been able to sustain their viticultural activities and have disappeared due to the very low grape prices set by the dominant wine producers (del Pozo, 2014; Overton & Murray, 2013). Research interview participants frequently mentioned these challenges associated with the concentration of Chile's wine industry. For instance, Álvaro Muñoz from the cooperative of small-scale producers Cooperativa Vitivinicola Loncomilla explained that:

> In Chile, there are three very important wine producers which use their size to abuse the smaller-scale producers ... these three control the prices of the grape market ... they all continue to pay less and less and have dropped the price to one that is not fair ... There are a lot of injustices in the sector. (Interview, May 2017)

In this context, small-scale and medium-scale grape and wine producers have searched for avenues to escape their vulnerable positions. Fair trade certified wine has represented one of these avenues and, since the early 2000s, fair trade certifications have expanded in the Chilean wine sector. By 2015, fair trade certified wine represented 33.4% of all Chilean products sold under a fair trade label (Wijnant et al., 2015). An important driving factor for the expansion of fair trade certified wine in Chile is the purchasing policies of Nordic countries (Denmark, Finland, Sweden and Norway). Under government-controlled alcohol purchasing monopolies, these countries have prioritised wines with ethical and sustainable production labels. This has created important markets for fair trade certified wine and has encouraged Chilean wine producers to implement fair trade certifications (Kleine, 2008; Malo & Mori, 2003; Wijnant et al., 2015). However, it is important to note that despite the expansion of fair trade certified wine in Chile, fair trade wine remains a minor segment of Chile's total wine production (Williams, 2019).

Fair trade certified grape and wine producers in Chile have entered into either the FLOCERT Fairtrade or IMO Fair for Life systems of certification, while small-scale handcraft producers tend to use the WFTO certification (Wijnant et al., 2015; Williams, 2019). Although there are some variations between FLOCERT Fairtrade and IMO certifications, both offer two different fair trade models: the cooperative model and the plantation or hired labour model. In February 2019, the fair trade price for non-organic FLOCERT Fairtrade certified wine grapes was €0.28 per kilogram (kg), with an additional €0.05 per kg paid as the fair trade premium. Certified organic and Fairtrade wine grapes received a higher price of €0.33 per kg plus the additional €0.05 per kg in premium (FLOCERT, 2019). Under the hired labour model, certified companies commit to decent working conditions for their employees and protect employees' rights following International Labour Organization Conventions. These rights include the right to join a union, the right to a safe and healthy work environment, and the prohibition of any discrimination or the use of child labour. Under the hired labour fair trade model, employees of a certified company form fair trade committees and decide how the fair trade premium is used to benefit employees and the local community (Fair for Life, n.d.; FLO International, n.d.). It is worth noting that certified fair trade wine produced and sold within Chile is usually sold without any fair trade labelling. This demonstrates that fair trade wine continues to represent what Jaffee et al. (2004) identified as 'far trade' despite the fact that the growing middle-classes in countries such as Chile have the financial capacities to purchase ethically labelled products.

Source: Peter Williams

Figure 9.3   *Wine barrels at Miguel Torres Winery, Curico Valley*

In Chile's main viticultural zones of the Central Valley, nine producer groups have implemented fair trade certifications in wine and grape production. The fair trade certified groups outlined in Table 9.1 provided varied case studies for this research. For example, Miguel Torres represents a large-scale and long-established winery with Spanish ownership while Viñas Caupolicán, is an association of small-scale grape producers from the area. These cases provided interesting comparative studies of fair trade within the same zone. Figure 9.3 displays an example of the wineries in Curicó.

Bordering Curicó to the south, the Red del Vino (Wine Network), an association of small-scale producers in the Colchagua Valley provided important findings for this research (Figure 9.4). Red del Vino is an association involved in grape and wine production that is FLOCERT certified and has a tourism programme based on ethical production and *campesino* traditions. This provided a separate case to be compared and contrasted with the case studies in Curicó. Furthermore, a number of vineyards in Colchagua are implementing alternative ethical trade schemes, such as Fair for Life certified Montes Wines and Polkura Wines which is B-Corp certified.

KEY OPPORTUNITIES IN CHILE'S FAIR TRADE WINE NETWORK

A key opportunity of fair trade is the creation of niche markets supported by an ethical narrative to attract customers, while offering fairer and more stable grape prices for producers. This provides a clear opportunity for small-scale producers to escape their dependence on the frequently low and fluctuating prices offered in the open market in Chile. Small-scale grape growers who participated in field interviews explained the difficulties in making a profit in the conventional grape market due to low prices for grapes that often dipped well below the cost of production. Yenny Llanos from the Coalición Nacional de Viñateros de Chile described the vulnerable position of the grape producers in the open market of Chile; "There is not a relationship between the grape producers and the buyer, there is just abuse. The buyer sets a low price and the producer has to accept this, they do not have any power to negotiate" (interview, May 2017). This essentially means that these producers have faced low grape prices and growing debt over successive years.

Fair trade certified grape growers explained that the fair trade market provided them with fairer prices that surpass the production costs while providing a profit margin. José, a small-scale grape grower at the fair trade producer association Red del Vino, explained the difficulties of making a profit in the

conventional grape market and highlighted the positive impact the fair trade
certification has had on grape prices:

> The grape prices are not fair in Chile. The production cost for a kilogram of grapes is
> between 150–180 pesos, but sometimes we are forced to sell our grapes for 70–130
> pesos … we suffer large losses with these prices. Fair trade has had an impact, it
> pays more than the standard market prices. (Interview, April 2017)

Table 9.1   *Key producer groups of fair trade certification in the Chilean
wine sector*

Organisation	Description
Lautaro	Vinos Lautaro was formed by a group of 17 small-scale producers in the Sagrada Familia district, in Curicó, Maule Region, in 1997. Lauraro is considered a leader in fair trade in Chilean wine and begun exporting wine to Oxfam Belgium under fair trade conditions without certification from 1997. In 2009, Vinos Lautaro certified with FLOCERT.
Miguel Torres	Miguel Torres is a Spanish-owned winery that expanded its operations into Chile in 1979, establishing its base in Curicó. Torres in Chile became fair trade certified in 2010, under the Fair for Life label. Torres is also considered a leader in Chile's fair trade wine sector due to its relatively high profile for promoting the certification.
Esperanza para la Costa	Esperanza para la Costa was formed by 19 small-scale grape producers and was certified with the FLOCERT after an offshore earthquake devastated central Chile in 2010. This group produces traditional País grape for Miguel Torres under fair trade sale conditions.
Red del Vino	Red del vino was formed in 2004, by 19 small-scale producers in the Colchagua Valley. The group certified with FLOCERT in 2010. Red del Vino has also promoted alternative forms of wine tourism.
Caupolicán	Viñas Caupolicán was originally founded by 23 all women small-scale grape producers following grape price crashes in 2007. The organisation certified with FLOCERT in 2008. Its producers are based in the Sagrada Familia, Curicó, Maule.
Agrícola Vitivinícola Loncomilla	Cooperativa Agrícola Vitivinícola Loncomilla was formed in 1959 with government support to assist small-scale farmers in Loncomilla, Maule. The cooperative is certified with FLOCERT.
Emiliana	Viña Emiliana was established as one of Chile's first and largest organic certified wineries. In 2011, Emiliana certified with Fair for Life and in 2012 with FLOCERT, these certifications cover the winery's hired labour. Emiliana has vineyards in diverse regions of Chile, including in Colchagua and Casablanca.
Viña La Fortuna	Viña La Fortuna is located in Sagrada Familia, Curicó, Maule. The winery was one of Chile's first wineries to certify for organic production. In 2009, La Fortuna certified with FLOCERT under the hired labour model.
Casas Patronales	Casas Patronales is a relatively new winery formed in 2001. It was certified in 2013 with Fair for Life under the hired labour model. It has various vineyards in the Maule Region.

Source: Elaborated by the author using primary information.

Source: Peter B.F. Williams

Figure 9.4   Fair trade wine banner at Red del Vino, Colchagua Valley

Moreover, representatives from fair trade grape and wine producing associations described the key opportunity of the fair trade premium. For example, Victor Aguilera, Commercial Manager at Lautaro, explained that since certifying with fair trade, there have been positive changes for the organisation's grape-producing partners that extend beyond better prices:

> We have seen a complete change in the quality of life of our partners, there have been large improvements which do not only relate to the better incomes. Our producers have stated that they have experienced significant changes in themselves …

they have moved from being small-scale producers to owners of an export company. The changes for the families have also been very important. (Interview, May 2017)

The fair trade market has therefore provided an ethical niche market that represents an alternative to the unstable and low-paid conventional wine grape market controlled by a handful of powerful Chilean wine exporters. Primary research participants also discussed broader benefits that fair trade has created for groups of small-scale producers in Chilean viticulture. A number of small-scale producers described how fair trade had been an important support for them and their families. For instance, Luis, a small-scale grape producer and partner at the fair trade association Viña Caupolicán, explained how fair trade had supported him and improved the quality of life of his family: "I have noticed changes in my life since entering fair trade, life was a lot harder before fair trade ... after we became certified, our children have the opportunities to study, this is paid by the fair trade premium" (Interview, April 2017).

Over the last decade, the different international fair trade certifiers, Fairtrade International, Institute of Marketology (IMO) and Fair Trade USA, have integrated larger companies into the fair trade movement under the plantation or hired labour model previously described. The growing involvement of these larger companies and hired labour has sparked global debates about fair trade, including in Chile's fair trade wine sector (Herman, 2019). For those that supported this shift it is argued that fair trade is having a 'larger impact' by reaching more vulnerable workers and producers in the Global South (Fair Trade USA, 2012). Those against the inclusion of larger companies have maintained that this shift has removed small-scale producers from the central focus of fair trade (Equal Exchange, 2012; Renard, 2005). Nevertheless, a range of research participants mentioned the positive outcomes fair trade had created for the employees at larger-scale fair trade certified wineries. Research participants explained that fair trade had positive outcomes for employees in the viticultural network when there was a clear commitment to fair trade by these companies. A number of employees interviewed from fair trade certified wineries felt that the certification had been something positive for them and their colleagues.

The research also demonstrated that there have been some positive outcomes for small-scale grape producers resulting from the integration of larger wineries into the fair trade wine network in Chile. For instance, Secundina Vasquez, from Esperanza para la Costa, explained that the integration of large wineries into fair trade has created benefits for her and other fair trade certified grape producers. Secundina highlighted the positive relationship between the cooperative and Miguel Torres Wines:

> Our relationship with Miguel Torres is very good, we are not numbers to them, we are people … they involve us in their events about the products that we supply grapes for, and they introduce us to the clients … because of fair trade we receive a better price for our grapes, which means a better a quality of life. (Interview, June 2017)

Throughout the field research, it was evident that company engagement in fair trade has created some positive impacts and reached some vulnerable producers and workers in Chile. This positive impact was usually linked to the premium raised through fair trade For example, Roberto from the fair trade committee at winery La Fortuna – a fair trade certified winery – explained that fair trade had been successful in realising a range of positive outcomes for the employees;

> For us workers, the certification has been very important, the premiums have generated a great impact for us. We are taking very good advantage of the premium through different projects; from repairing bikes, to fixing teeth, to the solidary fund which helps workers … It is difficult to measure the changes that fair trade has caused in our lives, but it has helped us a lot. (Interview, May 2017)

Some of the wider literature claims regarding fair trade states that these certifications encourage benefits for communities generated through the social premium raised through fair trade that is designated towards projects for community social development (Méndez et al., 2010). The various fair trade certifications used by both small-scale producer groups and companies with hired labour generate this premium to be used in projects such as schools, health clinics, transport and infrastructure, which should encourage broad benefits in the local communities (Dragusanu et al., 2014; Jaffee et al., 2004). In Chile, research participants frequently claimed that fair trade creates broad community benefits. The first involves providing basic necessities for the producers or workers and their families and, once these basic needs are covered, the second vision is to support the community through social projects funded through the fair trade premium.

At the broader network level, field research did reveal some important differences between the conventional and fair trade wine network. In particular, over 30 of the 41 research participants highlighted shifts in the way the different actors interacted and changes in the governance of the fair trade wine network in Chile. These interviews highlighted a shift from the hierarchical-captive governance frameworks common in Chile's conventional wine network to possibly more relational governance. Gereffi and Lee (2012,

p. 25) demonstrated that relational governance is characterised by 'Frequent interactions and knowledge sharing based on mutual trust and social ties between parties...'. Power and value are also shared more evenly in relational governed chains (Gereffi and Lee, 2012). The links and relationships in the fair trade network were also noted to differ from those in the conventional wine network. For example, reciprocal and stronger relationships between the different actors had been created in the fair trade wine network.

Overall, the fair trade wine network was considered to be more inclusive, allowing upgrading for upstream (production-end) actors such as small-scale grape and wine producers, and it provides more space for producer cooperatives compared with the concentrated conventional sector. The fair trade wine network was seen to be more transparent and producers involved in fair trade certified wine felt that they had a good level of access to information about the network and how value was being shared. This is echoed by fair trade literature that highlighted improved transparency in fair trade networks in comparison with conventional trade (Dragusanu et al., 2014). However, fieldwork revealed that, in practice, these outcomes tended to vary. For instance, the interviews indicated that the differences between the conventional and fair trade wine networks were sometimes only slight as participants often argued that the fair trade network involved the same processes and involved many of the same actors as the conventional wine network.

KEY CHALLENGES IN CHILE'S FAIR TRADE WINE NETWORK

Field research also demonstrated a number of challenges and limitations during the implementation of fair trade. As exemplified by an unnamed academic from the Universidad de Chile who explained that there are limitations to how ethical certifications can solve the larger problems faced by small-scale producers in Chile's viticultural sector: "I am not sure if the certifications can help with the problems we have discussed ... my impression is that the problems are created by monopolist power in the wine sector, and this cannot be resolved with a certification" (Interview, February 2017). The interviews also found that some participants believed that fair trade had failed to improve the overall quality of life of the certified producers while also failing to solve the larger problems that these producers faced in Chile's wine sector. It became evident through the primary interviews that there are limitations to how ethical certifications can solve the larger problems faced by small-scale producers in Chile's viticultural sector and created by monopolist power in the Chilean wine sector. In this sense, fair trade wine in Chile remains too limited in scope to be able to address the larger problems experienced by small-scale grape producers in Chile, caused by the dominant positions of a select few powerful wine producers which control the grape markets and enforce low prices.

Likewise, interview participants discussed the restrictive options for small-scale producers when attempting to enter the fair trade certification. Participants discussed some of the problems in finding the demand for niche fair trade products as there are many instances where the commercial opportunities simply do not exist. Ingrid Allende from Fairtrade International explained that the costs of certifying can represent an important barrier for producers: 'An important barrier is the cost of the certification, it is around 2,000 Euros which is 1,500,700 Chilean Pesos for the first year. This is a barrier because there are associations which are just starting or very small and they do not have a lot of access to finance' (interview, March 2017). This represents a significant barrier for cooperatives. Some participants stated that this cost barrier frequently excluded small-scale producers from fair trade certification, to diminish the core principle of fair trade as an instrument to support vulnerable producers. For example, Gabriel Edwards, a medium-scale winemaker, stated that:

> I believe the main problem with fair trade is the cost of certifying, this takes away from the essence of fair trade as it is a high cost for smaller producers. There are many smaller producers which are fairer than the larger ones, but they cannot afford these certifications. (Interview, May 2017)

This is a clear failing of the fair trade network. By excluding the most vulnerable small-scale producers it is unclear how fair trade is able to address some of the ethical concerns among Northern consumers about these types of producer groups (Jaffee & Howard, 2010). Similarly, Gerardo Wijnant, fair trade consultant in Chile, explained that financial support, so that producers can access certifications, simply does not exist and that the Chilean state has not shown enough interest in supporting the expansion of fair trade:

> There is a shortage of available finance. This impedes the producers from fully taking advantage of the certifications. Also, there is low public sector recognition of fair trade which means that public agencies are failing to generate more projects … to help develop fair trade here. (Interview, March 2017)

There are also other barriers that restrict small-scale producers from becoming fair trade certified. In particular, participants discussed the importance of creating producer cooperatives so that producers can share the costs and administration involved in fair trade certification. However, there are important and context-specific challenges of forming producers' cooperatives in Chile. Raúl

Navarrete, General Manager at Vinos Lautaro, described a context specific challenge to forming producers' cooperatives in Chile:

> In Chile, a challenge is that the producers are nervous about working in coopera-
> tives. This came before the Pinochet era but was worsened during the dictatorship
> ... This has made it very difficult to encourage producer cooperatives, which has
> made it more difficult for small-scale producers to certify with fair trade. (Interview,
> May 2017)

In other cases, producer groups lacked knowledge about the fair trade certifications which created a marked barrier to becoming certified. Academic, Daniella Gac, from Universidad De Los Lagos, explained this barrier:

> There are some producers that don't know about these certifications, including in
> the cases where it would make a lot of sense that they use these certificates. This is
> an area where the public sector could help a lot by informing the producers through
> the institutions that support small-scale producers. (Interview, March 2017)

Research participants also discussed a number of negative or failed outcomes associated with the involvement of larger companies in Chile's fair trade wine sector. For instance, representatives from fair trade certified wine producing cooperatives explained that it signified a shift from its original purpose of supporting small-scale primary producers. These participants discussed how larger wineries have come to dominate the fair trade wine network that is excluding small-scale producer groups from these niche markets. Gerardo Orellana, from Red del Vino, described this challenge:

> I don't understand why a company should certify itself so that their workers receive
> minimal benefits. These benefits are the basic responsibilities of the company ...
> For us, the most negative change is that the large companies arrive with all of their
> resources and occupy a niche that was started to support small-scale producers.
> (Interview, April 2017)

Small-scale producers and representatives from the producer cooperatives largely believed that allowing the engagement of larger companies in fair trade had been a mistake. Instead, a number of participants described how fair trade is now largely being used as a marketing tool which has detached smaller-scale producers from the fair trade ethical niche market. Álvaro Muñoz from Cooperativa Vitivinicola Loncomilla explained this challenge:

> I believe that in some cases there are wineries that shouldn't be fair trade certified,
> especially the larger wineries. I feel they use the certification as a marketing tool
> more than a real conviction to improving the living conditions of their workers ...
> the benefits of fair trade are meant to go to the raw material producers. (Interview,
> May 2017)

Participants frequently stated that corporate integration had converted fair trade certification into an unfair system. Raúl Navarrete, General Manager at Vinos Lautaro, for instance, discussed the involvement of the larger companies in fair trade and explained how this engagement has failed to contribute to social justice and equality goals of fair trade. Instead, Raúl described how fair trade is now largely being used as a marketing tool, which has removed smaller-scale producers from the fair trade ethical niche market:

> It is not fair when larger wineries use fair trade because small-scale producer organisations like ours cannot compete with transnational wine exporters ... the inclusion of the large companies into fair trade does not contribute to social justice or equality. (Interview, May 2017)

A number of participants identified the lack of distinction between fair trade certification for small-scale producers and hired labour as an important failure of fair trade. As explained by Rodrigo Valenzuela, General Manager at Red del Vino, this creates confusion as there is ambiguity about what groups the fair trade certification are really supporting:

> It is unfair that our wine made by small-scale producers uses the same fair trade certification as the wines of the large producers ... I believe there is manipulation of information by the certifiers ... it is unfair that the consumer does not have the clarity of what kind of fair trade they are supporting. (Interview, March 2017)

There is therefore a clear risk that the ethical value of fair trade can be co-opted by corporate actors (Jaffee & Howard, 2010). In the case of Chile, there has been a clear insertion of larger-scale and high-end wine exporters which have entered the ethical niche market. These corporate actors have entered into the fair trade wine network as the ethical value created in this network represents an opportunity for profits. By exploiting this opportunity for profit, these corporate wine exporters are appropriating the ethical value intended for smaller-scale and more disadvantaged producers in the network. The appropriation of the ethical value of the fair trade wine network through the insertion of corporate capital provides a warning for other similar fair trade networks which are being established (Jaffee & Howard, 2010).

CONCLUSIONS: OLD WINE IN NEW BOTTLES?

This chapter has discussed the rise of the fair trade wine network in Chile. In doing so, it has focused on the conditions which drove the expansion of fair trade in Chilean viticulture, including a highly concentrated industry controlled by a small group of powerful corporate actors. In this uneven environment, small-scale grape growers and wine producers face increasingly asymmetric power relations and are forced to operate in poorly paid and unstable markets. In response, vulnerable producers have sought ethical niche markets supported by conscious consumers, primarily in the Global North. The fair trade wine market, first driven by Nordic markets which demand ethical and sustainable wine, has become an attractive option for these producer groups. As explored, some of the key opportunities of the fair trade wine network in Chile have been the fairer and more stable markets as well as fairer places to work. Likewise, the fair trade premium has created wider benefits for a handful of rural communities in Chile. At the broader network level, fieldwork identified that the fair trade wine network in Chile was a more inclusive network characterised by relational governance based on reciprocal and stronger relationships between the different actors.

However, the study also revealed some key challenges that offer broader warnings for other similar ethical value networks. In particular, the Chilean case demonstrated the scope of fair trade remained very niche in a sector with widespread inequalities. The research highlighted that fair trade was unable to address the wider problems created by the high concentration of the sector in the hands of a select few very large wine exporters. Likewise, the financial and administrative barriers to fair trade for the smallest-scale and most vulnerable producers means that the fair trade network can also worsen inequalities by excluding these actors from the ethical niche market. As outlined in this chapter, corporate actors have also been attracted to the fair trade network as this represents a new opportunity for profits. The growing insertion of larger-scale wine exporters into the fair trade network means that the value of fair trade is being increasing appropriated by these actors. The growing appropriation of the fair trade wine network by corporate actors means that, despite some clear exceptions, fair trade Chilean wine increasingly represents old wine – produced by the conventional wine exporters – in new bottles with fair trade labelling (Herman, 2019; Williams, 2019).

REFERENCES

del Pozo, J. (2014). *Historia del vino chileno: Desde la época colonial hasta hoy* (1st ed.). LOM Ediciones.

Dragusanu, R., Giovannucci, D., & Nunn, N. (2014). The economics of fair trade. *Journal of Economic Perspectives*, 28(3), 217–236.

Equal Exchange. (2012). Support the authentic fair trade movement. Retrieved 08 December, 2015, from http://equalexchange.coop/small-farmer-campaign

Fair for Life. (n.d.). About for life and fair for life. Retrieved 04 June 2019, from http://www.fairforlife.org

Fair Trade USA. (2012). Fair trade for all update. Retrieved 08 December 2015, from http://fairtradeusa.org/

Farinelli, F., Fernández-Stark, K., Meneses, J., Meneses, S., Mulder, N., & Reuse, K. (2017). *Use of knowledge-intensive services in the Chilean wine industry*. Economic Commission for Latin America and the Caribbean.

FLO International. (n.d.). Certifying fairtrade. Retrieved 4 June 2019, from https://www.fairtrade.net

FLOCERT. (2019). Minimum price and premium information. Retrieved 4 June 2019, from https://www.fairtrade.net/standards/price-and-premium-info.html

Gereffi, G., & Lee, J. (2012). Why the world suddenly cares about global supply chains. *Journal of Supply Chain Management,* 48(3), 24-32.

Given, L. (2008). *The SAGE encyclopedia of qualitative research methods*. SAGE.

Herman, A. (2019). Assembling Fairtrade: Practices of progress and conventionalization in the Chilean wine industry. *Environment and Planning A: Economy and Space*, 51(1), 51–68.

Jaffee, D., & Howard, P.H. (2010). Corporate co-optation of organic and fair trade standards. *Agriculture and Human Values*, 27(4), 387–399.

Jaffee, D., Kloppenburg, J.R., & Monroy, M.B. (2004). Bringing the 'moral charge' home: Fair trade within the North and within the South. *Rural Sociology*, 69(2), 169–196.

Kleine, D. (2008). Negotiating partnerships, understanding power: doing action research on Chilean Fairtrade wine value chains. *Geographical Journal*, 174(2), 109–123.

Malo, M.C., & Mori, T. (2003). Impactos del comercio justo del vino. Tres casos de empresas colectivas de productores en Chile. *Revista de Economía Pública, Social y Cooperativa*, 46, 265–289.

Méndez, V.E., Bacon, C.M., Olson, M., Petchers, S., Herrador, D., Carranza, C., & Mendoza, A. (2010). Effects of fair trade and organic certifications on small-scale coffee farmer households in Central America and Mexico. *Renewable Agriculture and Food Systems*, 25(3), 236–251.

Morel-Astorga, P. (2002). *Patterns of entrepreneurship, development of Chilean wine industry 1850-2000*. Lund Papers in Economic History. Department of Economic History, Lund University.

Organisation of Vine and Wine. (2020). Statistics advance search. Retrieved 29 November 2020, from http://www.oiv.int/en/statistiques/recherche

Overton, J., & Murray, W.E. (2011). Playing the scales: Regional transformations and the differentiation of rural space in the Chilean wine industry. *Journal of Rural Studies*, 27(1), 63–72.

Overton, J., & Murray, W.E. (2013). Class in a glass: Capital, neoliberalism and social space in the global wine industry. *Antipode*, 45(3), 702–718.

Overton, J., Murray, W.E., & Banks, G. (2012). The race to the bottom of the glass? Wine, geography, and globalization. *Globalizations*, 9(2), 273–287.

Renard, M.-C. (2005). Quality certification, regulation and power in fair trade. *Journal of Rural Studies*, 21(4), 419–431.

Wijnant, G., Raga, R., & Ramakers, R. (2015). *Identificación y caracterización del sector comercio justo y consumo responsable*. Proqualitas Consultora.

Williams, P.B.F. (2019). *Creating ethical markets or marketing ethics? A critical exploration of ethical value networks in Chilean and Peruvian viticulture and oenology*. PhD thesis, Victoria University of Wellington.

10 Ethical value networks of organic food in Argentina: trajectories, trends and tensions

Navé Wald

INTRODUCTION

Organic food is conceptualized in this chapter as an Ethical Value Network for incorporating social and ecological philosophies that stipulate more sustainable and low-input farming methods (Bidwell et al. 2018; Overton et al. 2019). Similar to fair trade networks, organics have gradually evolved from a grassroots movement to a certified standard-based system, and this has presented some benefits, for instance in relation to quality. It has also presented challenges, notably around barriers for participation, especially for small producers (Bidwell et al. 2018).

This chapter, which is adapted from a working paper (Wald 2015a), identifies trajectories, trends and tensions within the organic food sector in Argentina, with much attention devoted to the certified organic sub-sector, using literature and official data from SENASA (National Agrifood Health and Quality Service). This sub-sector is contrasted with that of non-certified organic food, which represents different characteristics and values. This juxtaposition raises some critical and ethical questions regarding organic food and Ethical Value Networks.

The organic sector in Argentina has grown substantially over the last few decades. That growth was facilitated by increased institutional capacity with the 1995 creation of the Argentinian Movement for Organic Production (MAPO) (Marcos 2013) and the introduction of a comprehensive national-level legislation in 1999, which gave the Ministry of Agriculture (then the Secretary of Agriculture) the regulative and promotional responsibility over the sector (Mateos and Ghezán 2010). Within this context, the emphasis was primarily on expanding the sector and improving its competitiveness on the global market. Indeed, the certified organic sector in Argentina is best characterized by its focus on export markets, with nearly 99% of all certified organic produce being exported mainly to the European Union and the United States.

Statistical data, however, account only for certified organic products, ignoring the myriad experiences of non-certified producers and informal ethical value networks. The politics surrounding certification and the financial barrier it presents to some are important issues worthy of further examination. The tendency of official certification to exclude economically marginalized small-scale producers has been identified in Argentina (Marcos 2013), and in practice there exists an unofficial and often politicized parallel organic sector.

CERTIFIED ORGANIC FOOD PRODUCTION IN ARGENTINA

The origin of the organic sector in Argentina is attributed to the establishment of the Centre for Studies of Organic Crops in 1985, which was the country's first association oriented towards organic agriculture. At that time there was no national legislation or guidelines and those involved acted according to their own initiative and understanding of what constitutes organic farming (IICA 2009). Those early actors – producers, consumers and researchers – were predominantly of a middle class background and had a shared aspiration for a different socio-productive model that would be more socially just and environmentally sustainable. During this initial period, organic commercial chains were developed through personal contacts, and relied on trust between producers and consumers (Mateos and Ghezán 2010).

During the 1990s, the organic sector went through a process of professionalization and regulation. The organic movement received much impetus following the second International Federation of Organic Agriculture Movements (IFOAM) congress, held in Vienna in 1990. Delegates to the congress returned with news about a global supply shortage of organic food and that served as a driver for some producers to convert from conventional to organic production. Favourable agro-ecological conditions coupled with traditionally low use of agro-chemicals in conventional farming meant the conversion to organic farming was fairly easy and without a need for significant adjustment or investment (FAO/ITC/CTA 2001).

The expanding sector prompted regulatory action by the government, but beyond some concessions in export taxes, organic production has not received much support from state authorities (Foguelman 2007). Organic plant production was first regulated in 1992, followed by organic animal production in 1993 (Malanos 2013). The national regulatory framework was based on the existing guidelines of the IFOAM and the European Community (EC). This allowed Argentina to become a provisional third-country to the EC[1] the same year (confirmed in 1996), which enabled the exportation of organic goods.

This, in turn, facilitated a rapid expansion of the organic sector during the second half of the 1990s (FAO/ITC/CTA 2001).

This expansion led to the creation of MAPO in 1995, an organization which united the different actors along the domestic organic food chain, including producers, certifiers, investigators and traders (Marcos 2013). Among MAPO's main objectives were the promotion of organic production by small and medium-size farmers and the improvement and enlargement of local markets, as well as wider representation of the organic sector (Foguelman 2007). Its activities include myriad interventions and campaigns, including lobbying for organic legislation, participation in fairs and conferences, running training sessions, supporting research and more.

In 1999 the Congress in Argentina passed the National Organic Law (25.127/1999). This Law set the standards for ecological, biological and organic food production in the country. These include systems where animal and plant farming and gathering are managed in an ecologically sustainable manner, which avoid the use of synthetic chemicals and other toxic materials, maintain or enhance biological diversity, soil fertility and water resources, as well as provide the physical and ecological conditions for animals to express the basic characteristics of their innate behaviour (Art. 1). The Secretary of Agriculture was responsible for the promotion of organic production (Art. 6) and its regulation through SENASA (Art. 4) (Mateos and Ghezán 2010). This legislation was later complemented by Decrees 97/2001 and 206/2001, and in 2012 an official label for organic products (Resolution 1291/2012) was introduced.

The organic sector is managed and supported by public as well as private and non-profit entities. Those organizations provide, among other things, technical expertise and certification. Several organizations also focus on improving the visibility and competitiveness of the sector in the global market. Indeed, the certified organic sector in Argentina is best characterized by its export orientation, with nearly 99% of all certified organic produce being exported (De Nicola and Qüesta 2011). The main markets of destination are those of the more affluent countries within Europe, the US and, to a much lesser extent, Japan. Figure 10.1 reflects the rapid growth of organic exports, with much of the growth taking place between 2005 and 2008, and then again from 2015. There is no indication, however, for the size and growth of the organic sector in terms of its commercial value.

Between 2001 and 2019, organic harvested area and grazing land increased by 11 and 17%, respectively, and organic production volume has increased more than threefold (Figure 10.1). However, over the same period the number of certified organic producers has fallen by nearly a quarter, from 1664 to 1269 producers and the median certified farm size increased by nearly 70%. These trends suggest a concentration of production has taken effect. This is worrying because the government perceives the organic sector as an avenue for economic and social development to be achieved for and by predominantly small family producers (Ministry of Agriculture 2020). However, there is much scope here for further research since farm size alone may not reflect the economic value of production. For example, the provinces of southern Patagonia have a much larger median farm size than the national figure, but those farms are used for animal grazing, whereas high value products such as fresh fruit and wine come mostly from provinces with a much lower median farm size.

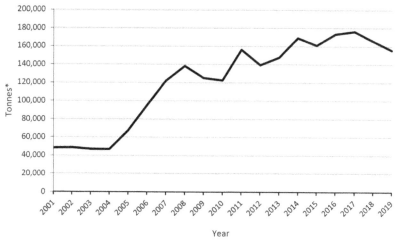

Note: Also includes liquids measured in litres
Source: SENASA annual reports 2001–2019

Figure 10.1   Exports of organic products from Argentina, 2001–2019

Indeed, wine and fruit, both organic and non-organic, constitute important food commodities in Argentina and thus provide interesting cases for the development of the certified organic sector in terms of both fresh and processed products.

Organic Wine

Argentina is the fifth largest wine producing country in the world, accounting for about 5% of global wine production (OIV 2019). Established during the colonial era by missionaries who brought vines from Europe, the history of Argentina's wine industry reflects tensions between quantity and quality. Wine producing regions are spread throughout the country but concentrated mainly to the west, with Mendoza the main centre of production (Figure 10.2).

Figure 10.2   Wine regions of Argentina

Wine in Argentina was suited to the local taste and historically was of low quality, high in alcohol and very sweet (Stein 2007). Vineyards and wineries used outdated equipment and techniques, unsuited for the control needed to produce quality wine (Morris 2000). The focus was on high volume, low-cost production for the domestic market. During the 1980s and 1990s, changes in consumers' tastes, as well as shifts in the political economy at both global and local levels, sent the wine industry into crisis. Many vineyards were abandoned and businesses bankrupted. The survival of the industry was in doubt and it needed to reinvent itself in order to survive (Corby 2010).

Faced with changing economic conditions and decreasing local demand, a number of wine makers decided to shift their focus towards export markets. This required producing better quality wine. For Stein (2007), this was Argentina's 'wine revolution', which entailed, among other things, replanting vineyards with better grape varieties, investing in new technologies, establishing new commercial outlets and hiring international wine experts as advisors. The high value of the peso and the influx of foreign capital were instrumental in implementing this new vision for the industry, but many small and medium-size producers (of grapes and wine) could not afford the necessary investment. Consequently, a process of centralization and vertical integration in the wine industry became increasingly evident (Corby 2010; Stein 2007).

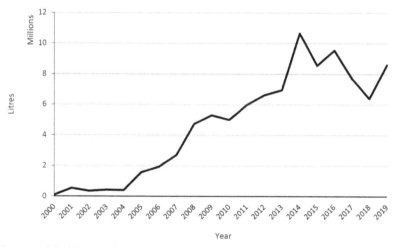

Source: SENASA annual reports 2000–2019

Figure 10.3   *Certified organic wine production in Argentina, 2000–2019*

The wine industry in Argentina, therefore, went through a transition from high quantity and low quality production for the domestic market to lower quantity and higher quality production (primarily, but not exclusively) for export markets. While differentiation and specialization in particular grape varieties (predominantly Malbec) were identified as important in this transformation (Morris 2000), the literature on Argentina's 'wine revolution' (Stein 2007, 2010) and restructuring (Corby 2010; Maclaine Pont 2011; Morris 2000) tends to make no reference to organic wine, either as a potential export niche or as a possible avenue for small producers.

Organic wine is, nevertheless, one of the main exported processed organic products in Argentina. As evident in Figure 10.3, organic wine production in Argentina enjoyed impressive growth between 2005 and 2014, followed by some instability. Similar to other organic products, nearly all the organic wine is exported, and, in 2019, 76% of that wine (about 6.4 million litres) went to Europe.

In spite of the growing importance of the organic wine sector in Argentina, there has been little research on it. Zilber et al.'s (2010) case-study of an organic winery is an exception, but it contains a limited amount of information. That study, nevertheless, reaffirms a number of attributes of the organic sector more widely. A manager of a vineyard owned by a foreign investor noted that the two main reasons this investor chose Argentina as a suitable location for organic wine making were the relatively low labour costs and that land is relatively uncontaminated with synthetic fertilizers and chemicals. The first factor is important because organic farming is more labour intensive and the second because the conversion to organic farming is faster and cheaper (Zilber et al. 2010). Moreover, while a discourse of environmental sustainability was evident in this case, it seems competitiveness on the global market and prospects of exporting high value wine to wealthy markets were also important.

Organic Fruit

Like the wine industry, the trajectory of the fresh fruit sector in Argentina has also been affected by changes in the global and local political economy. As a result of the Great Depression of the 1930s, the central government in Argentina decided to promote policies aimed at regenerating regional economies within the national territory (Girbal-Blacha and Ospital 2005; Ospital 2013). This meant greater attention and allocation of resources from the state to various agricultural sectors outside the Pampa region. Fruit farming was an important part of this scheme and different crops were developed in different regions. Fruit production was promoted primarily for supplying the domestic market, but its export potential was also identified as important (Ospital 2013).

Half a century later, new neoliberal political-economic circumstances involving liberalization of the economy and improved technologies of long-distance transportation of fresh produce, enhanced the export of fresh fruit from Argentina to lucrative markets in the northern hemisphere. At the centre of this growing export sector were three fruit crops grown in two peripheral areas: apples and pears from northern Patagonia and lemons from the north-western province of Tucumán (Rau 2010). The establishment of agro-industries for processing fruit has also accompanied the expanding cultivation of these products. Together, those developments have had a notable and multifaceted effect on the regions where these activities take place.

As in the case of the viticulture and wine industry, the expansion of fruit value chains is a result of economic deregulation that facilitated needed capital investment for transforming previously small and inefficient operators into competitive players on the global stage. This transformation also led to socio-spatial changes in the agrarian structures of regional economies. Lemons and pip fruit were initially grown by small farms, but since the 1990s, a process of centralization of production has been notable in both sectors. Large producers and multinational companies increased their shares in these sectors while small producers struggled to make necessary investments for improving production and commercialization (Alvaro and Trpin 2013; Cavalcanti and Bendini 2001; Landriscini 2014; Rivas and Zamora 2010).

To survive in this challenging environment, small producers had to adapt, and one strategy was to create alternative spaces for their social and economic reproduction. These spaces may include establishing cooperatives or associations, selling in local markets, participating in initiatives of social economy and more. Government agencies have also been engaged in supporting small-scale family farmers, providing technical assistance and capacitation, micro-credit schemes, supporting local fairs and more (Landriscini 2014). Organic production was also a potential alternative for marginalized or struggling agricultural producers whose subordination to global market forces threatens their livelihoods, but realizing this potential is no simple task.

Since 2000, organic fruit production has increased more than fivefold, and the area of organic orchards has increased in a similar manner from nearly 2100 hectares to almost 9300 hectares in 2019 (peaking at over 10,600 ha in 2017). In 2019, organic fruit production reached a new record in Argentina, reaching almost 50,000 tonnes (Figure 10.4). This figure, however, does not include processed goods made of fruit, such as concentrated juices, dried fruit and wine.

Pears are the main organic fruit crop, followed by apples. The cultivation of these crops is almost entirely concentrated in the northern Patagonian provinces of Río Negro and Neuquén. Together, these crops account for most of the organic fresh fruit production (over 94% in 2019). Most of the increase in the volume of organic pears and apples took place during the first decade of the 21st century, with a generally stable production in the following decade. Similar to other organic products, nearly all pears and apples are exported, predominantly to the EU and the US.

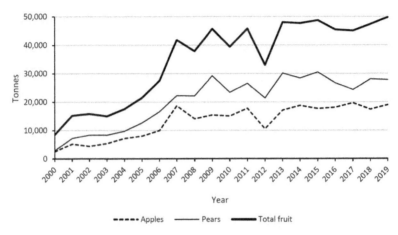

Source: SENASA annual reports 2000–2019

Figure 10.4   Certified organic fruit production in Argentina, 2000–2019

Studies examining the fruit sector in Argentina have identified a number of issues relating to processes of intensification and vertical integration of export-oriented food chains. However, this (admittedly small) body of litera-ture does not address organic food chains in a meaningful way. It is likely that since both the conventional and organic fruit sectors are export-oriented, some of the issues associated with the former are also relevant to the latter, but there is much scope for further research on organic fruit chains in Argentina.

TENSIONS WITHIN ORGANIC FOOD PRODUCTION IN ARGENTINA

The process of concentration of production, as noted, is evident in both con-ventional and organic farming. There are a number of contributing factors, but one that is notably related to the organic sector is certification. According to the Organic Law, certification of products is to be done by specialized public or private entities (Art. 8). Certification in Argentina is based on a third-party certification system, where independent companies have the role of assessing whether production systems comply with the legal requirements, which are predominantly set by IFOAM. This system, according to Marcos (2013), effectively means that not all producers are able to receive certification due to its cost. Therefore, this regulatory process constitutes an economic barrier that can only be met by well-capitalized companies or associations that can afford the necessary technological investments and the cost of the certification process.

The exclusionary nature of organic certification has been identified in the literature, and it has been attributed to the neoliberal commodification of organic production. This is epitomized in the shift from the self-regulatory systems of organic certification in the 1970s and 1980s to the implementation of the third-party system in the 1990s (Nelson et al. 2010). This certification system resulted in a mainstream organic sector that has been criticized for depoliticizing the ideals of the organic movement, undermining aspects of ecological and social justice in favour of capturing economic rents (González and Nigh 2005; Guthman 2004). The extensive and expensive bureaucracy of certification and the neoliberal capitalism it serves have alienated small-scale producers (economically and sometimes ideologically) and have triggered grassroots initiatives that wish to create arguably more genuine alternative sustainable food systems. Together with a focus on short food chains (farmers' markets, farm gate sales and so forth), moving beyond mainstream organics has also included alternative labelling methodologies. Instead of inventing them anew, these methodologies correspond to the industry's earlier experience of first-party peer review strategies of organic certification and are typically based on the IFOAM standards and/or national regulations. Emphasis is given to educational processes, social control over the whole food chain, low cost to those involved and transparency (Fonseca 2004). Such alternatives, commonly known as Participatory Guarantee Systems (PGSs), have been gaining increasing purchase among producers and civil society entities and official recognition by national governments, especially in Latin America and the Global South. However, with ISO standards being ignored, a PGS is not suitable for the certified organic export sector and this, in fact, appeals to PGS advocates who wish to strengthen local food systems (Nelson et al. 2010, 2016).

In Argentina, the exclusion of small-scale producers has been an important issue on the Advisory Commission for Organic Production's agenda. Those supporting family farmers (public agencies, NGOs and other civil society organizations) have contested the marginalized position of many producers within this certification system, and have made calls for alternative systems to be developed. These would include PGS certification and would only be applicable to the domestic market. However, this forum is dominated by representatives of actors (government agencies, MAPO, the association of certifiers and the large organic producers) who believe that having more than one certi-fication system would put the international credibility of Argentina's organic production at risk (Mateos and Ghezán 2010), and particularly the country's highly valued status as a third-country to the EU (Marcos 2013).

The effective exclusion of many small-scale producers from obtaining organic certification, however, does not mean there is no small-scale organic production in Argentina. Rather, there seems to be a dual system that, on the one hand, has officially certified products and, on the other hand, has alter-native non-certified organic products (Marcos 2013). It would be difficult to quantify the non-certified sector due to lack of data, but its main value may have less to do with volume and more with a set of ethics counter to those underpinning the neoliberal market economy.

In Argentina, as in other parts of Latin America and across the world, this set of ethics is associated with concepts such as 'social and solidarity economy' (SSE) and 'popular economy'. While SSE is by no means a new phenomenon – co-operatives and mutual-aid organizations have had a long history – its presence in Latin America has become increasingly prevalent since the 1990s as neoliberal restructuring led to increased unemployment and poverty (Caruana and Srnec 2013). In Argentina, the re-emergence of the SSE was particularly noticeable in the aftermath of the 2001 economic crisis, but social mobilization and many autonomous organizations had already taken shape during the 1990s.

Rural Grassroots Movements in Argentina

Less known than their urban counterparts were rural movements that have contested the marginalized position of small to medium-size producers within many rural economies. In the mid-1980s, public policies in Argentina began using terms such as 'rural poor' and 'small producers', with the term 'family farming' coming into use later as a more general term favoured by both policymakers and civil society organizations (Manzanal and González 2010). Family farming refers to a socio-productive category of agricultural producers, but the heterogeneity of this group makes this term problematic. In fact, this term covers a diversity of actors and identities, including *minifundis-tas*, peasants, landless peasants, *colonos*, family farmers, indigenous people, urban farmers and more. These types of actors, some of which already have unclear or contested definitions, emphasize different characteristics, from economic-technical aspects (land size, level of capitalization, mode of produc-tion, etc.) to more socio-cultural dimensions ('way of life', ethnicity, tradition, etc.) (Caballero et al. 2010).

Notwithstanding the inherent diversity of family farming, the subordinate position of many small producers vis-à-vis agribusiness and the market has generated resistance at the grassroots, as well as recognition by the state in the form of public policies. The ongoing struggle of small producers gave rise to new strategies of action aimed at improving the income level of families along with generating wider social, economic and political change. Among these strategies are alternative forms of agricultural production and commercialization, which include farmers' and peasant markets (known as *ferias francas*), networks of fair trade, networks and events of barter, owner-operated democratic cooperatives and more (Caballero et al. 2010; Paz et al. 2013; Wald 2015b). These production and commercialization strategies form part of the SSE; but given their relation to food, the politics and values of many participating actors often resonate with discourses of food sovereignty and agroecology. In such instances, emphasis is not only on environmentally sustainable production, but also on forming short food chains where intermediaries cannot take advantage of geographically and socially isolated producers and where food provision for local communities takes precedence.

CONCLUSIONS

The nexus between organic food production, ethical value chains and scale is, therefore, multifaceted and contested both politically and socially. The state has a regulatory framework of internationally recognized standards and has devoted resources for promoting organic farming. Organic certification, however, is largely only attainable by, and suitable for, predominantly capitalized agribusinesses or farmers, and their production is primarily export-oriented. This raises questions regarding the driving forces behind this model of organic food production, the ethics underpinning it and the degree to which this represents an alternative to mainstream intensive farming. This also raises questions regarding agricultural producers who cannot obtain certification under existing requirements, who are often small-scale family producers. Whether this situation reflects complementary or conflicting agendas is open to debate. However, agribusiness and export-oriented capitalized farmers, on the one hand, and many small- to medium-sized capital-poor producers who promote food sovereignty and agroecological production, on the other hand, do not share the same values and sometimes are engaged in conflicts over territory and other resources.

Rather than seeing Argentina as having a dual organic food chain, it is perhaps more accurate to speak of a spectrum of organic food chains. On one end of the spectrum are food chains of certified/large-scale/capitalized/global producers, while on the other end are food chains of non-certified/small-scale/non-capitalized/local producers. It should be asked whether all such chains are 'ethical'. Notwithstanding this organic food chain spectrum, from a public policy perspective, organic food production is seen as a vehicle for economic development not only for agribusiness but also for small producers. It is also seen to contribute more generally to rural development by promoting food sovereignty, preventing rural migration and tackling structural poverty in the countryside (Ministry of Agriculture 2020).

While there is much scope for research into both sub-sectors, official statistical data of the certified organic sector in Argentina demonstrates that this sub-sector has been experiencing notable growth over the last 15 years or so. This growth has been accompanied by the gradual development of a regulatory framework and designated public policies. The latter has assisted the sector to create links with offshore markets, predominantly in wealthy countries, a process that seems to have been intentional from the outset and has strongly oriented the sector towards exportation. Data also suggest a gradual concentration of production where fewer farmers on larger farms are producing more food. Whereas the environmental values of organic farming may be upheld, this trend counters some social and economic values and potential benefits.

There are a number of factors contributing to this trend, and one such factor is the unaffordability of organic certification to small producers. While not much is known about the non-certified sub-sector in quantitative terms, qualitatively this sub-sector tends to reflect environmental as well as anti-capitalist values. The existence of these sub-sectors and the differences between them raise ethical questions regarding organic ethical value networks. The dominant model of the global certified organic food chain, in which Argentina is predominantly a supplier, might be compatible with environmental ethical concerns. However, ethical concerns regarding socio-productive and economic equity remain.

NOTE

1. Third-country equivalence status indicates a non-European Union (EU) country has a regulatory framework compatible with that of the EU, which is important for enhancing trade in goods and services.

REFERENCES

Alvaro, B., & Trpin, V. (2013). Condiciones productivas y exigencias de calidad en la fruticultura de la Patagonia Argentina. *Región y Sociedad*, 25(58), 239–273.
Bidwell, S., Murray, W.E., & Overton, J. (2018). Ethical agro-food networks in global peripheries, Part I: The rise and recommodification of fair trade and organics. *Geography Compass*, 12(4), online DOI: 10.1111/gec3.12366 11pp.
Caballero, L., Dumrauf, S., González, E., Mainella, F., & Moricz, M. (2010). Los procesos organizativos de la agricultura familiar y la creación de ferias y mercados de economía social. *Otra Economía*, 4(7), 26–41.
Caruana, M.E.C., & Srnec, C.C. (2013). Public policies addressed to the social and solidarity economy in South America: Toward a new model? *Voluntas*, 24(3), 713–732.

Cavalcanti, J.S.B., & Bendini, M.I. (2001). Hacia una configuración de trabajadores agrarios en la fruticultura de exportación de Brasil y Argentina. In N. Giarracca (Ed.), *Una nueva ruralidad en América Latina?* (pp. 339–362). CLACSO.

Corby, J.H.K. (2010). For members and markets: Neoliberalism and cooperativism in Mendoza's wine industry. *Journal of Latin American Geography*, *9*(2), 27–47.

De Nicola, M., & Qüesta, T.M. (2011). La producción orgánica certificada en Argentina en el marco de las convenciones cívicas. *Revista de Economía del Instituto de Economía Agraria*, *58*(1), 115–128.

FAO/ITC/CTA (2001). *World markets for organic fruit and vegetables: Opportunities for developing countries in the production and export of organic horticultural products.* FAO/ITC/CTA, http://www.fao.org/docrep/004/y1669e/y1669e0h.htm#bm17 (accessed 19 October 2020).

Foguelman, D. (2007). MAPO and the Argentinian organic movement. In W. Lockeretz (Ed.), *Organic farming: An international history* (pp. 217–224). CABI.

Fonseca, M.F. (2004). Alternative certification and a network conformity assessment approach. In A.P. Lernoud and M.F. Fonseca (Eds.) *Workshop on alternatives on certification for organic production: Proceedings* (pp.10–15). IFOAM/Grolink.

Girbal-Blacha, N.M., & Ospital, M.S. (2005). 'Vivir con lo nuestro': Publicidad y política en la Argentina de los años 1930. *European Review of Latin American and Caribbean Studies*, *78*, 49–66.

González, A.A., & Nigh, R. (2005). Smallholder participation and certification of organic farm products in Mexico. *Journal of Rural Studies*, *21*(4), 449–460.

Guthman, J. (2004). Back to the land: The paradox of organic food standards. *Environment and Planning A*, *36*(3), 511–528.

IICA (2009). *La producción orgánica en la Argentina: Compilación de experiencias institucionales y productivas.* Instituto Interamericano de Cooperación para la Agricultura.

Landriscini, G. (2014). La fruticultura del Alto Valle de Río Negro y Neuquén. Un complejo agroalimentario en reestructuración: Concentración económica, mediación estatal y estrategias de agentes subalternos. In A. Rofman & A. García (Eds.), *Economía solidaria y cuestión regional en Argentina de principios de siglo XXI: Entre procesos de subordinación y prácticas alternativas* (pp. 171–199). Rofman.

Maclaine Pont, P.C. (2011). Who grows the grapes? The changing relationship of quality in Argentine wine production. *Journal of Wine Research*, *22*(1), 1–17.

Malanos, N.L. (2013). La producción agropecuaria orgánica en Argentina. *Revista Pilquen*, *13*, 2–5.

Manzanal, M., & González, F. (2010). Soberanía alimentaria y agricultura familiar: Oportunidades y desafíos del caso argentino. *Realidad Económica*, *255*, 51–67.

Marcos, M.F. (2013). El consumo de alimentos orgánicos en redes de comercio justo: El caso del galpón de Chacarita. Paper presented at the *VII jornadas Santiago Wallace de investigación en antropología social, UBA*, Buenos Aires, 27–29 November, available at https://www.aacademica.org/000-063/246.pdf (accessed 19 October 2020).

Mateos, M. & Ghezán, G. (2010). El proceso de construcción social de normas de calidad en alimentos orgánicos y la inclusión de pequeños productores: El caso de Argentina. Paper presented at the *ISDA conference*, Montpellier, 28 June – 1 July, available at https://hal.archives-ouvertes.fr/hal-00566243/document (accessed 10 October 2020).

Ministry of Agriculture (2020). *Plan estratégico Argentina orgánica 2030*, Ministry of Agriculture, Livestock and Fisheries, available at http://www.mapo.org.ar/

web2017/wp-content/uploads/2020/05/Plan-Estrat%C3%A9gico-Argentina-Org %C3%A1nica-2030-FINAL.pdf (accessed 1 October 2020).

Morris, A. (2000). Globalisation and regional differentiation: The Mendoza wine region. *Journal of Wine Research*, *11*(2), 145–153.

Nelson, E., Tovar, L.G., Rindermann, R.S., & Cruz, M.A.G. (2010). Participatory organic certification in Mexico: An alternative approach to maintaining the integrity of the organic label. *Agriculture and Human Values*, *27*(2), 227–237.

Nelson, E., Tovar, L.G., Gueguen, E., Humphries, S., Landman, K., & Rindermann, R.S. (2016). Participatory guarantee systems and the re-imagining of Mexico's organic sector. *Agriculture and Human Values*, *33*(2), 373–388.

OIV (2019). *Statistical report on world vitiviniculture.* International Organisation of Vine and Wine Intergovernmental Organisation. Available at http://oiv.int/public/ medias/6782/oiv-2019-statistical-report-on-world-vitiviniculture.pdf (accessed 29 September 2020).

Ospital, M.S. (2013). Políticas públicas para la fruticultura en Argentina, 1930-1943. *América Latina en la Historia Económica*, *20*(1), 78–97.

Overton, J., Murray, W.E., & Howson, K. (2019). Doing good by drinking wine? Ethical value networks and upscaling of wine production in Australia, New Zealand and South Africa. *European Planning Studies*, *27*(12), 2431–2449.

Paz, R., Jara, C., & Nazar, P. (2013). Economía social y agricultura familiar: La experiencia de la feria de Villa Río Hondo (Argentina). *Cayapa: Revista Venezolana de Economía Social*, *13*(25), 53–74.

Rau, V. (2010). Trasnacionalización productiva y calidad del empleo en la fruticultura argentina de exportación. Paper presented at the *VI Congreso del CEISAL*, Toulouse, 30 June – 3 July, available at https://hal.archives-ouvertes.fr/file/index/docid/ 503862/filename/VictorHoracioRau.pdf (accessed 19 October 2020).

Rivas, J.J., & Zamora, A.E.B. (2010). El complejo agroindustrial limonero de la provincia de Tucumán (argentina): Ejemplo de producciones no tradicionales y de desaparición de los pequeños productores. *Boletín de la Asociación de Geógrafos Españoles*, *53*, 67–88.

Stein, S. (2007). Grape wars: Quality in the history of Argentine wine. In G. Campbell & N. Guibert (Eds.), *Wine, society, and globalization: Multidisciplinary perspectives on the wine industry* (pp. 99–117). Palgrave Macmillan.

Stein, S. (2010). New markets and new strategies in Argentina's wine revolution. *Economics, Management, and Financial Markets*, *1*, 64–98.

Wald, N. (2015a). *Alternative sustainable and ethical value chains in Argentina: Organic foods, geographical indications, and fair trade.* Ethical Value Networks Working Paper Series. Victoria University of Wellington.

Wald, N. (2015b). In search of alternatives: Peasant initiatives for a different development in northern Argentina. *Latin American Perspectives*, *42*(2), 90–106.

Zilber, S.N., Friel, D., & Nascimento, L.F.M. (2010). Organic wine production: The case of Bodega Colomé in Argentina. *International Journal of Wine Business Research*, *22*(2), 164–177.

11 Ethical value networks of geographical indications and fair trade in Argentina

Navé Wald

INTRODUCTION

This chapter explores Geographical Indications (GIs) and Fair Trade[1] as two forms of ethical value food networks in Argentina. Those networks are global and thus inherently geographical in the sense that production, commercialization and consumption, and the relationships between them take shape across space. The ethical aspect of these food networks is rooted in claims regarding those relationships, either within or between groups along the network. Being 'ethical' adds value to the products and differentiates them from competing products on the market, which justifies a higher price tag and presents an opportunity for producers to increase their income (Overton et al. 2019).

While GIs and Fair Trade can be considered ethical value networks, there is no certainty or guarantee they will always be so in practice. There is, therefore, much need for a critical examination of such networks, addressing issues of control, participation and governance, among other things (Overton et al. 2019). In the Argentinian context, critical attention is devoted in this chapter to these networks especially regarding the wine industry. With that, there is much scope for further exploration of the contexts and landscapes where these ethical value networks operate, and of specific products therein. The juxtaposed analysis of GIs and Fair Trade in Argentina reveals a number of similarities and differences, as well as directions for further research.

GEOGRAPHICAL INDICATIONS IN ARGENTINA

The economic rationale for using GIs is that, like trademarks, there are information asymmetries between sellers and buyers and these could be mitigated by recognized signals that mark quality. GIs, unlike trademarks, are a type of collective property rights and as such are available to new producers, as long as they are located within the demarcated geographical area and meet the stipulated requirements (Rangnekar 2004). The listing of a GI requires setting boundaries for the production area and for the allowed production methods in order to establish consistency and quality. The formulation of this GI code of practice should involve local producers and other stakeholders (Galtier et al. 2013).

The appeal of GIs is rooted primarily in their ability to contribute to regional development and the socio-economic benefits that might be generated. However, as important as the attributes of GIs may be, such arguments are primarily based on the potential of GIs. Realising this potential, however, is no simple task. At best, there is only anecdotal evidence that indicates GIs create real benefit to producers in developing countries. Otherwise, it is difficult to isolate the effect of GIs from other contributing factors such as technological advancements (Jena and Grote 2010). As noted by Yeung and Kerr (2011, p. 360), GIs 'do not sell themselves'. Economically successful examples of GIs are often associated with sustained and large-scale marketing efforts, as well as legal action, which of course require resources many communities and local authorities do not have.

In contrast to Europe's long trajectory of regional differentiation of food and beverages, GIs began to attract interest in Latin America only in the 1990s. As in other parts of the world, the use of GIs in Argentina is seen as a particularly useful strategy for small-scale family producers trying to differentiate their production in order to survive in a highly competitive and integrated market, controlled by large agribusiness (Guedes and Silva 2014).

Moreover, many well-known foodstuffs associated with Latin American territories do not originate there. Beef, sheep, sugarcane, coffee and vines, for example, were brought into these territories by the European colonizers, and that presents challenges for registering GIs. In Argentina, during the late 19th and early 20th centuries, the colonial 'estancia' model evolved, in some areas, to include freehold family farms. These farmers, many of whom were Italian and other European immigrants, formed a new agrarian social group of middle class rural producers, who established local agro-industries. Over time, 'imported' food, knowledge and cultures adapted to, and were changed by, the new social and natural environments into which they were introduced. This process generated food products, especially dairy and meat, which although not removed from their European roots, have assumed new and differentiated identities and have become part of a new productive and consumerist culture. However, familiar European product names were also widely used and that created tensions when geographic names began to be protected in Europe under property rights legislation (Schiavone 2010).

Disputes about geographical names, that because their wide use may be considered 'generic' and thus cannot be protected, still remain. Although domestic industries, such as that of cheese, may be disadvantaged by such legislation (Schiavone 2010), Argentina has adopted a legislative framework that closely resembles that of the European Union (EU). Thus, legislation in Argentina includes the EU's distinction between wine and food products, exclusion of services and application of Designation of Origin (DO) and Geographical Indication (GI) as two distinctive categories of territory-based protected names (Guedes and Silva 2014). DO is subject to two main conditions: (a) the agricultural product originates in a particular geographical area and (b) the quality or characteristics of that product stem from the human and natural elements of the geographical environment in which it is being grown and processed. The first condition for receiving a GI recognition is identical to that of DO, but the second condition is different, requiring a link between a product's quality or other characteristics and the area in which it is being produced and/or processed. Essentially, DO is a more strict legal expression of *terroir*, while GI may be applied to a wider range of products as it does not require the whole value chain to be located within the designated area. Instead, for GIs it is sufficient to have only one stage of the production process carried out within the region, even if the raw materials are produced elsewhere (Josling 2006).

Argentina has been a signatory of the Agreement on Trade-Related Aspects of Intellectual Property Rights (TRIPS) ever since it came into effect in 1995. Within a few years TRIPS was translated into national-level legislation with one legal framework for wine and another for other agricultural food products. The objective of Law 25.163/1999 for wine and other alcoholic vinous beverages (modified in 2004 by Law 25.966) was to create a system for the recognition, protection and registration of geographic names that distinguish the origin of wine and other grape-based alcoholic drinks within the national territory. The execution of this legislation is the responsibility of the National Institute of Viticulture (Instituto Nacional de Vitivinicultura – INV) (Article 36), an independent agency related to the Ministry of Agriculture.

In addition to the categories of GI and DO, the above includes Indication of Provenance (IP) as another category. While in some countries this category is equivalent to that of GI, in Argentina this category is used for wines of inferior quality – known as 'table wines' or 'regional wines'. GI and DO, therefore, are reserved for wines of a certain higher quality (Molina 2020). According to INV data, 101 GIs exist in Argentina, of which nearly three quarters were granted in 2002, and less than 15% have been gazetted since 2010. In a way, these do not represent many different wine regions. Rather, this is a tiered system whereby GIs are given to territories at different scales. For example, a province may have its recognized GI, while different territories within that province may have their own GIs. Similarly, a number of provinces may have a collective GI (for example, Cuyo, which includes the provinces of Mendoza, San Juan and La Rioja). This allows wines made from combining grapes grown in territories with different GIs to assume the single GI of the larger territory, and this is particularly important for a DO certification, where raw materials and production must all be situated within the designated territory as noted previously.

Only two wine producing areas, Luján de Cuyo and San Rafael, have received DO recognition, and both have previously had a GI recognition and both are located in the main wine producing province of Mendoza. This clearly suggests that, relative to GI, DO certification is much more difficult to obtain, but also that a GI status could be used as a step towards DO. However, there is no indication of how these forms of product differentiation affect price premiums, and the popularity of the GI system suggests it is more useful than a DO.

GIs for food products are regulated by Law 25.380/2000 and its application is the responsibility of the Secretary of Agriculture, Livestock and Fisheries within the Ministry of Agriculture (Champredonde et al. 2014). This body is trusted with assisting, verifying, controlling and protecting the system under which GIs are granted and operated. Another role is to liaise with international bodies as the technical and administrative authority in Argentina.

The uptake of GIs and DOs for foodstuffs has not been as notable as it has been for wine. To date there are three recognized DOs and five GIs in Argentina. The DOs include Creole goats of North Neuquén (Chivito Criollo del Norte Neuquino), salami of Tandil (Salame de Tandil), and blond quince paste of San Juan (Dulce de Membrillo Rubio de San Juan). The GIs include Patagonian lamb (Cordero Patagonico), 'typical' salami of Colonia Caroya (Salame Típico de Colonia Caroya), melon of Media Agua, San Juan (Melón de Media Agua, San Juan), Platense artichoke (Alcauciles Platenses), and Yerba mate. Each product has its own official label. There are also more products, such as olive oil and honey, certification for which is in process (Cendón and Bruno 2018).

The production of these items involves predominantly small-scale family producers and much emphasis is given to artisanal processing techniques and traditional farming methods. Moreover, the process of obtaining certification requires the cooperation and commitment of a number of producers, which in the case of the creole goats of North Neuquén, enhanced the social cohesion within the designated geographic area, improved levels of income, valorized local knowledge and impacted positively on the natural environment (Centeno 2008).

Obtaining GI/DO recognition is a collective process that requires producers to come together and work with other agencies and organizations. In Argentina, government institutions, local authorities and academics were always involved to some degree in these processes. Different groups may be interested in GI/DO for the wider economic benefits that may be created beyond those directly involved in the food network. In Argentina, a wider economic and social impact materialized through activities and events such as fairs and festivals that promote local foods and tourism (Cendón and Bruno 2018). To date, GI/DO foods have had mainly a local impact. Most of the products are sold locally or in the region where they originate. Commercialization at the national level is not common, mostly for lack of consumer brand awareness beyond the areas of production (Cendón and Bruno 2018). However, the GI/DO recognition of those foods is quite recent and promotion efforts, such as tourism events which are mostly for the domestic market, could change that over time. Unlike wine, it is difficult to see how most of these networks could become global.

FAIR TRADE IN ARGENTINA

Early experiences of fair trade activism in Europe in the late 1960s were rooted in political actions against neo-imperialism and manifested in establishing trade networks with countries that were politically excluded from mainstream trade. These actions merged with other, arguably less radical, initiatives of non-governmental organizations (NGOs) that pursued more equitable links between producers in the Global South and consumers in the Global North (Renard 2003). Criticizing the exploitation inherent in the world economy and advocating for 'trade not aid', activists envisioned fair trade as a strategy for sustainable development of marginalized producers in the South that relies on producer-consumer solidarity and trust (Raynolds 2000). Thus, the fair trade movement ought to create "a *moral economy* of alternative development" (Goodman 2004, p. 893, emphasis in original).

In subsequent decades, the movement grew and evolved from focusing primarily on importing handicrafts, coffee and tea through parallel trade networks and selling them in special stores managed by volunteers/activists (Renard 2003), into a fast expanding sector with products worth several billions of dollars (Raynolds 2014). The Fair Trade movement uses voluntary certification programmes for the purpose of setting and guaranteeing certain standards for adequate and ethical social, economic and environmental conditions for producers in the Global South. Certification systems often involve multiple stakeholders and are mostly driven and organized by NGOs (Raynolds 2017).

Two important and interconnected pillars of fair trade politics and certification are valuing producers' knowledge and promoting democratic organization, with a particular focus on independent smallholders and hired workers. Only democratically organized cooperatives or associations and plantations where workers are represented through democratic and independent unions can receive Fairtrade certification (Goodman 2004; Raynolds 2000). However, unlike what constitutes organic farming, empirical findings suggest that the ability of the certification process to generate a clear understanding among producers of what is fair trade has been limited (Murray et al. 2006). A systematic review of studies on the impact of Fairtrade certification on agricultural producers and workers found inconclusive evidence for an increase in household income and no evidence for higher wages for workers. This does not mean certification cannot be beneficial but rather, success is not guaranteed, and while certification could be a contributor, there are other important contextual and specific factors at play (Oya et al. 2018).

Values in the Fair Trade movement converge on contesting inequalities in the conventional market, but there is some divergence in terms of promoting more local or short chains vis-à-vis global ones. The 'mainstreaming' of fair trade, where multinational corporations become stakeholders, has been a thorny issue. Staricco (2019) noted that while initially academic literature about Fairtrade International was mostly positive, in more recent years scholars have become increasingly critical of its actions on several issues. Raynolds (2014, p. 503), for instance, noted that "The certification of large scale enterprises raises a series of challenges to Fairtrade's domestic ideals of producer/ consumer 'connections' and trade 'partnerships'."

Fair Trade in Argentina

In Argentina, Fair Trade certification has had a relatively short trajectory, with the wine-making Cooperative La Riojana being the first organization to obtain certification in 2006. Sales volumes of Fair Trade certified products from Argentina have been small, but the country's wine and honey industries were identified as having a considerable potential for increasing their respective shares in Fair Trade markets. Argentinian Fair Trade producers could also have an important role in providing off-season fresh produce in Northern Hemisphere markets (Salerno and Gonzalez 2013).

In Argentina, while Fair Trade certification is seen as a market strategy in different industries, there has not been much focus on the issues that require 'fairness' or a move towards a more ethical value network. Academic research focuses mostly on the wine sector, where issues relating to its reliance on seasonal hired workers have been identified (e.g. Staricco 2015), but there is much scope for further examination of fair trade beyond its economic logic and in sectors other than wine.

As in other parts of the world, the processes of certification, auditing and promotion in Argentina have been carried out by private and civil society organizations. Fair Trade certification and capacitation received a notable expansion in 2010 following a partnership between Fundación Fortalecer[2] and the Multilateral Investment Fund (FOMIN), a member of the Inter-American Development Bank (IADB). Formed in 2000, the Foundation's objective is to improve the competitiveness of small and medium-size producers by offering a variety of services (Solari 2013), and it forms part of the Argentinian Agrarian Federation (Federación Agraria Argentina – FAA). This partnership, which ended in 2014, was instrumental in establishing Fair Trade certification in Argentina (Cosiorovski-Gonzalez et al. 2015).

In this effort of capacitating producers towards complying with the established international requirements, it became evident to the technical staff of the Foundation that there were producers that met the required standards but could not get certified for exporting. This prompted the Foundation to develop a recognized Fair Trade framework for the domestic market (Solari 2013). It is not entirely clear what barriers prevented producers from exporting their products or what were the domestic standards, but one reason seems to be that the Foundation certifies producers that adhere to the Fairtrade standards but whose products were not included in the Fairtrade International list of goods, such as milk products. The Foundation has effectively created an additional certification scheme under the name of Recognized Fair Ventures (Emprendimiento Justo Reconocido – RFV), including an official label.

As part of the effort to increase the commercialization of Fair Trade products within the country, in November 2012 Fundación Fortalecer signed a deal with Cooperativa Obrera, the owner of more than a hundred supermarkets nationwide (Salerno and Gonzalez 2013). However, from the consumers' perspective, Fair Trade certification is not well established in Argentina, and so its effectiveness as a strategy for product differentiation and commercialization has been largely dependent on external markets (Cosiorovski-Gonzalez et al. 2015). Nevertheless, when the IADB-funded project ended, so did the work of the Foundation in this area, including its certification initiative.

In 2019, the Fair Trade Coordinating Association of Argentina and Uruguay was established as a body representing over 800 Fairtrade certified producers of wine, olive oil and honey. This civil association comprises members of the Latin American and Caribbean Fair Trade Small Producers and Workers Network (CLAC), which is part of the global Fairtrade International network. According to the CLAC's website, this Coordinating Association has identified the development of fair trade in the national markets as a strategic area requiring attention. This resonates with the efforts of Fundación Fortalecer to establish Fair Trade chains within the national economy in Argentina, and it reflects concerns regarding the export-orientation of the sector. This vision challenges the inherent North/South divide in Fair Trade schemes. While commendable, the experience of Fundación Fortalecer suggests this is difficult to achieve and it remains to be seen whether short ethical food chains of Fair Trade products can offer producers the premiums they ought to provide. The option of selling locally Fair Trade products reconfigures the geography of Fair Trade from a contested North/South divide (see Staricco 2019) to a local/global divide. However, this does not guarantee avoiding the power imbalanced between producers, traders, retailers and consumers, which could be replicated locally.

Tensions in Fair Trade Wine in Argentina

Fairtrade wine is a telling example of tensions within the Fair Trade movement, especially in relation to the heterogeneity of actors and to the local/global divide. Wine was added to the list of Fair Trade products in 2003, and after then its volume grew tremendously. The wine industry has received critical examination as a particular case of Fair Trade value chains, serving as an example for their mainstreaming, departure from the guiding values of transparency, democracy and empowerment, as well as for their conventionalization and bureaucratization (Herman 2019a).

In spite of not having many Fair Trade certified wine organizations, Argentina is still one of the largest producers of Fair Trade wine in the world. Among those certified organizations, nearly a half are foreign owned and belong to international groups (e.g. Paso Alto [France] and Bodega Palmer [Austria]), while most others are also export-oriented producers of fine wine. Only one actor includes small and medium size grape growers (Uvasol) (Staricco and Ponte 2015) and better reflected stated fair trade values. All these producers have the necessary resources and experience for participating in certified global Fair Trade value chains, something that is beyond the means of many other producers (Herman 2019b).

There are three types of Fairtrade certified organizations in Argentina: Small Producer Organization (SPO), Hired Labour (HL) and Trader. SPO certified producers, of which there are only two in Argentina, are arguably a more ideal entity in terms of ethics, especially if structured as a cooperative. HL certification is mostly suitable for large-scale companies that rely on a hired workforce. The HL standards are meant to improve or guarantee the working conditions of workers, and in Argentina this is the dominant category of certification in the wine industry, which is indicative of the type of producers that make quality wine for export (Staricco 2015).

Existing labour laws in Argentina meant that wine producing and trading companies already met most of the Fairtrade stipulated requirements for working conditions at the time of applying for certification (Staricco 2015). Historically, the wine industry in Argentina relied heavily on unskilled seasonal workers, especially for harvest. When the wine industry expanded around the turn of the 20th century, such workers were in short supply, as both creole and new immigrants were reluctant to engage in wage-labour. This was the main reason behind the creation of the *contratista* system, where workers lived on the land they cultivated with their families, but without owning it and with the landlord supplying all the necessary tools and other resources (Salvatore 1986). Essentially, *contratistas* were in between hired rural workers and lease holders. Since the 1990s, this system became decreasingly dominant and increasingly undesirable due to the Argentinian 'wine revolution' (Stein 2007) and the reorientation towards export of quality wine led to centralization and vertical integration in the industry (Corby 2010). The wine revolution and the capitalization of the wine industry – supported by a wide neoliberal economic restructuring – favoured a seasonal and flexible hired labour force. Fairtrade certification has the potential of protecting those workers, but Staricco (2015) found that some of the Fairtrade standards, such as direct contracting and permanent work, are not being sufficiently enforced by accreditors, resulting in a missed opportunity for effecting change.

Similarly, in examining the yerba mate industry in northeast Argentina, Bowles (2013) found that small-scale family producers, known for their self-organized network of farmers' markets (*ferías francas*), often ignore the rights of the hired workers who do much of the harvest in their small-scale yerba plantations. Those organized small-scale family producers use a non-certified fair trade system to sell their yerba mate. In this instance, 'fair trade' refers to how the product is being sold rather than to how it is being produced. This example demonstrates that official certification has merit in terms of conveying some degree of certainty over production conditions, although improved incomes is another matter. This finding also resonates with Salerno and Gonzalez's (2013) observation that farmers with hired labour find the implementation of Fairtrade standards far more difficult compared with those utilizing only family labour, as the changes required from the former group are much more significant. While labour laws in Argentina provide workers some protection, the need for labour flexibility in agriculture is notable among both family-size and large producers. A focus on waged labour as part of Fair Trade initiatives is thus important, but not easily resolved in the context of agricultural production that is labour-intensive and seasonal. Fair Trade initiatives, therefore, should be closely and critically examined, but not automatically discarded.

CONCLUSIONS

Geographical indications and Fair Trade are both strategies for promoting rural development through adding value and achieving a competitive advantage for food producers. Both also contain an ethical ethos (Overton et al. 2019). The effect of these schemes is meant to go beyond merely improving incomes for small and medium size producers, to tackle social and economic inequalities. Both also require a process of certification that entails a degree of standardization as well as the formation of collaborative relationships between different stakeholders. In Argentina, producers that have benefited from those schemes are predominantly capital-rich and export-oriented wine makers. Domestic consumers are generally not aware of GIs and fair trade certifications. For some time fair trade marketeers in Argentina have wished to focus also on the national market as a strategic avenue for products.

There are also some interesting differences between GIs and Fair Trade. For example, GIs are organized and recognized by state authorities, whereas as Fair Trade certification is done through civil society organizations. In Argentina, this has implications for the continuity of Fair Trade support, capacitation and certification. Whereas both types of certification are not well recognized by domestic consumers, excluding wine and yerba mate, products with GI/DO recognition in Argentina are not well known outside of their immediate areas of production. While more small-scale producers may participate in those initiatives, the main benefits seem to involve promoting domestic tourism and social events and the products are not export-oriented.

Therefore, similar to ethical value chains of certified organic food, GIs and Fair Trade in Argentina are advantageous mostly for export-oriented producers, who also tend to be large-scale and capitalized. The potential for a more meaningful rural development, which would include other types of producers, does exist but to date there is little indication of its materialization.

NOTES

1. Following Valiente-Riedl's (2013) distinction, 'fair trade' refers to the concept, while 'Fair Trade' (capitalized) is a general term for the diversity of philosophies and practices that some believe will make trade fair. 'Fairtrade' (one word) is a trademark for a product label of a particular set of standards and certification process.
2. Meaning in English 'to strengthen' or 'to build'.

REFERENCES

Bowles, J.S. (2013). Exploring the dialectic of labor rights and food sovereignty in everyday work conflicts of Argentina's Yerba mate country. Paper presented at *Food Sovereignty: A Critical Dialogue*, Yale University, 14–15 September, https://www.tni.org/files/download/47_bowles_2013_0.pdf (accessed 15 October 2020).

Cendón, M.L., & Bruno, M.P. (2018). Indicaciones geográficas en Argentina: Aportes metodológicos para el estudio de sus potencialidades y limitantes. *RIVAR*, *5*(14), 106–127.

Centeno, M.P. (2008). Caso 8: Chivito Criollo del Norte Neuquino, Argentina. In H. Riveros, E. Vandecandelaere, & F. Tartanac (Eds.), *Calidad de los alimentos vinculada al origen y las tradiciones en América Latina: Estudios de casos* (pp. 158–179). FAO-IICA.

Champredonde, M., Vitrolles, D., Casabianca, F., & Cerdan, C. (2014). La Pampa como indicación geográfica para diferenciar carnes vacunas en Argentina y en Brasil: Motivaciones y limitantes. *Agroalimentaria*, *20*(38), 35–52.

Corby, J.H.K. (2010). For members and markets: Neoliberalism and cooperativism in Mendoza's wine industry. *Journal of Latin American Geography*, *9*(2), 27–47.

Cosiorovski-Gonzalez, J., Champredonde, M. & Salerno, M. (2015). The challenge of Argentina Fairtrade certification for small producer organizations. Paper presented at the *5th Fair Trade International Symposium*, Milan, Italy, 29–31 May, https://www .researchgate.net/publication/280234482_The_challenge_of_Argentina_Fairtrade _certification_for_small_producer_organizations (accessed 14 October 2020).

Galtier, F., Belletti, G., & Marescotti, A. (2013). Factors constraining building effective and fair geographical indications for coffee: Insights from a Dominican case study. *Development Policy Review*, *31*(5), 597–615.

Goodman, M.K. (2004). Reading fair trade: Political ecological imaginary and the moral economy of fair trade foods. *Political Geography*, *23*(7), 891–915.

Guedes, C.A.M., & Silva, R. (2014). Agri-food geographical indications, policies, and social management: Argentina, Brazil, and the Spanish experience in the European context. *Análise Social*, *49*(2), 408–429.

Herman, A. (2019a). Asymmetries and opportunities: Power and inequality in Fairtrade wine global production networks. *Area*, *51*(2), 332–339.

Herman, A. (2019b). Governing Fairtrade: Ethics of care and justice in the Argentinean wine industry. *Social and Cultural Geography*, 1–22.

Jena, P.R., & Grote, U. (2010). Changing institutions to protect regional heritage: A case for geographical indications in the Indian agrifood sector. *Development Policy Review*, *28*(2), 217–236.

Josling, T. (2006). The war on *terroir*: Geographical indications as a transatlantic trade conflict. *Journal of Agricultural Economics*, *57*(3), 337–363.

Molina, M.S. (2020). Las indicaciones de origen geográfico de vinos en la legislación argentina. *Revista de la Facultad de Derecho*, *49*, 1–45.

Murray, D.L., Raynolds, L.T., & Taylor, P.L. (2006). The future of fair trade coffee: Dilemmas facing Latin America's small-scale producers. *Development in Practice*, *16*(2), 179–192.

Overton, J., Murray, W.E., & Howson, K. (2019). Doing good by drinking wine? Ethical value networks and upscaling of wine production in Australia, New Zealand and South Africa. *European Planning Studies*, *27*(12), 2431–2449.

Oya, C., Schaefer, F., & Skalidou, D. (2018). The effectiveness of agricultural certification in developing countries: A systematic review. *World Development*, *112*, 282–312.

Rangnekar D. (2004) *The socio-economics of geographical indications: A review of empirical evidence from Europe.* Issue Paper No. 8. ICTSD, UNCTAD.

Raynolds, L.T. (2000). Re-embedding global agriculture: The international organic and fair trade movements. *Agriculture and Human Values*, *17*(3), 297–309.

Raynolds, L.T. (2014). Fairtrade, certification, and labor: Global and local tensions in improving conditions for agricultural workers. *Agriculture and Human Values*, *31*(3), 499–511.

Raynolds, L.T. (2017). Fairtrade labour certification: The contested incorporation of plantations and workers. *Third World Quarterly*, *38*(7), 1473–1492.

Renard, M.-C. (2003). Fair trade: Quality, market and conventions. *Journal of Rural Studies*, *19*(1), 87–96.

Salerno, M. and Gonzalez, J. (2013). Procesos de implementación y certificación de comercio justo (fairtrade) en Argentina. Paper presented at the *6th International Conference on Local Food Systems (SIAL)*, Florianopolis, Brazil, 21–24 May, https://inta.gob.ar/sites/default/files/script-tmp-salerno_gonzalez_procesos_de _implementacin_y_certific.pdf (accessed 21 October 2020).

Salvatore, R.D. (1986). Labor control and discrimination: The contratista system in Mendoza, Argentina, 1880-1920. *Agricultural History*, *60*(3), 52–80.

Schiavone, E. (2010). Saberes, migraciones y nombres de los alimentos: Los genéricos y las denominaciones de origen. Paper presented at the *European Association of Agricultural Economists (EAAE) 116th Seminar*, Parma, Italy, October 27-30, http://ageconsearch.umn.edu/bitstream/95232/2/148%20completo.pdf (accessed 21 October 2020).

Solari, S. (2013). *Comercio justo: Una alternativa de producción sustentable y orientada al beneficio de los trabajadores. Experiencias de productores y organizaciones que implementaron los principios del comercio justo en Argentina*. Fundación Fortalecer.

Staricco, J.I. (2015). *Towards a fair global economic regime? A critical assessment of fair trade through the examination of the Argentinean wine industry*. PhD thesis, Copenhagen Business School.

Staricco, J.I. (2019). Class dynamics and ideological construction in the struggle over fairness: A neo-Gramscian examination of the Fairtrade initiative. *Journal of Peasant Studies*, *46*(1), 96–114.

Staricco, J.I., & Ponte, S. (2015). Qualit regimes in agro-food industries: A regulation theory reading of fair trade wine in Argentina. *Journal of Rural Studies*, *38*, 65–76.

Stein, S. (2007). Grape wars: Quality in the history of Argentine wine. In G. Campbell & N. Guibert (Eds.), *Wine, society, and globalization: Multidisciplinary perspectives on the wine industry* (pp. 99–117). Palgrave Macmillan.

Valiente-Riedl, E. (2013). *Is Fairtrade Fair?* New York: Palgrave Macmillan.

Yeung, M.T., & Kerr, W.A. (2011). Are geographical indications a wise strategy for developing country farmers? Greenfields, clawbacks and monopoly rents. *Journal of World Intellectual Property*, *14*(5), 353–367.

12 From the Indonesian fragrant highlands to the Netherlands: ethical value networks for Kerinci cinnamon

Theresa Sila Wikaningtyas and Warwick E. Murray

INTRODUCTION

The concept of ethical value chains emerged as a response to conventional trade that has put a strain on small producers in the resource periphery. This concept however, has not been widely adopted in the global spice industry. Indonesia is the leading producer of cinnamon, accounting for 66% of the world's supply. The industry itself has long been an important source of income for the people of Kerinci, the largest cinnamon producing area in Indonesia.

Using a qualitative case study, this chapter investigates the nature and evolution of ethical value chains of Kerinci cinnamon. The chapter illustrates that ethical value chains have evolved through the establishment of a farmers' organisation, adoption of organic farming and organic certification, as well as pending geographical indications registration. The central question posed in this research was: what is the nature and evolution of the adoption of ethical value chains for Kerinci cinnamon? From this flowed a number of sub-questions: (1) How is the concept of ethical value chains being implemented in the case of Kerinci cinnamon? (2) What are the factors that prompted chain actors to participate in the ethical value chains? (3) What have been the perceived benefits of the implementation of ethical value chains for the relevant actors, such as farmers, buyers and intermediaries? The work shows that the factors that prompted the adoption of the ethical practices varied among farmers, buyers/exporters and intermediaries, but there was a common goal of improving the livelihood of farmers and realising more equitable commodity trade.

ETHICAL VALUE NETWORKS IN INDONESIA

Organic agriculture is the 'ethical' form of trade that has been more widely practised in Indonesia. According to David and Ardiansyah (2017), the organic movement in Indonesia began in the early 1970s in response to the Government of Indonesia's (GoI) 'Green Revolution' campaign, when Wahana Lingkungan Hidup (WALHI), an environmental NGO, protested against the excessive use of chemical inputs in agriculture, which characterised the government's campaign. Following that, Bina Sarana Bakti, a foundation dedicated to natural farming was established in 1984 (Ariesusanty, 2011) and became the pioneer of organic agriculture in the country. In 1992, Aceh Gayo coffee became the first certified organic product in Indonesia. This was later followed by the establishment of the national network of organic agriculture (Jaker-PO) in 1998 and the Indonesia Organic Alliance (AOI) in 2002. Currently, AOI has over 100 members, comprising 79 organisations and 39 individuals from 20 provinces in Indonesia (AOI, 2012).

There has been support coming from the GoI regarding the implementation of organic agriculture: evident in the establishment of the National Standard (SNI) for Organic Food No. 01-6729-2002 in 2002, which currently is on its third revision (David & Ardiansyah, 2017). Certified Indonesian organic products may bear the 'Organik Indonesia' logo providing they comply with the production standards and are certified by the authorised certifying bodies.

Furthermore, in 2001 the GoI launched an ambitious programme called 'Go Organic 2010'. This programme aimed to promote organic agriculture and make Indonesia one of the biggest organic exporters in the world by 2010 (Prajanti & Soesilowati, 2012). The programme failed to achieve its main objectives due to poor management. Khudori (2014) stated that there was a lack of commitment with regard to implementation, considering the only concrete action taken by the government was to provide subsidy in the form of organic fertilisers. In a case study of the Go Organic 2010 programme implementation in Semarang, Central Java, differing views on managerial issues between that of the farmers, the government and the private sector challenged the roll-out of the programme (Prajanti & Soesilowati, 2012). Nonetheless, some positive impacts were noted: increased consumer awareness of organic products; increased demands for organic food; expanded certified organic land; and increased numbers of organic producers.

Aside from organic certification there have been other attempts to construct EVeNs in Indonesia. For example, the GI protection of Arabica Kintamani coffee from Bali has increased its reputation, placing the coffee in the speciality coffee class and, as a result, buyers have started paying a premium price (Mawardi, 2009; Durand & Fournier, 2017). It has also prompted a restructuring in smallholder coffee systems, with prioritisation of farmers' cooperatives over traditional structures, signifying integration at the upstream level (Neilson, 2008). Rural development impacts have also been observed in the case of GI for Kintamani Coffee, with infrastructure such as village roads, processing units and electricity being developed by the government as a means to promote coffee agro-tourism in Bali (Mawardi, 2009).

The adoption of ethical value chains in Indonesia has had its challenges. One of the most significant challenges is the issue of governance, as seen in the case of GI for Muntok White Pepper (Durand & Fournier, 2017). The process of getting GI for Muntok White Pepper involved minimum engagement of the relevant stakeholders. Generally, there is low public awareness of the significance of ethical standards, resulting in low demand and unwillingness to pay for products (Arifin, 2013; Yusida & Suwondo, 2014). Lastly, due to the high cost of certification, rights are usually held by exporters. As a result, more farmers are now engaged in contract farming. This highlights the issue of who benefits from product differentiation and how to ensure that benefits are received by the intended beneficiaries. The studies on adoption of ethical value chains in Indonesia also highlight the importance of intermediaries such as NGOs and academics or research institutions. These institutions are acknowledged as important agents to help ensure transparency, implementation of sustainability principles, and facilitators of capacity building and public awareness-raising (Mawardi, 2009; Arifin, 2013).

THE CASE STUDY AREA: KERINCI, SUMATRA, INDONESIA

As noted previously, Indonesia is the major exporter of cinnamon – providing around 66% of global supply (Iskandar et al., 2012). Much of this comes from a district in Sumatra, called Kerinci. Although, in general, cinnamon production does not contribute greatly to the Indonesian national economy, this crop is an important livelihood in Kerinci. Kerinci cinnamon (*Cinnamommum burmannii*) does not only possess economic value, the spice also has cultural values and is revered as an ancestral plant.

Kerinci is at an altitude of between 500 and 1500 metres above sea level, located within the Bukit Barisan Mountain Range, which includes the highest volcano in Sumatra, Mount Kerinci (3805 m). More than half of Kerinci, or an area of 1990.89 km^2 (BPS Kerinci, 2016), forms part of the Kerinci Seblat National Park (KSNP). The Ministry of Forestry in Indonesia promulgated the KSNP as a national park in recognition that it serves as the habitat of the endangered Sumatran Tiger and as a vast source of water and biodiversity for the surrounding communities (Dephut, 2010). This park is also listed as part of the UNESCO Tropical Rainforest Heritage of Sumatra (UNESCO, 2004).

Covering an area of 3808.50 km² (BPS Kerinci, 2016), Kerinci is the smallest district of Jambi Province (Figure 12.1). It is located almost 400 km from Jambi City, the capital of the province, and is accessible by land and air transportation. Under normal conditions, a journey from Jambi City to Kerinci takes around 10–12 hours by car. There are only three flights per week going to and from Kerinci; road travel is still the preferred mode of transport for most people. The remote location of the district, its mountainous terrain, and the National Park status of over half its area create some unique rural development challenges. These challenges include poorly developed infrastructure, poor access to ports that connect the district to other parts of Indonesia, and the ever-present competition between development and conservation endeavours.

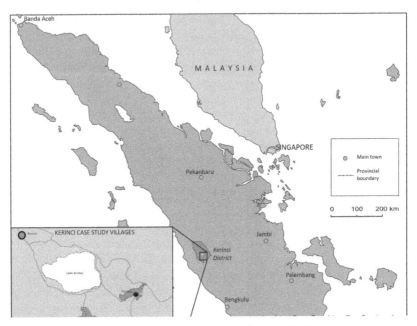

Figure 12.1   Kerinci cinnamon producing district, Jambi province,
*   Indonesia*

For the duration of one of the author's (Sila's) stay in Kerinci, she was based in Talang Kemuning, a village located approximately 40 km, or a one hour drive, from the centre of the district. Talang Kemuning is primarily a cinnamon farming community, with almost every household owning at least a block of rice paddy or dry land which they use for the cultivation of cinnamon or other cash crops. She gained access to this village and to the farming community through assistance provided by Mitra Aksi, a local Civil Society Organisation

(CSO) in Jambi that conducted an agricultural capacity building programme in the community in the period from 2013 to 2015. She utilised three data collection methodologies for this case study – semi-structured interviews, field observations and the collection of information from secondary resources.

Kerinci Cinnamon as a Global Commodity

The history of the spice trade in Indonesia has been closely linked to the history of colonialism in Southeast Asia. Spices were what had drawn traders, especially from Europe, to the archipelago. Brown (2003) noted that the 15th century marked the blossoming of the international spice trade in Indonesia, at that time known as Nusantara, with the increasing demands of Maluku spices from its two biggest markets, namely China and Europe. Meanwhile, in Sumatra, the main spice commodity traded during this period was black pepper.

The trade relations with traders from south Asia and China brought about religious influence, particularly Islam, to Indonesia (Brown, 2003). To the Indonesian traders, their conversion to Islam provided them with commercial as well as spiritual benefits. European merchants and political leaders were dismayed by the fact that the Indonesian spice trade links with Europe were dominated by Muslim intermediaries, prompting them to begin a journey to Asia in search of the source of spices and later to colonise the Indonesian archipelago and the neighbouring regions.

European imperialism in the Indonesian archipelago culminated in the Dutch colonisation of Indonesia, which lasted for well over three centuries. Headquartered in Amsterdam, in the year 1619, the Dutch East India Company, popularly known in the Indonesian context as VOC (Vereenigde Oost-Indische Compagnie), established a capital in the port city of Batavia, a city known today as Jakarta (Vickers, 2013). Batavia became the centre of VOC's trading network in Asia and from this point on and for the next 200 years VOC monopolised the spice trade in the region (Vickers, 2013), and successfully took over the positions of its rivals, namely the British and the Portuguese, as well as eradicating the home-grown Indonesian traders (Meilink-Roelofsz, 2016).

Unlike other Indonesian spice commodities, there is virtually no academic resource that has specifically focused on the history of cinnamon cultivation in Kerinci. There are, however, some short discussions on Kerinci cinnamon in the few papers that have focused on cinnamon agroforestry (Wibowo, 1999; Suyanto et al., 2007). These papers noted that the cultivation of Kerinci cinnamon began in the early 19th century, during the Dutch colonial era. Suyanto et al. (2007) noted that the cinnamon species that were growing in Kerinci were native and traditionally harvested from the forest along the Bukit Barisan mountain range. Meanwhile, Wibowo (1999) suggests that the Dutch colonial administration endorsed this traditional harvesting in order to meet European demands of the spice. Following the development of roads by the Dutch administration and population growth in Kerinci, people began cultivating the cinnamon in their fallowed swidden (Suyanto et al., 2007). As previously noted, cinnamon is now the major crop in Kerinci and the majority of farmers cultivating this spice are smallholders.

Kerinci Cinnamon: Harvesting, Quality and Place

Kerinci cinnamon plants are cultivated in the highlands of Kerinci district (Hasanah et al., 2003). To yield a good quality harvest, the plants need to grow on light, rich sandy loam soil. At higher altitudes, the cinnamon trees grow slower but produce thicker and better quality bark (Figure 12.2). Although the cultivation method is similar to Ceylon cinnamon, Kerinci cinnamon is harvested and processed differently. Harvesting conditions and methods of production often determine the quality of cinnamon (Senanayake & Wijesekera, 2003). The post-harvest processing methods of cinnamon differ according to the age of the tree and the final use of the product. If the age of the tree is 10 years or younger, the bark is used to make sticks. For this purpose, each bark sheet is cut into strips 2.5 cm in width. Meanwhile, if the bark comes from a tree that is over 15 years old, it is made into quills so they do not need to be cut into smaller widths. All bark needs to be dried under direct sunlight; a process that usually takes around 3–4 days. To maintain cleanliness, farmers need to line the ground with tarp sheets so that the bark does not come into direct contact with the ground. The cinnamon is then sorted according to grade, which depends on a number of factors, such as: type (scraped, un-scraped, quills, sticks and chips), appearance, and volatile oil content. These factors play an important role in quality and uniqueness, and thus underpin claims to place specificity pursued in potential GI registration.

CONVENTIONAL AND ETHICAL VALUE CHAINS FOR KERINCI CINNAMON

Participants were asked about the challenges they have faced with regard to cinnamon farming and trading in conventional chains. The two most pressing issues were low farm gate prices and farmers' imperfect knowledge of sustainable practices and international markets, with the latter contributing to the persistence of the former. NGO representatives also suggested a significant constraint was the absence of farmers' organisations and thus the persistence of information asymmetry. This study found that in the case of Kerinci cinnamon, ethical value chains have evolved through the establishment of a farmers' organisation and the adoption of organic certification. There is a GI programme in evolution which offers some promise with respect to these challenges.

Source: Sila Wikaningtyas

Figure 12.2   A young cinnamon tree, Kerinchi

TAKTIK Farmers' Organisation

Ethical value chains would not have materialised without the establishment of farmers' organisation TAKTIK (Tani Sakti Alam Kerinci) – established in mid-July 2013. Its mission is to "actualise environmentally friendly agriculture that is free from exploitation, by creating a fair marketing system for farmers" (TAKTIK, 2013, p. 1). It is worth noting that prior to the official establishment of TAKTIK, the initiators had attempted to form a farmers' group known as Asosiasi Petani Organik Kerinci – APOK (Kerinci Organic Farmers' Association). The TAKTIK organisation was first established by a group of farmers from five villages in Kerinci district; Talang Kemuning, Bintang Marak, Tanjung Syam, Sungai Hangat and Selampaung. By the end of 2013, the organisation had expanded its membership to include farmers from three additional villages, these being Air Mumu, Pondok and Kebun Lima. A local NGO based in Jambi, Mitra Aksi, was instrumental in establishing the organisation.

Membership of TAKTIK is voluntary, with straightforward membership prerequisites. Farmers from the eight villages mentioned above may become permanent members of this organisation by filling in a registration form and paying a one-time registration fee of IDR 50,000 (around US$5). Ordinary members are not required to pay the registration and monthly fees, but then they may not elect or be elected as members of the organisation's board. By 2014, 1014 farmers were registered as members of the organisation (VECO Indonesia, 2014) with this number increasing to around 1200 by 2015 (NGO Representative 1, interview 2016).

TAKTIK's buyer is a spice trading and exporting company based in Jakarta, called ATN. The relationship between TAKTIK and ATN commenced in 2015 and takes the form of joint-operations (Buyer 2, interview 2016). As such they have moved from a mere trading relationship to a closer connection in which both parties have relatively equal bargaining power. This relationship entails the provision of substantial financial resources, warehouse equipment and capacity-building activities by ATN for TAKTIK members and officials (Figures 12.3 and 12.4). The new value chains are shorter and seem to be more beneficial to farmers as well as more sustainable than conventional value chains.

Organic Certification

Cinnamon farming in Kerinchi today is primarily conducted in accordance with the principles of organic farming. Cinnamon trees can grow naturally in Kerinci and they need very little maintenance. It is the cash crops that the farmers cultivate using intercropping methods that are usually not organic.

The use of chemical fertilisers and fungicides may pose a risk of contamination. Prior to the establishment of TAKTIK, cinnamon farmers in Kerinci did not practise organic and sustainable agriculture, relying heavily on the use of chemical fertilisers and fungicides to maintain their smallholdings. However, in 2015, they began to practise organic farming specifically as a means to add value (NGO Representative 1, interview 2016). Farmers are required to implement a number of organic farming techniques and principles, such as ensuring organic and non-organic plants do not grow on the same farm; using non-GMO cultivation techniques; conserving soil; water resources and native plants and animals; using organic fertilisers and pesticides/fungicides; and practising integrated waste management (TAKTIK, 2013).

Source: Sila Wikaningtyas

Figure 12.3   Workers sorting and packing cinnamon sticks at TAKTIK's warehouse

For TAKTIK members, the process of acquiring this certification began when they received training from VECO Indonesia and Mitra Aksi in 2014, with the purpose of preparing the farmers to obtain Rainforest Alliance (RA) certification. According to one NGO representative, this was conducted as part of a trade arrangement that they had entered into with Cassia Coop, a Belgian-owned cinnamon exporting company based in the district. The attempt to obtain the RA certificate was not successful because several of the 500 farms inspected at random did not meet the RA standard. However, with support from ATN and VECO International TAKTIK has continued to strive to obtain organic certification for the farms belonging to its members.

Figure 12.4   Cinnamon quills at Kerinchi awaiting transport to Jakarta

Geographical Indications

Kerinci cinnamon has its own unique properties, although generally consumers have little awareness of this. According to MPIG-K2J (2015), Kerinci cinnamon contains more than 5% essential oil and more than 80% Cinnamaldehyde (an organic compound unique to Cinnamon, which gives the spice its flavour and odour). This characteristic is what makes the quality of Kerinci cinnamon widely considered better than that produced by neighbouring regions. The first step to claiming GI rights was to establish an agency that represents the Kerinci cinnamon community. The agency, called Masyarakat Perlindungan Indikasi Geografis Kerinci (MPIG-K2), has a membership consisting of a number of stakeholders and office bearers, including cinnamon farmers, traders and processors, representatives of local authorities, traditional leaders, and representatives from various District Offices.

The registered name for Kerinci cinnamon is *Kayumanis Koerintji.* *Kayumanis* is the Indonesian word for cinnamon, while *Koerintji* is the old spelling of Kerinci. There is an increasing degree of recognition for the term "Koerintji cinnamon" in global cinnamon markets (Madan & Kannan, 2003). Three types of cinnamon products can each receive GI registration, these being dried cinnamon quills of four different quality grades, each of which has its own attributes; cinnamon sticks; and cinnamon powder. Not many research participants were aware of this potential GI, and those who had heard of it knew relatively little about the principles.

Fair Trade Principles

In the case of TAKTIK and ATN's business practices, adherence to the WFTO's ten fair trade principles was observed. Here, two are mentioned: first, principle one, *creating opportunities for economically disadvantaged producers*. This was the underlying principle of the partnership between TAKTIK and ATN. The partnership enables Kerinci farmers to obtain more secure income through more effective cinnamon agribusiness. More secure and regular income from cinnamon also means that it has a long-term poverty reduction potential for the farming community and for the Kerinci district in general. Second, fair trade principle three, *fair trading practices*. As a company with relatively strong financial capability, ATN recognised TAKTIK's need for financial support and, as a result, ATN has been providing TAKTIK with funding to purchase production equipment, and made advance payment to TAKTIK's business unit in order to help with its operational costs. Prices were agreed between TAKTIK and ATN, and were calculated in such a way that took into account the cost of labour and added values. Furthermore, workers were also paid at a socially acceptable rate.

FARMERS' PARTICIPATION AND OUTCOMES OF CINNAMON ETHICAL VALUE CHAINS

The case study found that the factors prompting Kerinci cinnamon farmers' participation in ethical value chains can be analysed through two sets of ideas: first, the factors that prompted the establishment of the farmers' organisation; and second, the factors that prompted the farmers to join that organisation. First and foremost, the most significant occurrence has been the formation of the TAKTIK organisation, and the research participants were asked to share their reasons for joining. The majority stated that they did so because they were invited by someone they knew (a family member, friend, or relative) who was already a registered member. With regard to the uptake of sustainable agriculture, farmers became interested in practising organic farming because organic products were promoted as more lucrative compared with conventional crops. Clearly, social and community factors, rather than knowledge concerning ethical value, play an important role in influencing Kerinci farmers to become members of TAKTIK and consequently to adopt the ethical practices.

First, there was a consensus among the farmers about what they perceived as the most prominent benefit of the ethical value chains – higher farm-gate prices. There was also a promise of a guaranteed price. But with this lies a question about the sustainability of the system. Are the high prices TAKTIK pays sustainable and what determines this or otherwise? Having learned that in some cases the premium from ethical certification did not directly benefit the smallest producers (Ruben & Fort, 2012; Valkila, 2014), we argue that the transfer of premium to farmers should be scrutinised. There is also a question of whether TAKTIK can maintain the quality standards that are imposed. This is crucial because upholding quality is the basis of earning the premium.

Second, the adoption of ethical value chains has brought about positive change in the local community, providing employment, especially for women farmers. Being able to work at TAKTIK has given each of them a more stable income on top of their funds from wider farming.

Third, there have been ecological benefits. Even though Kerinci cinnamon is inherently organic, inorganic inputs had been used for intercrop cultivation as mentioned. Farmers used chemical fertilisers and insecticides before they learned that they can use organic input and get a better quality harvest. Practising organic farming has helped farmers rejuvenate the quality of the soil.

There are potential benefits of GI protection for Kerinci cinnamon as it could boost the local economy through the sales of value added products. However, there needs to be a clear and transparent mechanism of transferring the benefits of a GI back to the community. In terms of potential costs however, the findings suggest that marginalisation could be a potential drawback from GI protection. GI protection only applies to cinnamon from four sub-districts in Kerinci – the GI protection has the potential to marginalise cinnamon farmers from other areas in Kerinci.

CONCLUSION

EVeNs in Kerinci cinnamon evolved as the result of the intervention of intermediaries, principally TAKTIK. This institution has clearly played a critical role and should be considered a model. Participation by farmers has resulted through the role of this and other bodies. Farmers themselves were also influenced by a 'neighbourhood adoption' effect and price signals.

This evolution of ethical chains adoption has created social, economic, and environmental benefits for farmers, as well as for buyers, allowing them to market their products as environmentally-friendly and socially-just. In the case of organic certification, prices have been at a premium. Fair trade certification has also brought a range of benefits for growers. The proposed GI is promising given the unique qualities of Kerinchi cinnamon. Nevertheless, these benefits are not guaranteed and care will need to be taken to ensure their sustainability and that they are distributed in a just manner. This latter point calls for a crucial oversight role of the local government and civil society organisations as well as a role for academics in conducting research that monitors outcomes.

REFERENCES

AOI (2012). *Aliansi Organis Indonesia: Tentang AOI*. Retrieved 18 January 2017, from http://organicindonesia.org/0302-aboutus-isi.php?id=590#.WH7fzOZ96Uk

Ariesusanty, L. (2011). Indonesia: Country report. In *The world of organic agriculture, Statistics and emerging trends* (pp. 137–139). FiBL and IFOAM. Retrieved from https://shop.fibl.org/fileadmin/documents/shop/1546-organic-world-2011.pdf#page =137.

Arifin, B. (2013). On the competitiveness and sustainability of the Indonesian agricultural export commodities. *ASEAN Journal of Economics, Management and Accounting*, *1*(1), 81–100.

BPS Kerinci. (2016). Geografi dan Iklim. Retrieved 10 August 2016, from https:// kerincikab.bps.go.id/web%202014/index.php?hal=subject&id=1.

Brown, C. (2003). *A short history of Indonesia: The unlikely nation?* Allen & Unwin.

David, W., & Ardiansyah, A. (2017). Organic agriculture in Indonesia: Challenges and opportunities. *Organic Agriculture*, *7*, 329–338.

Dephut (2010). *Kerinci Seblat National Park*. Retrieved from http://www.dephut.go.id/ INFORMASI/TN%20INDO-ENGLISH/tn_kerinciseblat.htm.

Durand, C., & Fournier, S. (2017). Can geographical indications modernize Indonesian and Vietnamese agriculture? Analyzing the role of national and local governments and producers' strategies. *World Development*, *98*, 93–104.

Hasanah, M., Nuryani, Y., Djisbar, A., Mulyono, E., Wikardi, E., & Asman, A. (2003). Indonesian Cassia (Indonesian Cinnamon). In P.N. Ravindran, K.N. Babu, & M. Shylaja (Eds.), *Cinnamon and cassia: The genus cinnamomum* (pp. 185–198). CRC Press.

Iskandar, S., Jauhari, H., Mulyana, A., Dewata, E., Yamin, M., & Marwa, T. (2012). *Analysis of Determinant Factors Influencing Cinnamon Export and Prices in Indonesia*. MIICEMA 2012, Palembang.

Khudori (2014). Jokowi-JK dan Go Organic. tempo.co. Retrieved 20 January 2017, from https://www.tempo.co/read/kolom/2014/09/23/1662/Jokowi-JK-dan-Go -Organic.

Madan, M.S., & Kannan, S. (2003). Economics and marketing of cinnamon and cassia: A global view. In P.N. Ravindran, K.N. Babu, & M. Shylaja (Eds.), *Cinnamon and cassia: The genus cinnamomum* (pp. 285–310). CRC Press.

Mawardi, S. (2009). *Advantages, constraints and key success factors in establishing origin- and tradition-linked quality signs: The case of Kintamani Bali Arabica coffee geographical indication, Indonesia*. FAO.

Meilink-Roelofsz, M.A.P. (2016). *Persaingan Eropa dan Asia di Nusantara. Sejarah Perniagaan 1500—1630* (translated T.K. Bambu). Komunitas Bambu.

Neilson, J. (2008). Global private regulation and value-chain restructuring in Indonesian smallholder coffee systems. *World Development*, *36*(9), 1607–1622.

Prajanti, S.D.W., & Soesilowati, E. (2012). The policy effectiveness of 'Go Organic': A study on implementation and efficiency of organic vegetable cultivation in Semarang Municipality. *International Journal of Sociology Study*, *2*(6), 468–482.

Ruben, R., & Fort, R. (2012). The impact of fair trade certification for coffee farmers in Peru. *World Development*, *40*(3), 570–582.

Senanayake, U., & Wijesekera, R. (2003). Cinnamon and cassia—The future vision. In P.N. Ravindran, K.N. Babu, & M. Shylaja (Eds.), *Cinnamon and cassia: The genus cinnamomum* (pp. 285–310). CRC Press.

Suyanto, S., Tomich, T., & Otsuka, K. (2007). The role of land tenure in development of cinnamon agroforestry in Kerinci, Sumatra. In *Voices from the forest: Integrating indigenous knowledge into sustainable upland farming* (pp. 743–753). RFF Press.

TAKTIK (2013). Formulir inspeksi internal lahan petani (Internal farm inspection form). Unpublished, Kerinci.

UNESCO (2004). *Tropical rainforest heritage of Sumatra*. UNESCO.

Valkila, J. (2014). Do fair trade pricing policies reduce inequalities in coffee production and trade? *Development Policy Review*, *32*(4), 475–493.

VECO Indonesia. (2014). Laporan Populer VECO Indonesia 2014. Retrieved 11 October 2016, from https://issuu.com/vecoindonesia/docs/laporan_populer_2014 _veco_indonesia.

Vickers, A. (2013). *A history of modern Indonesia*. Cambridge University Press.

Wibowo, D.H. (1999). The 'cinnamon connection' and government failure in conservation management: Lesson learned from deforestation in the Kerinci-Seblat National Park. https://www.dropbox.com/s/9fiunjh255qd8gn/chapter%2012%20sila %20cinnamon%20wm%20may%206.docx?dl=0.

Yusida, E., & Suwondo, J.P.R. (2014). Is fair trade really a solution to create fairness in agricultural trade? Case in Indonesia. *International Journal of Trade, Economics and Finance*, *5*(3), 277–284.

13 Coffee and conflict in Timor-Leste: a role for ethical certification

Kelle Howson

INTRODUCTION

As Asia's newest and poorest country, Timor-Leste (Figure 13.1) faces significant development challenges. While oil and gas reserves have served as the cornerstone of the country's development strategy since the end of Indonesian occupation in 2002, the rehabilitation and upgrading of the coffee sector has also been seen as key to Timor's future prosperity (Government of Timor-Leste, 2011). Coffee provides income to a large section of the country's rural population, predominantly smallholders (Inder et al., 2013; Khamis, 2015; Lundahl & Sjoholm, 2012). Left to grow largely uncultivated on traditionally-held land during the Indonesian occupation, its organic-by-default status has proved an attractive selling point to large international buyers. Coffee upgrading and export has been a key focus of international development partners and donors. USAID and its implementation partner NCBA CLUSA[1] have been especially active in supporting Timor-Leste's smallholder coffee cooperative to consolidate operations, and to export coffee to the US. In particular, this arrangement has aided in attaining Fairtrade International certification for Timor-Leste's main coffee cooperative, *Cooperativa Café Timor* (CCT) and in facilitating a supply relationship through a network led by Starbucks.

However, coffee production in Timor-Leste, and the organisation that became CCT, have a dark history, interwoven with colonisation, conflict and exploitation. Since independence, the challenge of coffee upgrading and development has been twofold. Alongside the inequitable conditions that have come to characterise the globalised coffee market since the dismantling of the International Coffee Agreement in 1989 – of extreme buyer power, dependency and uneven development – the local Timorese coffee network is hampered by the legacy of historical relations of control and oppression (Khamis, 2015; Shepherd & McWilliam, 2013). Independence and Fairtrade certification have reconfigured the production network for Timorese coffee, but producers there have faced particularly steep barriers to upgrading, underpinned by local contingencies. This chapter seeks to situate the ethical value network of Fairtrade coffee production which has CCT at its centre, within the postcolonial, post-conflict conditions in which it is embedded, in order to gain insight into how those conditions influence the configuration of the network, and ultimately its outcomes for smallholder producers, in terms of governance and realisation of ethical value.

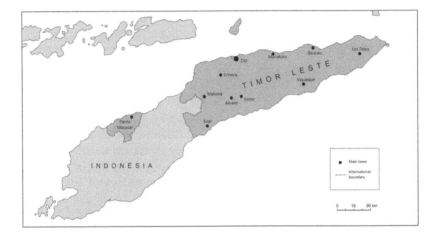

Figure 13.1   Timor-Leste

First the chapter gives an overview of the intersecting histories of coffee, colonialism and conflict in Timor-Leste. It then briefly discusses the contribution of coffee to economic rehabilitation and growth in the country. Then it describes the emergence of the Timorese coffee ethical value network, drawing on fieldwork conducted in 2014, as well as a review of more recent reports, to analyse the extent to which ethical certification is able to afford producers greater agency and a more equitable share of value from their production network.

COFFEE AND COLONIALISM IN TIMOR-LESTE

The history of plantation agriculture in Timor-Leste is deeply linked to colonialism and violence. Coffee production was used as a tool of economic control and subjugation during both the Portuguese and Indonesian eras. Hierarchal governance structures and path dependencies institutionalised during these coffee regimes continue to inform structural vulnerabilities experienced by the large proportion of Timor-Leste's rural population that still depend on coffee exports for survival.

Although coffee was first introduced to Timor in 1815 by the Dutch, its emergence as a vital export coincided with the decline of available sandalwood in the mid-19th century (Roque, 2010). The commercialisation of coffee was coordinated by successive Portuguese governors, beginning with Alfonso de Castro, who oversaw an increase in exports from 22 tonnes in 1860, to 145 tonnes in 1865 (Shepherd & McWilliam, 2013, p. 330). From 1879 to 1892, coffee exports were regularly above 1000 tonnes (Clarence-Smith, 1992, p. 15). In the following decades, coffee accounted for about half of Timor's exports, reaching over 2000 tonnes by 1963 – 73% of exports by value (Khamis, 2015).

Castro's agricultural system was informed by a similar scheme to that adopted in the Dutch East Indies 30 years prior. The Culture System, or *cultuurstelsel* was a colonial means of organising the local land and workforce around monocultural smallholdings. This involved a forced labour regime that monopolised land for production of sugar and coffee, implemented by local authorities, who were rewarded with tax breaks on their own production. This was an effective method of increasing GDP, whist also extending "an unprecedented level of colonial surveillance and control" (Li, 2007). Governance structures regulating coffee planting and farming in Timor-Leste in the late 19th century remain relatively opaque. This is due in large part to the complexity of relationships of enforcement and taxation. The colonial government relied on rural indigenous leaders (*Liurai*) to enforce the agricultural regime (Nixon, 2013). Portuguese colonial narratives cast *Liurai* as ruthless tyrants, ready to exploit their people in pursuit of coffee wealth (Roque, 2010; Shepherd & McWilliam, 2013).

The *Liurai* were positioned as agents within a system of forced agricultural labour, enforced in turn through chiefs of subsidiary groups – *suco* – and reportedly underpinned by violent means such as 'head-hunting' (Shepherd & McWilliam, 2013). In the late 19th and early 20th centuries, coffee production in Timor-Leste was strategically transitioned to large-scale plantations, and away from smallholders. This was due in part to increasing difficulties in these supply relations. As the Portuguese attempted to solidify their authority and control over production through military excursions in the indigenous kingdoms, leaders engaged in widespread rebellion, selling large amounts of coffee on the black market to Chinese buyers or corrupt officials (Shepherd & McWilliam, 2013). The colonial administration began to lose significant amounts of revenue. This gave rise to a number of military 'pacification campaigns' aiming to subdue the population and maximise production and profit (Weatherbee, 1966). These campaigns often secured agricultural slaves for the coffee industry. *Liurai* were also obliged to provide waged workers for

Portuguese-owned plantations. Shepherd and McWilliam (2013) point out that wages were "only sufficient to ensure survival." The most notable of the commercial plantations established at this time was the Soceidade Agrícola Patria e Trabalho (SAPT) in Ermera district, which covered almost 2000 hectares of previously smallholder-owned land by 1908 (Shepherd & McWilliam, 2013, p. 333).

Agricultural programmes, especially involving coffee, were a vital tool of the Portuguese subjugation of the Timorese population in the latter half of the 19th century. While the historiography is limited, Shepherd and McWilliam (2013) provide a comprehensive commentary, and identify Foucauldian patterns of "… routine surveillance, control, and discipline of human bodies," linked to the introduction of commercial coffee production in the territory (p. 328). The use of military force, forced labour, and the co-optation of indigenous political systems enabled the Portuguese governors to establish coffee cultivation as a tool of socio-economic dominance.

Timor-Leste gained its independence from Portugal in 1975, only to be promptly annexed by Indonesia in a bloody invasion. The new occupier, like its predecessor, employed simultaneous programmes of military and economic suppression to consolidate control. Under Indonesian rule, the coffee sector was 'decapitalised,' and the potential of coffee production and economic development stymied (Nevins, 2003). This was despite the occupation's outward developmentalist rhetoric and encouragement of cash-cropping. While this rhetoric to some extent helped to placate the international community amid concerns about the wellbeing of the Timorese people, food insecurity remained a serious issue, in the decade following the invasion, an estimated 100,000 East Timorese died – the majority from starvation (Shepherd & McWilliam, 2013, p. 343).

Nevertheless, cash-cropping was supported by international development partners and aid organisations. However, little investment went into quality upgrading. During the 1980s, Timorese coffee trees fell into an acute state of neglect, due in large part to a policy of low-grade production for the Indonesian instant coffee market. Commentators have noted that the Indonesian occupation succeeded in establishing a coffee monopsony when SAPT was formally transferred to a company called PT Denok Hernandes Indonesia by decree from the Indonesian Governor. Damian Grenfell (2005), claims that PT Denok was a vehicle for "senior Indonesian army officers to raise money for the armed forces and for corrupt self-interest" (p. 83). PT Denok was a subsidiary company of PT Batara Indra – the only company at the time with a licence to export Timorese coffee (Oxfam, 2003, p. 3). The Indonesians continued to make use of networks of rural indigenous coffee collectors, and Chinese buyers. Farmers were forced to sell through PT Denok, and punished harshly if they sought other channels (Khamis, 2015). Oxfam reported that the administration installed a "well-controlled and government supervised" collection mechanism "disguised as a cooperative" (Oxfam, 2003), called *Puskud Timor Timur*, which coordinated procurement for remuneration well below market averages. During the period of occupation, farmers in neighbouring West Timor received six times the price that East Timorese producers were paid for their coffee, with East Timorese losing \$2.50 per kg (Khamis, 2015).

Coffee trees were allowed to grow wild during the period of Indonesian aggression – under forest canopies and along roadsides. Little to no capital went towards technical support or training in cultivation, and quality and yields fell dramatically.

> [The Indonesian Government] were interested only in extracting income through the quantity of cheap coffee they could accrue for forward sale ... as a result, interest in coffee cultivation amongst the East Timorese generally decreased. Farmers acting as caretakers simply began to harvest beans annually from the previous large planta-tions as well as from their own small-holdings (Oxfam, 2003, p. 4)

Farmers ceased to prune, or to clear land, and trees were allowed to grow too old. Knowledge of cultivation techniques declined at this time. Beans of vari-able quality were blended together, meaning that knowledge of bean selection, efficient transportation and exact processing was unnecessary (Shepherd & McWilliam, 2013). By 1994 yields had fallen dramatically. One inadvertent consequence of the lack of investment in agricultural management, however, was the absence of pesticides, herbicides, and chemical fertilisers in produc-tion. The fact that all of Timor-Leste's coffee remained, by default, organic, was to have a significant influence on the direction of the sector (Khamis, 2015).

COFFEE AND DEVELOPMENT IN TIMOR-LESTE

In 1992, under international (and particularly US) pressure to open up markets and allow for competition, the Indonesian military relinquished *Puskud*. This allowed USAID to take a central role in the coffee industry (Grenfell, 2005), outsourcing implementation of its development project to US company NCBA-CLUSA (or 'the NCBA'), as the United States government did not formally recognise Indonesian sovereignty in Timor. The NCBA established a presence in Dili in 1994, sought to develop the coffee industry through technical support and management training, and in 2001 oversaw the transfor-mation of Puskud into Cooperativa Café Timor (CCR); for which it acted as buyer (Grenfell, 2005). The NCBA's entry into the Timorese coffee industry took place within the context of increasing international demand for premium, quality differentiated coffee, including organic coffee. At the turn of the millennium the Timorese coffee industry was beset by manifold challenges, including a grave infrastructure deficit, exacerbated by the destruction wrought by outgoing Indonesian forces in 1999, who destroyed 70–80% of buildings, as well as other key public infrastructure, and severely disrupted agriculture (Khamis, 2015). However, newly exposed to tumultuous deregulated global markets, Timorese coffee producers possessed the comparative advantage of organic status. Growing consumer demand for ethical products had piqued the interest of powerful coffee buyers in Timor's organic coffee supply, and in turn the NCBA hoped to tap into a differentiated premium niche.

Timor-Leste's 20 year Strategic Development Plan, released in 2011 (Government of Timor-Leste, 2011), lays out an ambitious roadmap for economic development with a strong emphasis on smallholder agriculture. At the time of the report's release the country's population stood at 1.1 million, with roughly three quarters living in rural areas. The rural population experiences particularly significant challenges including higher levels of food insecurity (in 2011, rural households experienced shortages of staple foods for 3.8 months of the year), and lack of access to basic services, including health and education (p. 107). Bolstering agriculture remains a crucial intervention for rural economic development in Timor-Leste. A 2013 report showed the coffee sector to be the principal source of income for approximately a quarter of households (Inder et al., 2013, p. 4). However, those who rely on coffee for their primary income are amongst the most vulnerable sectors of the population to poverty (Inder et al., 2013; Lundahl & Sjoholm, 2012). The development of the coffee sector has the potential to deliver targeted development outcomes and sustainable livelihoods for those most susceptible to extreme poverty. To unlock this potential, the Strategic Development Plan set a target of doubling coffee production by 2020 following the rehabilitation of 40,000 ha of coffee plantations. The plan notes that, in 2011, Timor-Leste was exporting roughly 12,500 tonnes of coffee, accounting for 80% of non-oil exports.

In 2001, CCT obtained Fairtrade certification from (then) Fair Trade Labelling Organisations International (FLO, now Fairtrade International), and the NCBA began to broker deals with US buyers, most notably Starbucks, for Fairtrade organic certified Timorese coffee. In 2005, shortly after independence, the NCBA claimed to be the largest private enterprise in Timor-Leste, dominating the export of premium coffee (although other organisations still bought low quality product for instant blends). The NCBA ensured quality control by vertically integrating as much of the pre-export production process as possible. The organisation bought coffee in its lowest-value form (unprocessed red cherry) from farmers along the roadside, and tightly oversaw processing at four wet-processing plants (Grenfell, 2005). CCT was fully dependent on the NCBA as a buyer, processor and broker. Although development partners, ethical consumers, and officials of the new state hopefully viewed CCT as a vehicle for the generation of ethical value to impoverished, malnourished and traumatised rural populations, the organisation also sat at the confluence of historical oppression and power imbalance. It came into being as a colonial system of forced and underpaid labour, and was maintained by the Indonesian occupation as a regime-sustaining monopsony, underpinned by both violence and neglect. The key ethical selling point for Timorese coffee derived from that neglect, and transforming top-down instruments of production and distribution established under colonial rule to generators of ethical value, has proved challenging and controversial.

Notably, to achieve its targets, the 2011 Strategic Development Plan prescribed a move away from organic production in the short term. Although it promised a much-needed foothold in the global marketplace, organic coffee was expensive, producing lower yields, and hard to scale up. Stakeholders questioned whether it was a strategy better suited to established producers with existing capital, as opposed to one of the most underdeveloped coffee sectors in the world (Khamis, 2015). The Strategic Development Plan's target of doubling coffee production appeared not to have been met in 2019. Government statistics show export volumes fluctuating dramatically year-on-year, to a relatively low point of just over 7000 tonnes in 2018 and 2019. Despite this, export value has climbed at a steady pace, from roughly US$6 million in 2004, to over US$18 million in 2019. Indonesia remained the largest importer of Timorese coffee by both volume and value in 2019. It bought nearly twice the volume of the next two largest importers combined – the US and Canada. However, Indonesia continues to import non-premium bulk coffee. While export value to Indonesia reached nearly $5.5 million in 2019, Canada was close behind with $4.15 million, and export value to the US stood at $3.9 million. The inverse relationship between volume and value growth indicates that efforts to upgrade coffee quality and to establish premium value networks have been somewhat successful, though such dramatically declining yields are not in line with the Plan. The question of the share of export value that is retained to benefit rural communities is of crucial importance.

CAPTURING ETHICAL VALUE: GOVERNANCE AND UPGRADING IN CCT'S EVEN

Very soon after Timor-Leste gained independence, a large portion of the country's smallholder coffee producers were subsumed into a global ethical value network, facilitated by USAID and the NCBA. The transformation of Puskud into CCT occurred at a time when coffee consumers in the Global North were becoming increasingly concerned with provenance, quality and social and environmental impact. The Indonesians had left a legacy of dependency, neglect, extraction and destruction. However, parts of this legacy became elements of the ethical selling point of Timorese coffee. In 2019, CCT had 24,000 farmer members, and according to the NCBA, is Timor-Leste's largest private sector employer, and one of the world's largest suppliers of certified organic coffee (NCBA-CLUSA, 2020). However, while the ethical value network was rapidly consolidated and certified, farmers in Timor-Leste continue to face high barriers to realising the full benefits, both in terms of increased agency and representation, and increased value share.

In qualitative interviews with CCT management in 2014, the cooperative's Fairtrade status was framed predominantly as a required hurdle for market access and, by extension, something of a headache. One CCT representative felt that the requirements of Fairtrade did not reflect the reality farmers were facing in Timor-Leste, describing them as 'silly' and 'nonsense'. As the interviewee explained, Fairtrade served as "a niche marketing arrangement. Some buyers want Fairtrade coffee, the principal one being Starbucks – they always buy Fairtrade now." However, the benefits of Fairtrade's minimum practice standards were cast in a dubious light when the participant recounted a case in which the cooperative was incentivised to lay off women workers, rather than providing Fairtrade's required number of toilets for the workforce at its processing plant: "We thought, what nonsense – we're not going to do that. So unfortunately we've replaced a number of women workers with machines." While cooperative governance is central to Fairtrade's standards for small producers, CCT's governance structures remained hierarchical even after Fairtrade certification. Farmers could access representation through delegates at an annual general meeting. But largely the cooperative functioned simply as a "roster of suppliers" (Laughton, 2007). Although officially farmers were required to produce a membership card in order to sell cherry to the CCT truck, three interviewed farmers claimed to sell to the CCT truck without being members. Farmers were generally dissatisfied with the price they received from CCT, saying that it was not sufficient to meet production and living costs, and that CCT was not supporting them enough.

It is important to note that at the time of field research, CCT/NCBA was the only organisation that bought coffee in its raw (red cherry) form in Timor-Leste, to be 'wet-processed' at scale, into high quality product. This monopsony had a number of structural consequences for farmer-power. Cherry needs to be processed within 24 hours of harvesting, therefore farmers rely on the CCT truck to collect cherry at the correct time. This can be a problem for farmers in more rural or remote areas. If they are unable to sell cherry in time, the only other option is to 'dry process' it with wooden equipment at home, resulting in 'dry parchment' – an inferior product which cannot be sold to the premium market. While a kilogram of dry parchment fetches a higher price at farm gate than a kilogram of cherry, volume is significantly reduced, and moreover farmers must rely on intermediaries to transport product to collection hubs. Therefore returns for dry parchment are well below returns for red cherry. Ultimately, smallholder farmers wanting to sell red cherry must sell to CCT/NCBA.

Another key barrier to both production upgrading and participatory governance within CCT was found to be lagging capability, underpinned by (1) high rates of illiteracy in rural areas;[2] (2) information asymmetries within the cooperative structure; and (3) insufficient access to training and resources (Inder et al., 2013; Laughton, 2007). A 2013 study found that only 14% of CCT's members had received training in production methods, and moreover, that training had had little to no impact on yields. The authors observed: "Support and training will be better received if it builds on the existing social capital in the community, and considers all the needs of the household and the community, rather than seeing farmers purely as producers of a commodity" (Inder et al., 2013, p. 36). Some industry stakeholders interviewed in field research, including CCT members, had little knowledge of CCT's Fairtrade certification, the Fairtrade standards, or the Fairtrade-mandated cooperative governance structures. This knowledge and information gap both provides evidence of, and reinforces, a lack of farmer agency within cooperative structures, which fails Fairtrade's principles of representation and transparency.

However, despite documented challenges in instituting governance and practice standards, Fairtrade has facilitated one significant material benefit for farming communities in Timor-Leste. With the Fairtrade organic premium, CCT/NCBA has been able to establish a network of clinics providing primary healthcare to Timor-Leste's rural population. CCT offers free healthcare to its 24,000 members, and their families – reaching remote communities with both fixed and mobile services. CCT, using Fairtrade premium funds and direct backing from Starbucks, is now the largest private health provider in the country (NCBA-CLUSA, 2016), a significant impact made possible by the formation of an ethical value network for Timorese coffee, and the facilitation of key development partners.

However, in this network configuration, farmers are largely unrepresented in multi-nodal income streams. CCT's purchase of red cherry and central processing mechanisms act as a form of quality control, and therefore farmers are discouraged from setting up collective processing hubs in coffee growing districts or improving their processing capacity at home. While CCT pays the market or Fairtrade floor price for raw coffee, and while selling red cherry is the only economically viable option for many farmers, this model combined with CCT's monopsony also creates a captive and dependent supply relationship with little option for value chain upgrading for smallholders. A 2007 study was highly critical of CCT/NCBA's subsumption of value-added nodes in the Timor coffee EVeN, which barred farmers from income from processing, arguing it was against the spirit of the Fairtrade principles. The study quoted one farmer, Justino, who said: "Farmer options need to be broader than either selling coffee cherry or processing coffee the hard way" (Laughton, 2007, p. 129).

Within this picture of lock-in to low-value activities, what impact has ethical value network participation had on farmer's livelihoods, and on rural poverty alleviation? Updated evidence is required, especially given the recent drop in export volume and corresponding spike in export value. However, based on 2014 field research I calculated that farmers received approximately US6c per espresso sold at Starbucks, or 1.6% of the final retail price, when they sold red cherry to CCT. Coffee producers in Timor-Leste had much lower yields compared with producers elsewhere in the Asia-Pacific region. This derives in large part from the organic strategy which has been a key motivator in the formation and governance of CCT's production network. Organic status provided Puskud and then CCT with a rapid foothold in international markets, but it locked farmers into the unproductive status quo created by the Indonesian military. Inder and colleagues' (2013) survey found that non-CCT member households earned on average US$200 per year from coffee, making up on average over 50% of their income. A household selling an equivalent amount exclusively to CCT would make $260 in the same year – or 70c a day, still well below the extreme poverty line. While selling red cherry to CCT at a Fairtrade price does differentiate cooperative members from their non-cooperative counterparts, this model serves to institute a tiered system of inclusion and exclusion, as well as limiting upgrading opportunities. This supports the recommendation of the Strategic Development Plan – that the country should move away from organic coffee as a rural development strategy (Government of Timor-Leste, 2011; Khamis, 2015). Although Fairtrade farmers earned marginally more than non-Fairtrade farmers, their income remained inadequate, and the ethical value network actually functioned as a barrier to greater income generation.

CONCLUSION

Fairtrade organic certification and the ethical value network it has created for smallholder coffee producers in Timor-Leste has succeeded in providing sustainable market access and, perhaps most importantly, rural healthcare services. However, the network remains highly concentrated and asymmetric, locking in suppliers to captive and extractive relations for the benefit of a lead firm monopsony. This is partly due to the embeddedness of the local network in a hierarchical colonial legacy, which the international and contextually dis-embedded fair trade system will always struggle to address or account for. CCT is a cooperative that has grown out of a violent forced collection mechanism, and while farmer-ownership is now much better institutionalised, legacies of that remain visible in a lack of trust, transparency and participation. Moreover, the more recent involvement of Starbucks and what in many ways appears to be their functional agent, the NCBA, allows the lead firm to secure a reliable supply of low-cost organic coffee to satisfy market demands. Organic status and the cost, technology and knowledge required to process the product, serve to preclude farmers from capturing a greater share of value. Thus, while farmers have benefited somewhat from ethical value creation as a result of this network formation, this value remains insufficient for significant poverty alleviation and broader progress.

NOTES

1. The National Cooperative Business Association and the Cooperative League of the United States of America.
2. In 2013 it was reported that over half of those aged 45 and older in coffee producing areas had no formal education (Mendez, 2013).

REFERENCES

Clarence-Smith, W.G. (1992). Planters and smallholders in Portuguese Timor in the nineteenth and twentieth centuries. *Indonesia Circle. School of Oriental and African Studies Newsletter*, *20*(57), 15–30.

Government of Timor-Leste. (2011). *Strategic development plan 2011-2030*. Dili.

Grenfell, D. (2005). Reconstructing the coffee republic: Development and colonialism in Timor-Leste. *Development Bulletin*, *68*, 83–86.

Inder, B., Cornwell, K., & Lloyd, D. (2013). *Coffee, poverty and economic development in Timor-Leste*. Monash University.

Khamis, S. (2015). Timor-Leste coffee: Marketing the 'golden prince' in post-crisis conditions. *Food, Culture & Society*, *18*(3), 481–500.

Laughton, K. (2007). Has fair trade lost its way? Practice anomalies in Timor-Leste's coffee industry. *The International Journal of Environmental, Cultural, Economic and Social Sustainability*, *3*(3), 123–134.

Li, T.M. (2007). *The will to improve: Governmentality, development, and the practice of politics*. Duke University Press.

Lundahl, M., & Sjoholm, F. (2012). Improving the lot of the farmer: Development challenges in Timor-Leste during the second decade of Independence. *IFN Working Paper*, *929*. Research Institute of Industrial Economics.

Mendez, E.A. (2013). *Performance evaluation of the USAID/Timor-Leste Consolidating Cooperative and Agribusiness Recovery Project*. USAID.

NCBA-CLUSA (2016). Starbucks sells single source coffee from East Timor's Cooperativa Café Timor. *Global Programs*. https://ncbaclusa.coop/blog/starbucks-sells-single-source-coffee-from-east-timors-cooperativa-cafe-timor/ (accessed 3 December 2020).

NCBA-CLUSA (2020). *Building an inclusive economy together: 2019 Annual report*. Washington DC: NCBA-CLUSA. https://ncbaclusa.coop/content/uploads/2020/05/2019-Annual-Report-for-web.pdf (accessed 2 December 2020).

Nevins, J. (2003). Restitution over coffee: Truth, reconciliation, and environmental violence in East Timor. *Political Geography*, *22*(6), 677–701.

Nixon, R. (2013). *Justice and governance in East Timor: Indigenous approaches and the 'new subsistence state'*. Routledge.

Oxfam (2003). *Overview of the coffee sector in Timor-Leste*. Oxfam New Zealand.

Roque, R. (2010). The unruly island: Colonialism's predicament in late Nineteenth Century East Timor. *Portuguese Literary and Cultural Studies, 17*(18), 303–330.

Shepherd, C.J., & McWilliam, A. (2013). Cultivating plantations and subjects in East Timor: A genealogy. *Journal of the Humanities and Social Sciences of Southeast Asia and Oceania/Bijdragen tot de Taal-, Land-en Volkenkunde, 169*, 326–361.

Weatherbee, D.E. (1966). Portuguese Timor: An Indonesian dilemma. *Asian Survey, 6*(12), 683–695.

14 Water and sustainability in South Africa's fruit value networks

Nora Lanari

INTRODUCTION

Despite increased concerns over environmental sustainability and climate change, academic inquiries informed by Global Value Chain and Global Production Network approaches have largely ignored the environmental dynamics underpinning globalised agriculture and trade. This chapter joins recent efforts to address this gap (Baglioni and Campling 2017; Irarrázaval and Bustos-Gallardo 2019; Krishnan 2017). It examines changes in water management on export-oriented fruit farms in South Africa's Western Cape and interrogates associated sustainability claims.

Water is a useful lens to study the link between globalised agricultural production and environmental sustainability as it is essential for crop production and the economy more broadly, fulfils a range of ecological functions, has considerable cultural value, and is a basic human need (Gupta and Pahl-Wostl 2013). Water management practices, therefore, are part of the wider processes of water governance that need to balance often competing priorities. The Western Cape and its export-oriented horticulture industry is an ideal case study for this research as water is scarce, crucial for economic development, and continues to be unequally distributed along racial lines due to the country's apartheid legacy (Figure 14.1).

THE WESTERN CAPE AND AGRICULTURE

The Western Cape is the southernmost Province of South Africa (see Figure 14.1) and agriculture is a key sector in the Province: in 2015 it contributed to almost one quarter of the national Agriculture, Forestry, and Fisheries sector, over 4% of the Gross Domestic Product (GDP), and 45% of national agricultural exports. It is dominated by horticultural production, mainly fruit for export, which makes up 52% of the annual agricultural production value of the Province (Midgley et al. 2016). As a result, much of South Africa's fruit industry is concentrated in the Western Cape. The Province has good meso-climatic conditions to grow fruit, especially apples and pears (Hortgro 2017). However, it lacks abundant water resources and struggles with effective water management and governance. This poses a challenge for fruit growers wanting to participate in global value networks.

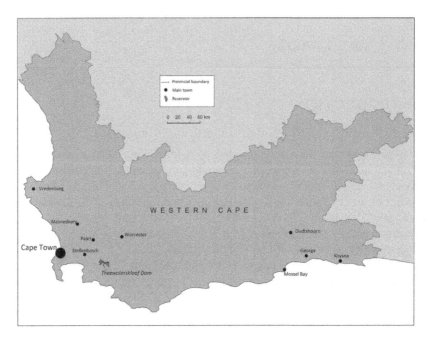

Figure 14.1   Western Cape, South Africa

Global agricultural value networks are governed by private and social stand-ards[1] and, for some time, water has been of concern within these, particularly in terms of its quality and how it can compromise food safety. More recently, retailers have become interested in water quantity and on-farm water resource management (Morgan 2017). This is because of a realisation how wider (catchment) processes impact individual growers and the value chain. In the study area, the recent 2015–2018 drought, for example, has led to fears over security of supply of fresh fruit to global markets. As a result, retailers are engaging in questions of water management more directly, including through private and social standards.

The research presented here is part of a larger project investigating the influence of global agricultural value networks on water management and water governance (see Lanari 2019). Fieldwork was conducted over the course of 2017 at the peak of a four-year drought in South Africa's Western Cape. It included semi-structured interviews with 76 stakeholders, including fruit farmers, industry agents, buyers for retailers, and representatives of different levels of government and from non-governmental organisations. This was complemented by an analysis of South African water and agricultural policy, as well as of private and social governance mechanisms required by Global North retailers, such as GlobalGAP or Fairtrade.

WATER IN ETHICAL VALUE NETWORKS

Consumers in the Global North are increasingly interested in the conditions under which commodities are produced and sourced. Often, these attributes (e.g. worker welfare, food provenance, environmental stewardship) are not observable at the point of purchase (Henson and Reardon 2005). Private and social standards have become a way to communicate these conditions to buyers (e.g. supermarkets) and consumers, both through audit processes and product labels. As such, private and social standards have become a new governance mechanism in global value chains and production networks besides public regulation implemented by governments (Tallontire 2007).

In agri-food value networks, standards have developed as a response to new regulatory controls over food safety, mostly in Europe and particularly in relation to Maximum Residue Levels (MRLs) of chemicals applied during the growing process (Henson and Humphrey 2010). In parallel, concerns about power asymmetries in global trade have put a spotlight on social issues, such as the welfare of farm workers and livelihoods for small-scale farmers, which have become the core of many standards promoting ethical trade (Barrientos 2000). Of late, environmental concerns beyond health and safety have also started to feature in public and private standards.

Water, until recently, only featured in private and social standards in terms of its quality and how that links to food safety. Water quality is a concern throughout the global fruit value network because irrigation water is one source of pre-harvest microbiological contamination of fresh produce (Ijabadeniyi and Buys 2012). If microbiological contamination occurs and is not detected before the produce reaches the end consumer, it can lead to an outbreak of foodborne illnesses, such as those caused by E. coli or Salmonella (van Pelt et al. 2018). Because of the global reach of fresh produce value networks, such as those governing fruit, outbreaks are rarely confined to the country of origin. For example, in June 2011, Germany and France reported two linked E. coli outbreaks that were traced back to contaminated fenugreek seeds imported from Egypt. The outbreak affected 14 EU countries plus the US and Canada (EFSA 2011, WHO 2011). Water quality is therefore closely linked to food safety assurances and carries not only a health risk but also a reputational risk (Sojamo 2016). For commercial fruit growers embedded in global value networks, complying with food safety and other standards is key to gaining and maintaining access to lucrative export markets.

More recently, realisation about the large water footprint of export crops has moved concerns about water quantity and water resource management to the top of global lead firms' sustainability agenda. The World Economic Forum's Global Risk Report has driven much of this private sector concern by listing the world's water crises within its top five global risks since 2012 (WEF 2012–2020). For global lead firms (e.g. European supermarkets), it has led to a realisation that (a) these large water footprints pose a reputational risk which needs to be managed (Sojamo 2016), and (b) wider (catchment) processes at the production scale can jeopardise agricultural operations, potentially affecting security of supply to global markets (Hepworth 2012).

As a result, lead firms – often the most powerful actors in global value networks – are taking this "water question" (Vos and Boelens 2014, p. 205) more seriously. Private and social standards, such as GlobalGAP and Fairtrade, have started to include requirements about water use and on-farm water management beyond quality (Morgan 2017). One social standard, the Alliance for Water Stewardship has even been developed with an exclusive focus on water (AWS 2014). Water-related requirements have thus largely been raised, developed, and pushed through by Global North stakeholders, such as private and social standards and supermarkets, while they most directly impact producers in the Global South (Vos and Boelens 2014).

Water management, however, is typically complex and of a localised nature. In practice, on-farm water use and management cannot be easily disassociated from wider catchment processes (Vos and Boelens 2014). To add complexity, water is essential for life and there is no substitute. Unlike other environmental sustainability concerns covered by private and social standards (e.g. carbon), water abstraction and pollution have localised effects that cannot be mitigated elsewhere (Perry 2014). Hence, water is a key issue, not only in terms of environmental sustainability but also in terms of social justice.

EXPORT FRUIT AND WATER IN SOUTH AFRICA'S WESTERN CAPE

South Africa offers interesting dynamics to study the interactions between environmental sustainability concerns and the phenomenon of Ethical Value Networks. The country transitioned from its apartheid regime to a multiracial democracy in the early 1990s. Apartheid – meaning "separateness" in Afrikaans (Ross 2008, p. 123) – was a system of overt institutionalised racial segregation that justified social, political, and economic discrimination against non-whites (Feinstein 2005). With democracy came also a new economic policy and South Africa's post-apartheid macro-economic plan included neoliberal market restructuring with a focus on trade liberalisation and export-orientation as a model of development (Marais 2011). For the horticulture industry, this resulted in a complete deregulation that removed single-channel marketing boards, which coincided with the expansion of powerful European supermarkets in the late 1990s. This has embedded South African growers into global networks of production and supply, sparking a considerable amount of research into the ethics and sustainability of value chain participation. Because of the country's history of apartheid, much of this work has investigated how the embedding of fruit growers into global value networks interacts with this social and economic legacy. A particular focus has been on farm labour and working conditions (e.g. Alford 2016; Du Toit 2005), economic and social upgrading (e.g. Barrientos and Visser 2012), and ethical trade (e.g. Hughes et al. 2013).

Environmental concerns have only featured on the fringes of these investigations, including regarding water. This is despite the fact that water use and management are important issues in the production of export crops in South Africa, not only in terms of environmental care but also in terms of social justice. In fact, during apartheid, access to water played a key role in the government's policies of separate development (Tempelhoff 2017). Under the pretence of enabling the development of the different South African groups according to their own traditions, black South Africans were confined to the homelands, which constituted a meagre 13% of the total land area. Most of that land was unforgiving with little access to water resources, curtailing any attempts to commercialise black agriculture. White South African farmers, in contrast, were given preferential access to vast stretches of fertile and well-watered land (Marais 2011; Ross 2008).[2] As a result, the apartheid government enforced a dualistic agrarian structure that endures today (Bernstein 2013; Hall 2004). The country's export-oriented horticulture industry developed out of these dynamics of colonialism, discrimination, and segregation in the early 20th century (Feinstein 2005; van Koppen et al. 2009). Today, the industry is characterised by large-scale, capital- and labour-intensive farms that remain predominantly owned by white South Africans.

Thanks to its southern hemisphere location, the South African fruit industry operates in counter-seasonality to European fruit growers, making it an ideal supplier of fresh fruit to European supermarkets during northern hemisphere winters. Much of this export-oriented fruit industry is located in the Western Cape. And while the Province offers ideal meso-climatic conditions to grow fruit, it is also characterised by a Mediterranean climate. Consequently, the Western Cape experiences an inverse relation between winter rainfall patterns and summer production demands (Midgley et al. 2016). This adds complexity to on-farm water management and means that fruit production in the Western

Cape relies on the mobilisation and storage of water resources to ensure the regular availability of enough clean water to supply global markets. This was made apparent during the 2015–2018 Cape Drought. During the drought, the City of Cape Town almost ran out of water (popularly referred to as "Day Zero", see e.g. Onishi and Sengupta 2018). This also greatly impacted the surrounding fruit production regions, whose water allocations were heavily restricted (Meintjes 2017). Many dams that fill up in winter to provide water for fruit production during the dry summer months came dangerously close to being completely emptied, including Theewaterskloof Dam (see Figure 14.2), one of the Province's largest and most important dams.

Source: Nora Lanari

Figure 14.2   *Theewaterskloof Dam, Western Cape, close to empty in October 2017*

Water-related Requirements for Fruit Growers in Private and Social Standards

The minimum requirement for South African fruit growers to take part in global export markets is GlobalGAP; a private standard that covers a range of aspects, from health and safety, over worker welfare to environmental management aspects (GlobalGAP 2019). It is often the basis of retailer specific standards. For example, since 2017, growers can obtain the Tesco NURTURE certification as an add-on module to the GlobalGAP IFA Version five audit process (GlobalGAP 2017). In addition, many growers comply with social standards, such as Fairtrade. Fairtrade is the foremost standard to certify ethical trading practices and mainly concerns itself with securing a fair wage/ fair trading prices for commodities (McEwan et al. 2017). Both GlobalGAP and Fairtrade now include aspects relating to water resource management and Table 14.1 includes further details regarding their water-related requirements (not including those pertaining to water quality). A 'Major Must'/'Core' requirement must be complied with to obtain the certification, while a 'Minor Must'/'Development' requirement may be worked towards over time (Fair Trade International 2014; GlobalGAP 2018).

As Table 14.1 shows, both standards have a range of requirements regarding on farm water use and management. Most of these requirements focus on record keeping, efficiency, and optimisation of irrigation water use (from now on referred to as REO-requirements) and easily integrate into the existing approaches of audit-based compliance models. In that vein, GlobalGAP states that farmers need to "ensure efficient use and application" (see CB. 5.2.2 in Table 14.1) of water, while Fairtrade wants farmers to "make efficient and rational use of water sources" (see 4.3.10 in Table 14.1). To do so, Fairtrade requires the "use of the best... technology for irrigation... to optimize quantities of water applied" (see 4.3.12 in in Table 14.1). GlobalGAP expects farmers to "keep records of the usage of crop irrigation/fertigation water..." (see CB. 5.2.3 in Table 14.1) and to calculate "crop irrigation requirements... based on data. Data... must be maintained" (see CB. 5.1.1 in Table 14.1). The focus on REO-requirements has had one specific effect on fruit growers in the Western Cape: most, if not all of them, have moved to high-tech irrigation systems.

High-tech irrigation systems are usually composed of water conveyance and application technology as well as a monitoring system (Evans and Sadler 2008). In the study area, growers either use short-range micro-jets or drip irrigation systems on their farms to distribute and apply water (see Figure 14.3). In addition, neutron probes and/or continuous water loggers measure soil moisture content. This information feeds into a computerised system that not only informs irrigation scheduling and administers irrigation water but also records this data. Computerised systems have become an important support tool for scientific irrigation scheduling and considerably reduce human error, i.e. by opening and closing valves automatically or sending out alerts when pipes block or burst. Overall, this creates very high-tech irrigation systems on individual farms that facilitate compliance with REO-requirements of private and social standards as they can easily be assessed and 'ticked-off' during audits.

Both within GlobalGAP and within Fairtrade there is one obligation that moves beyond the three REO-requirements. The second half of control point CB. 5.2.1 in GlobalGAP and control point 4.3.11 in Fairtrade focus on

Table 14.1   Examples of water-related requirements in private and social standards

Standard	Control point	Requirements regarding water management (not including water quality)	Level
GlobalGAP Version: 5.1 Source: GlobalGAP (2018)	CB. 5.1	*Predicting Irrigation Requirements*	Minor Must
	CB. 5.1.1	[...] crop irrigation requirements are calculated based on data (e.g. local agricultural institute data, farm rain gauges, drainage trays for substrate growing, evaporation meters, water tension meters for the percentage of soil moisture content). [...] Data to demonstrate how irrigation needs were determined must be maintained.	
	CB. 5.2	*Efficient Water Use on Farm*	Major Must
	CB. 5.2.1	[...] risk assessment that identifies environmental impacts of the water sources, distribution system and irrigation and crop washing usages. In addition, the risk assessment shall take into consideration the impact of own farming activities on off-farm environments, where information is [...] available. [...]	
	CB. 5.2.2	[...] written and implemented action plan, approved by the management within the previous 12 months, which identifies water sources and measures to ensure efficient use and application.	Major Must
	CB. 5.2.3	[...] keep records of the usage of crop irrigation/fertigation water that include the date, cycle duration, actual or estimated flow rate, and the volume (per water meter or per irrigation unit) updated on a monthly basis, based on the water management plan and an annual total.	Minor Must
Fairtrade Standard for Hired Labour	4.3.9	*Sources of irrigation water* [...] knows where water used in irrigation and processing of Fairtrade crops comes from. An inventory of sources is available.	Core

Standard	Control point	Requirements regarding water management (not including water quality)	Level
	4.3.10	*Optimizing water use* [...] implements procedures to make efficient and rational use of water sources. These procedures include prediction of volumes of water needed to irrigate the crop, measuring (or estimating) volumes of water extracted from sources and volumes actually used in irrigation and processing, providing maintenance to the water distribution system and adopting, as applicable, methods to recirculate, reuse and/or recycle water.	Core
	4.3.11	*Sustainable use of water* [...] keeps informed about the status of the water sources in the area. In case local environmental authorities or other entities consider that water sources are being depleted, are in a critical condition or under excessive usage, your company engages in a dialogue with the authorities or local initiatives in order to identify possible ways to be involved in in research or solution finding.	Development
	4.3.12	*Optimizing irrigation systems* [...] makes use of the best accessible (or locally available) technology for irrigation and processing in order to optimize quantities of water applied.	Core

Source:
Fair Trade
International
2014

water-related processes beyond the individual farm-gate. GlobalGAP frames
this in terms of risk: "the risk assessment shall take into consideration the
impact of own farming activities on off-farm environments" (see CB. 5.2.1
in Table 14.1), emphasising how growers face water-related risks when
inadequate water security because of wider (catchment) processes jeopardise
their operations; but simultaneously, growers generate water risk when their
operations threaten water and water sources within the production region
(Hepworth 2012). While this is part of a 'Major Must' in GlobalGAP, it is
qualified with a caveat of "where information is … available" (CB. 5.2.1).
Fairtrade explicitly focuses on *sustainable* water use within control point
4.3.11. Where water sources are being depleted or in a critical condition, it
wants growers to engage "in a dialogue with the authorities or local initiatives
… to identify possible ways to be involved in research or solution finding"
(see 4.3.11 in Table 14.1). In addition to highlighting the two-way water risks,
Fairtrade emphasises the need for growers to be part of the solution. This is a
'Development' requirement that growers have to work towards over the course
of their Fairtrade membership. Overall, these requirements present a promising
move away from tick-box exercises of audit-based compliance models towards
approaches based on continuous improvement.

Source: Nora Lanari

Figure 14.3   Microjets on an apple orchard in Western Cape

DISCUSSION AND CONCLUSION

Water-related requirements in private and social sustainability standards overwhelmingly focus on the three REO-requirements: record keeping, efficiency, and optimisation of irrigation practices. These three requirements easily fit into existing audit-based compliance models and can often only be achieved by adopting high-tech irrigation systems. Boelens and Vos (2012) argue that, in this vein, private and social standards can be understood as 'techniques of visibilisation' that highlight certain aspects of production and obscure others, forming "an effective technique to control discussions on what is regarded as 'sustainable agriculture' and how to assess it" (Vos and Boelens 2014, p. 214), i.e. by keeping records, improving efficiency, and optimising irrigation water use through high-tech irrigation systems. This feeds into a common critique of private and social standards: they are often defined in technocratic terms that normalise scientific knowledge (Friedmann and McNair 2009). This can result in uniform values and definitions regarding water, which disregard how irrigation water use is embedded in institutional, cultural, and political economic contexts (Vos and Boelens 2014).

In the study area, the focus on REO-requirements coupled with the move to high-tech irrigation systems has had several tangible effects. First, high-tech irrigation systems are expensive. Only the more prosperous farmers can afford them. This puts up additional barriers for smallholders to produce for global supermarkets, while large-scale farmers further consolidate their market share (Fuchs et al. 2009; van der Meer 2006). Second, because private and social standards redefine what is regarded as sustainable agriculture – in this case in terms of irrigation water use – farmers using less sophisticated irrigation systems are often seen as less sustainable (Vos and Boelens 2014). In the study area, this feeds into what Movik (2009, p. 11) terms a "poverty -environment-degradation" narrative, which implies that emerging uses (i.e. black livelihoods) are not only non-productive but also causing environmental degradation, further increasing barriers to market participation for mostly smallholders. It results in the third effect, where large-scale export-oriented growers and their highly efficient water use are considered to be environmentally sound, which in turn allows them to project a positive image to the wider community about their water use (Lanari 2019). All three dynamics are problematic, but the last one is particularly salient for this chapter.

By positively highlighting farmers' compliance with REO-requirements, other aspects of water use in commercial horticultural production are obscured. In particular, it obfuscates concerns about inequities within the current system of water allocation. In the Western Cape, access to water resources for productive activities remains highly unequal. White landowners have predominantly been able to retain privileged access to water resources, despite the political re-orientation post-apartheid, while the black and coloured communities predominantly remain without access to land and water (Movik 2009, 2014). All of this is arguably a key component of sustainable agricultural production but is lost in translation when framing sustainability in terms of REO-requirements. This is because the understanding of sustainable water use as delimited by REO-requirements rests on the argument that there is little wastage of water with high-tech irrigation and that water is used productively, i.e. for high-value export crops. This technocratic articulation, however, side-lines the more fundamental question of water allocation, effectively removing commercial farmers from the hydro-political line of fire that is South Africa's water reform process (Peters and Woodhouse 2019). Thus, in a way, private and social standards have validated water resource use by export-oriented fruit growers and given it a sustainability stamp of approval without taking into account institutional, cultural, and political economic contexts. Ultimately, this contributes to reifying the dualistic agrarian structure predominant in South Africa.

Moreover, the sustainability claims associated with REO-requirements do not necessarily hold true. Unlike what is often presumed, increased irrigation efficiency and optimisation of water use at the farm level does not necessarily translate into increased water availability within the wider catchment. This is called the "paradox of irrigation efficiency" (Grafton et al. 2018) and refers to the fact that (a) less efficient irrigation systems often have ecological benefits as water can be recovered or reused downstream, thus becoming available to other water users (Ward and Pulido-Velazquez 2008); and (b) water savings at the farm level are usually reinvested into the production site, e.g. by irrigating additional hectares. This reduces runoff or subsurface recharge, which can then not be re-used elsewhere in the catchment, and therefore, highly efficient irrigation may actually increase water consumption (Perry and Steduto 2017). Thus, unlike what is often presumed, by increasing their irrigation efficiency, growers do not free-up water for other uses, but only for themselves. Private and social standards requiring efficiency and optimisation gains therefore do not reduce the overall water footprint of their growers.

The focus on REO-requirements and the move to high-tech irrigation systems can, in fact, make water scarcity both worse and more difficult to manage at the catchment scale (Perry and Steduto 2017). In the Western Cape, where dry spells and fully-fledged droughts are common and a large proportion of the population does not have access to running water, this is highly problematic and raises ethical questions. A focus on high-tech irrigation is, therefore, insufficient to address concerns regarding the sustainability of water resources, both locally and globally. Consequently, there is a serious need to re-examine the widely-held belief presented in private and social standards "that increased irrigation efficiency will relieve the world's water crisis" (Ward and Pulido-Velazquez 2008, p. 18219). Concerns regarding the sustainability of water resources are embedded in local institutional, social, and political economic contexts that need to be observed on the ground and addressed through sound water governance.

Private and social standards can support appropriate governance by moving away from REO-requirements and instead emphasise water-related requirements that connect growers and their irrigation water use to their catchments and their institutional, social, and political economic context (Vos and Boelens 2014). Moves towards continuous improvement, where private and social standards require growers to evaluate their water use within the catchment and collaborate with other water stakeholders are encouraging steps towards such a broader understanding. This approach not only evaluates how on-farm water use affects the catchment in hydrological terms, but also includes a social dimension. In South Africa, this is crucial considering ongoing inequities in terms of access to water resources as well as in terms of access to the benefits of water resource use (i.e. the ability to produce crops with the help of irrigation). We can find encouraging examples of such approaches in South Africa, often led by local stakeholders. They include Woolworths' Farming for the Future programme (King and Thobela 2014; Woolworths 2019) and SIZA's EnviroStandard (SIZA 2020), both of which seek to move away from compliance-based models to a continuous improvement approach that fits the local context.

NOTES

1. Private governance mechanisms describe product, labour, and environmental standards developed by lead firms and private organisations, such as GLOBAL G.A.P or Tesco NURTURE. Social governance mechanisms describe labour and environmental standards developed by civil society organisations, including non-governmental organisations (NGOs), charities, or trade unions, for example Fairtrade. This is in contrast to public standards, developed by governments, and more commonly referred to as regulation (Barrientos 2019).
2. This chapter makes reference to the black, coloured, and white people of South Africa to explain how the different racial groups' social construction throughout history influences present day dynamics (Feinstein 2005). Although these terms originate from apartheid-era race classification, for many South Africans, they are expressions of identity, including the otherwise-contested term coloured (McEwan et al. 2017).

REFERENCES

Alford, M. (2016). Trans-scalar embeddedness and governance deficits in global production networks: Crisis in South African fruit. *Geoforum*, *75*, 52–63.

AWS (2014). The AWS International Water Stewardship Standard v 1.0. Alliance for Water Stewardship, North Berwick, Scotland. Accessed 24 July 2020. http://assets .worldwildlife.org/publications/746/files/original/AWS-Standard-v-1-Abbreviated -print_(1).pdf?1418140260&_ga=1.52961640.1326916128.1480931991.

Baglioni, E., & Campling, L. (2017). Natural resource industries as global value chains: Frontiers, fetishism, labour and the state. *Environment and Planning A*, *49*(11), 2437–2456.

Barrientos, S. (2019). *Gender and work in global value chains.* Cambridge University Press.

Barrientos, S. (2000). Globalization and ethical trade: Assessing the implications for development. *Journal of International Development*, *12*(4), 559–570.

Barrientos, S., & Visser, M. (2012). *South African horticulture: Opportunities and challenges for economic and social upgrading in value.* Capturing the Gains Working Paper 12. University of Manchester.

Bernstein, H. (2013). Commercial agriculture in South Africa since 1994: 'Natural, simply capitalism'. *Journal of Agrarian Change*, *13*(1), 23–46.

Boelens, R., & Vos, J. (2012). The danger of naturalizing water policy concepts: Water productivity and efficiency discourses from field irrigation to virtual water trade. *Agricultural Water Management*, *108*, 16–26.

Du Toit, A. (2005). *Forgotten by the highway: Globalisation, adverse incorporation and chronic poverty in a commercial farming district.* CSSR Working Paper 101. Centre for Social Science Research, University of Cape Town.

EFSA (2011). Shiga toxin-producing *E. Coli* (STEC) O104:H4 2011 outbreaks in Europe: Taking stock. *EFSA Journal*, *9*(10), 1–22.

Evans, R.G., & Sadler, E.J. (2008). Methods and technologies to improve efficiency of water use. *Water Resources Research*, *44*(7), 3459–3465.

Fair Trade International (2014). *Fairtrade standard for hired labour.* Fair Trade International.

Feinstein, C.H. (2005). *An economic history of South Africa: conquest, discrimination and development.* Cambridge University Press.

Friedmann, H., & McNair, A. (2009). Whose rules rule? Contested projects to certify 'local production for distant consumers'. *Transnational Agrarian Movements Confronting Globalization*, *8*, 239–265.

Fuchs, D., Kalfagianni, A., & Arentsen, M. (2009). Retail power, private standards, and sustainability in the global food system. In J. Clapp & D. Fuchs (Eds.), *Corporate power in global agrifood governance* (pp. 29–60). MIT Press.

GlobalGAP (2017). *Tesco NURTURE module.* GlobalGAP. Accessed 24 July 2020. https://www.globalgap.org/uk_en/for-producers/globalg.a.p.-add-on/nurture -module/.

GlobalGAP (2018). *GlobalGAP - National interpretation guideline South Africa: Integrated farm assurance V5.1.* GlobalGAP.

GlobalGAP (2019). *GlobalGAP general regulations: Part I - General requirements V5.2.* GlobalGAP.

Grafton, R.Q., Williams, J., Perry, C., Molle, F., Ringler, C., Steduto, P., Udall, B., Wheeler, S.A., Wang, Y., Garrick, D., & Allen, R.G. (2018). The paradox of irrigation efficiency. *Science*, *361*(6404), 748–750.

Gupta, J., & Pahl-Wostl, C. (2013). Global water governance in the context of global and multilevel governance: Its needs. *Forms, and Challenges, Ecology and Society*, *18*(4), 53.

Hall, R. (2004). A political economy of land reform in South Africa. *Review of African Political Economy*, *31*(100), 213–227.

Henson, S., & Humphrey, J. (2010). Understanding the complexities of private standards in global agri-food chains as they impact developing countries. *Journal of Development Studies*, *46*(9), 1628–1646.

Henson, S., & Reardon, T. (2005). Private agri-food standards: Implications for food policy and the agri-food system. *Food Policy*, *30*(3), 241–253.

Hepworth, N. (2012). Open for business or opening Pandora's box? A constructive critique of corporate engagement in water policy: An introduction. *Water Alternatives*, *5*(3), 543–562.

Hortgro (2017). *20 Years of fruit freedom – A review*. Hortgro. Accessed 24 July 2020. https://hortgro.co.za/wp-content/uploads/2017/11/hortgro-booklet_digital.pdf.

Hughes, A., McEwan, C., & Bek, D. (2013). Retailers, supply networks and changing articulations of ethicality: Lessons from Flower Valley in South Africa. *Journal of Economic Geography*, *13*(2), 211–230.

Ijabadeniyi, O.A., & Buys, E.M. (2012). Irrigation water and microbiological safety of fresh produce; South Africa as a case study: A review. *African Journal of Agricultural Research*, *7*(35), 4848–4857.

Irarrázaval, F., & Bustos-Gallardo, B. (2019). Global salmon networks: Unpacking ecological contradictions at the production stage. *Economic Geography*, *95*(2), 159–178.

King, L., & Thobela, S. (2014). Woolworths farming for the future. *International Food and Agribusiness Management Review*, *17*(B), 161–166.

Krishnan, A. (2017). *Re-thinking the environmental dimensions of upgrading and embeddedness in production networks: The case of Kenyan horticulture farmers*. PhD thesis, University of Manchester.

Lanari, N. (2019). *The influence of global production networks on processes of water governance*. PhD Thesis, Coventry University.

Marais, H. (2011). *South Africa pushed to the limit: The political economy of change*. Zed Books.

McEwan, C., Hughes, A., & Bek, D. (2017). Fairtrade, place and moral economy: Between abstract ethical discourse and the moral experience of Northern Cape Farmers. *Environment and Planning A*, *49*(3), 572–591.

Meintjes, F. (2017). Cape growers face difficult times. *Eurofruit* blog, 9 August 2017. Accessed 18 August 2020. http://www.fruitnet.com/eurofruit/article/173042/cape-growers-face-difficult-times.

Midgley, S., New, M., & Methner, N. (2016). *A status quo review of climate change and the agriculture sector of the Western Cape Province – Final*. Western Cape Government.

Morgan, A. (2017). *Water risk in agricultural supply chains: How well are sustainability standards covering water stewardship – A progress report*. WWF-Germany.

Movik, S. (2009). *The dynamics and discourses of water allocation reform in South Africa*. STEPS Working Paper 21. Steps Centre.

Movik, S. (2014). A fair share? Perceptions of justice in South Africa's water allocation reform policy. *Geoforum*, *54*, 187–195.

Onishi, N., & Sengupta, S. (2018). Dangerously low on water, Cape Town now faces 'Day Zero'. *The New York Times*, 30 January 2018.

Perry, C. (2014). Water footprints: Path to enlightenment, or false trail? *Agricultural Water Management*, *134*, 119–125.

Perry, C., & Steduto, P. (2017). *Does improved irrigation technology save water? A review of the evidence.* FAO.

Peters, R., & Woodhouse, P. (2019). Reform and regression: Discourses of water reallocation in Mpumalanga, South Africa. *Water Alternatives, 12*(3), 1–16.

Ross, R. (2008). *A concise history of South Africa* (2nd ed.). Cambridge University Press.

SIZA (2020). *SIZA environmental standard. V 1.2.* Sustainability Initiative South Africa.

Sojamo, S. (2016). *Water-using corporations as agents of water security, management and governance: Exploring cases from stewardship initiatives in South Africa to global networks of power.* Aalto University.

Tallontire, A. (2007). CSR and regulation: Towards a framework for understanding private standards initiatives in the agri-food chain. *Third World Quarterly, 28*(4), 775–791.

Tempelhoff, J. (2017). The Water Act, No. 54 of 1956 and the first phase of apartheid in South Africa (1948–1960). *Water History, 9*(54), 189–213.

van der Meer, K. (2006). Exclusion of small-scale farmers form coordinated supply chains: Market failure, policy failure or just economies of scale? In R. Ruben, M. Slingerland, & H. Nijhoff (Eds.), *Agro-food chains and networks for development* (pp. 209–218). Springer.

van Koppen, B., Sally, H., Aliber, M., Cousins, B., & Tapela, B. (2009). *Water resources management, rural redress and agrarian reform.* Development Planning Division Working Paper Series 7. Development Bank of Southern Africa.

van Pelt, A.E., Quiñones, B., Lofgren, H.L., Bartz, F.E., Newman, K.L., & Leon, J.S. (2018). Low prevalence of human pathogens on fresh produce on farms and in packing facilities: A systematic review. *Frontiers in Public Health, 6*, 1–10.

Vos, J., & Boelens, R. (2014). Sustainability standards and the water question. *Development and Change, 45*(2), 205–230.

Ward, F.A., & Pulido-Velazquez, M. (2008). Water conservation in irrigation can increase water use. *Proceedings of the National Academy of Sciences, 105*(47), 18215–18220.

WEF (2012). *Global risks 2012: 7th edition.* World Economic Forum.

WEF (2013). *Global risks 2013: 8th edition.* World Economic Forum.

WEF (2014). *Global risks 2014: 9th edition.* World Economic Forum.

WEF (2015). *Global risks 2015: 10th edition.* World Economic Forum.

WEF (2016). *The global risks report 2016: 11th edition.* World Economic Forum.

WEF (2017). *The global risks report 2017: 12th edition.* World Economic Forum.

WEF (2018). *The global risks report 2018: 13th edition.* World Economic Forum.

WEF (2019). *The global risks report 2019: 14th edition.* World Economic Forum.

WEF (2020). *The global risks report 2020: 15th edition.* World Economic Forum.

WHO (2011). *EHEC outbreak: Update 13,* 10 June 2016. Accessed 24 July 2020. https://www.euro.who.int/en/countries/germany/news/news/2011/06/ehec-outbreak-update-13.

Woolworths (2019). *Farming for the future.* Woolworths. Accessed 24 July 2020. https://www.woolworths.co.za/content/article/farming-for-the-future/_/A-cmp100417.

PART III

Reflections

15 Value from virtue: the construction of provenance in ethical value networks

John Overton, Simon Bidwell and Warwick E. Murray

INTRODUCTION

The term 'virtue signalling' has come into vernacular use in recent years. It has been defined thus: "to take a conspicuous but essentially useless action ostensibly to support a good cause but actually to show off how much more moral you are than everybody else" (Urban Dictionary n.d.). We see some utility in adapting this concept to reflect on ideas in this volume, not with its more pejorative connotations of 'useless' and implications of conceit, but rather in its suggestions that virtue is something that can be displayed conspicuously to attract public approval and that virtue can be constructed and performed.

We suggest that the case studies in this book reveal various processes of 'virtue making': the construction of discourses of provenance that embed various ethical principles in supposedly virtuous food products in order to add value to them. 'Virtue' encompasses notions of high moral standards and behaviour which reflects these. Virtue ethics emphasises the moral character of people and their actions, rather than adherence to rules, or the consequences of actions.[1] In the context of agri-food networks, we contend, (apparent) virtue has economic value, manifested in the premium consumers will pay for virtuous products that align with the underlying moral principles they subscribe to. Making and displaying virtue, then, can be seen as a deliberate and strategic economic process to add value to products.

This chapter presents a theoretical reflection on the process of virtue making. It starts with our earlier notion of 'fictive place' as it applies to GIs but extends this line of thinking to the other two ethical constellations of sustainability and social justice. Here we move from notions of active 'place making' as an economic process, to explore the concept of provenance. We see provenance as more than just a record of the history of a product: it is also a process of building, disseminating and protecting such histories. Finally, we argue that such 'provenancing' is a key element of EVeNs, both needing the networks to construct and embed the narratives of authenticity, sustainability and social justice and reinforcing the networks in the process.

FROM FICTIVE PLACE TO FICTIVE VIRTUE

In earlier work on the global wine market, we developed the concept of 'fictive place' (Overton and Murray, 2016). This was seen in the way the wine industry actively engaged in place-making strategies in order to create and extract new forms of value and profit from wine. This was made possible by the association of place with wine quality, the way *terroir* imbued grapes with distinctive flavours and maintained traditions of particular vinicultural and viticultural practices. This relatively widespread acceptance that different places make wines with distinctive, even unique, characteristics has created potential values in place, particularly if claims of quality (and therefore claims to a price premium) can be associated with place. However, 'place' is not some absolute objective entity: it has to be defined and delimited then regulated and protected. 'Fictive place' concerns the way places are imagined, created and given value as a conscious process of commodifying nature and culture. In this process we see active story making and storytelling about place. Some places are seen to have certain soil characteristics or micro-climates that make special wines, or age-old traditions that are embedded in those places and the wines they make. These usually have some real and qualitative basis – soil types, heat balances and so on – but they are given additional layers of meaning in the way they build stories and claims about quality.

Fictive places, then, can be seen, mapped and experienced but critically they are imagined in ways which give them economic value, manifested in the enhanced price of bottles of wine. Interestingly, the narratives that are used to build stories of place often have ethical as well as environmental elements. So whilst much might be made of soils, geology or sunshine hours, we also see cultural dimensions, such as histories and traditions or tales of craft production and small family-run vineyards. These cultural elements then become the basis for arguing that such traditions and social forms should be preserved and protected. In the parlance of trade negotiations, these became forms of 'intellectual property': places in a sense were the repositories for cultural knowledge, for long-established reputational value and for distinctive cultural forms. Recognising certain places can thus be seen as a form of social justice and even sustainability: people's knowledges and traditions are confirmed, maintained and protected 'in place'.

Provenance underpins these processes. If places are to be given value, consumers not only need assurance that the desired products do indeed come from that place but also a 'spatial history' of the product (Morgan et al., 2006) – the stories and imaginaries of where the product comes from, its environment, and other geographical features that have shaped its identity. In addition, provenance involves 'social histories', particularly if culturally-based claims to quality are being made. Consumers can learn about who makes the wine and how. This may involve stories of generations-old winemaking methods being used in rural Italy or alternatively new and innovative winemaking communities in California or Chile. Provenance is what constructs and affirms the value of places in the global wine market.

What then becomes vital is how places and provenance are regulated. In order to protect producers in such places from others who would seek to appropriate such surplus, for example by calling their sparkling white wine 'Champagne' when produced in Australia, the USA or South Africa, places have to be delimited with boundaries, they have to be codified so that they have recognition by states, and they have to be 'copyrighted' so that others cannot use the same place name to sell their own products. Regulation of place involves giving consumers assurances that provenance is guaranteed – that the product comes from where it says it comes from.[2] It also has the function of protecting places and giving clarity – by gazetting place names, states and institutions recognise that these names cannot be used freely elsewhere in ways that mis-appropriate the value of place. Furthermore, such regulation has been globalised. As we have seen, global trade negotiations have incorporated (albeit reluctantly by some countries) the idea that places, in the form of Geographical Indications (GIs), are forms of intellectual property which are recognised, codified and protected worldwide.

The global spread of the GI mechanisms and laws has allowed the spread of fictive places. Although the *terroir* basis of wine place-making lies firmly in Europe, and France in particular with its AOC system, it is now seen in many parts of the world. Nearly all major wine-producing countries have instituted GI systems for wine, as we have seen in Chile and Argentina for example. They continue to spread through new trade agreements: as part of trade deals with the European Union, partners must recognise European place brands and are thus encouraged to institute and provide schedules of their own GIs. There has also been a proliferation of GIs beyond wine. *Terroir* narratives that work for wine, for example in the way certain soils and trace elements give grapes particular flavour profiles, can be applicable to cheese, apples, tequila, potatoes, rhubarb and a plethora of other agro-commodities as well as other products such as Turkish carpets or Indian textiles (Pochampally Ikat) which draw on production traditions associated with certain places (Bowen, 2010; Dogana and Gokovali, 2012; Jena and Groote, 2012).

Whilst place – and fictive place – have become established in global value chains, the studies in this volume suggest that the underlying themes can be extended to other ethical constellations. In particular, we see deliberate strategies of value-making in agriculturally based production that build particular narratives and regulatory frameworks to construct ethical value. These strategies are also 'fictive' in that they are based on real people, processes and materials but these are woven together and augmented in value through narratives that make claims about the virtuous nature of the resulting products. Such strategies can span fair trade – the promotion of products created through 'fair' and 'just' methods, conditions and remuneration – and various types of organic and sustainable production networks that deliver products which are 'healthy' for people and the environment.

Thus, these narratives work to construct 'fictive virtue' (not just 'fictive place'). Fictive virtue refers to the way narratives and assurances of ethical practices are mobilised to create added value. It goes beyond factoring in the added costs of production that fair or sustainable methods may involve, to create additional and differentiated demand. Virtue is, in effect, created and commodified as a new factor in production. This can be seen as a strategy to build competitive alternatives to race-to-the-bottom Fordist production. Rather than competing on the basis of undifferentiated mass-produced, low-cost products, it involves establishing niches where consumers will prefer, and pay more for, virtuous products. As with fictive place, we need to focus on the way stories and histories are made, contested and institutionalised to build and protect claims of virtue.

PROVENANCE AND 'PROVENANCING'

Just as we saw how stories of provenance were central to the creation of fictive places, so too do we suggest that provenance is a key element of these virtue-making approaches. In this sense, it is imperative that consumers receive information not only about where the products come from but also detailed – and reliable – information about how they were produced. Again, these involve spatial histories because place of origin ties the virtue narratives to specific locations and chains of distribution. However it is the social histories that take on more significance: these offer stories about producers' identities, production practices and lives, the methods of processing, packaging and transport, and the absence of harmful chemicals or additives. They act to personalise as well as place the product, associating it with particular people, cultures and personalities. They may also attach the products to non-human agents: microbes in the soil, bird and insect life, hedgerows and trees, humanely treated farm animals and so on. So, provenance gives indications of virtue – as seen for example in accounts of African-owned and run wineries with good working conditions and fair wages for workers in South Africa, or in the way the use of biodynamic preparations has enhanced the vitality of soils in Argentina.

Provenance makes value from putative virtues. In this sense provenance seems to be concrete, observable and verifiable. Provenance can be guaranteed through the use of codes of practice, it can be regulated and audited by state and non-state institutions, and it can be certified as meeting explicit virtue criteria, whether involving fair trade, social investment, organic production or food miles. Consumers seek such assurances of the integrity of the product and provenance provides evidence of virtue.

However, as we have learned in the chapters above, provenance in practice is not fixed and immutable despite the use of codes, certification and audits. Provenance is not just 'there'; provenance 'becomes'. Provenance is conceived, built, changed and contested. It is an active process of building and embedding the histories/stories, not only by highlighting aspects of production and trade but also by obscuring or glossing over others. Thus, we can suggest that provenance can almost be used as a verb ('to provenance' or 'provenancing'), not so much as the act of certifying provenance but instead the act of creating, refining and disseminating the 'social and spatial histories of a product'.

In widening the view of provenancing to encompass the creation of value through 'virtue-making', we can see the origin of a product and its transfer from place of production to the consumer, as involving several, sometimes overlapping, ethical discourses. They may span claims to health (both environmental and human from organic and/or sustainable methods of production); quality ('better' products get qualities from certain *terroir* and craft-like practices); sociocultural conservation (the protection of traditions and rural societies); and social justice (fair rewards and greater agency for marginalised producers and workers). They construct notions of virtuous goods that bring social and environmental benefits. In doing this, provenancing positions virtuous goods in the market in ways which seek to either displace mainstream (harmful) others or charge a premium over them.

Provenancing in practice may result in the adoption of a fixed and visible account of where a product came from, how it was produced and by whom, but in its conception and development it is far from rigid. Stories of origin involve imagination, creativity and skill. Stories are made. They knit together 'facts' (things which can be seen and verified) into narrative frameworks which present them as tales of virtue and quality. In doing so, they link 'evidence' from the places of production to ethical priorities in the places of consumption. Effective provenancing communicates clear stories and histories to those who seek information to guide their ethical buying choices. Yet in the process of construction, and in their continued existence, they will encounter debates and opposition. Those potentially disadvantaged by a particular ethical narrative – whether fair trade, appellation of origin or organic agriculture – often seek to oppose or confuse the provenancing narrative. In the field of GIs, there are examples of how some wine companies have gone to court to challenge and alter boundaries around gazetted wine regions (Banks and Sharpe, 2006) and in France regional appellation schemes have been subject to continual challenge and change (Barker, 2004). In other instances, we have seen how fair trade or organic labelling, for example, has been responded to by the generation of alternative schemes that imply similar virtues ('direct trade', 'sustainable production') but which may have weaker standards in practice.

As well as challenges, provenancing can involve considerable embellishment and even myth making. *Terroir* stories in the wine world are very well known – and sometimes parodied – in the ways they suggest how seemingly innocuous environmental features (such as underlying geology) make for unique and highly desired wines. Some critics are highly dismissive of the very notion of *terroir*: "In essence, *terroir* is bullshit. As such it is easily the most effective manure for vines, the most easily absorbed, the cheapest to create" (Gluck, 2009, p. 40).

Flexible and imaginative story-making and telling is important for provenance. Stories are added to and changed to test, spread and augment the narrative, and stories may be challenged and dismissed along the way. Stories and narratives of people, places and environments in time become discourses of virtue. Such discourses may continue to be contested and altered but they tend to become more fixed as they evolve. Discourses of virtue become established market niches. This is because the needs of the market require the fixing of narratives in place, through gazetting, mapping regulation and audit, and this acts to fix and ossify both the claims of provenance and the systems of regulation. We then see a move from the development of provenance – provenancing – to the protection of surplus by copyrighting and promoting the stories and reaping the royalties. Throughout, we have seen how ethical value networks have started often as flexible, creative, progressive and innovative efforts – many of which do not progress – to more rigid and orthodox discourses that are essentially conservative to protect the gains made. To understand how this happens, we need to turn to examine the relationship between provenancing and the various ethical value networks in which it operates.

PROVENANCE AND EVENS

We have argued above that provenance is not fixed and immutable – even though it tends to become more so over time if it becomes established. Provenance is made, explained, illustrated and reinforced. Provenancing must therefore work through ethical value networks to link conscious consumers (willing to pay an ethical premium) with supposedly ethical producers. On the other hand, the various ethical networks we have examined, in turn, require robust and continuing assurances of provenance to survive and spread.

Ethical value networks play a key role in conveying information as well as products. Value networks are usually defined in terms of the way they produce, assemble, process and transfer commodities from the points of production to the points of consumption. They involve complex webs of institutions that move goods along this chain and, in doing so, add and extract value, and regulate how products are processed, moved and presented to consumers. We also know that they are very important in conveying market information from consumers to producers (prices, preferences, feedback and so forth). However, we suggest that we should also appreciate their role in provenancing, in gathering and transmitting stories, assurances of, and demands for virtue in multiple directions through the networks.

So, if one answer to the question of what ethical value networks are, is that they are systems of constructing, performing, and profiting from virtue, what do the studies in this book tell us about how these systems work? First, we have seen how they depend both on a material infrastructure (packaging, labels, the physical and online environments where products are sold), and a discursive infrastructure (including formal regulations and standards but also the more informal concepts and rhetoric that make up provenancing narratives). As we highlighted in Chapter 2, the materialities of products themselves can affect their ability to 'speak' of their provenance (products that come in bottles have a clear advantage in this respect). Perhaps more fundamentally, actors with greater control of the material and discursive infrastructures (such as processors, retailers and advertisers, particularly in the Global North) are in the best position to shape and benefit from provenancing narratives.

This helps explain the generally frustrated expectations that indigenous producers with close connections to place and environment would have a competitive advantage in ethical markets (Bramley and Kirsten, 2007; Vandecandelaere et al., 2010). As Bidwell (Chapter 8, this volume) argues, the micro-geographies and 'beyond organic' practices of small Andean communities producing maize, quinoa or potatoes are rarely articulated or understood in extra-local markets where these products are seen as commodities, or at best, generic 'superfoods'. Meanwhile, as Overton and Murray (2016) discuss, marketers can mobilise relatively spurious connections such as those between "a Polynesian place name, a South American wine and a European tradition" (2016, p. 794) to give a sheen of authenticity to products that lack deep connections to place.

Beyond this general point about unequal access to the tools of virtue-making, we have seen how expansion into mass markets can drive tactical changes in provenancing narratives, which in turn reshape the character of ethical networks themselves. Goodman et al. (2012) discuss how the embrace of fair trade by large retailers in the 2000s was associated with a 'turn to quality' – a shift in emphasis from solidarity to taste and distinction. Previously, fair trade products had often featured images of the small producers and workers who benefited from the exchange networks. While subject to criticisms of spectacle making, this represented a gesture towards the producer–consumer reconnections the networks aimed to engender. As the narrative shifted to emphasise craft-like qualities, images highlighting product materials and tools became predominant. This shift occurred alongside a trend for existing successful cooperatives to capture a significant share of growing fair trade markets, while smaller and poorer groups faced increasingly high barriers to entry.

In another example, Overton et al. (2014) report that the development of New Zealand's geographical indications for wine has been influenced by concerns about confusion in international markets over the subtleties of indigenous places names (e.g. Waipara, Wairarapa, Waiheke). While New Zealand's local wine identities developed over a relatively short period, they nevertheless emerged through a shared understanding of place. A drive to target international markets – connected to increasing production volumes and corporate participation – resulted in decisions to create less *terroir*-based and authentic designations of origin, such as 'North Canterbury' instead of 'Waipara'.

Finally, a theme running throughout our studies of ethical value networks is that, rather than simply making social and spatial origins transparent, provenancing narratives can be turned back on people and places, shaping and constraining them. For example, Fairtrade International's adoption of the cooperative as the emblematic form of 'democratic' social organisation has driven small producers and communities to form cooperative-like arrangements in parts of the world where these have little institutional history or local legitimacy (Walker, 2015). Likewise, certified organic standards impose new disciplines and scrutiny on small farmers in the Global South. Rather than offering an easy competitive advantage to traditional practices, the high costs and exacting requirements of organics can leave farmers ever more tightly bound to market demands (Bidwell, 2020; Gómez Tovar et al., 2005; González and Nigh, 2005).

A useful analogy here is with Andolina et al.'s (2009) discussion of the cultural turn in development practice. In theory, this sought to pursue 'culturally appropriate development' by adapting development projects to the values and strengths of local cultures. In practice, it promoted 'developmentally appropriate culture', by selectively reinventing and approving aspects of local culture amenable to development. In a similar way, the processes of virtue making in ethical value networks can amplify and distort certain aspects of social, environmental and geographical provenance, while suppressing or obscuring others.

CONCLUSIONS

This chapter has drawn together threads running throughout this volume to develop a key theoretical insight about ethical value networks. Building on our previous work on fictive place, the chapter elaborates the broader concept of fictive virtue – the creation of added value through provenancing narratives that explain and assure the social and spatial histories of products. We have argued that the relationship between ethical value networks and virtue making is symbiotic: the process of virtue making depends on network elements such as market niches, social movements, institutions, and regulatory frameworks; while in turn the networks rely on discourses of provenance and virtuous practice to survive and thrive. Thus, rather than 'removing the veil' between producers and consumers (Hudson and Hudson, 2003) and revealing the 'true' conditions of production, ethical value networks actively construct stories of provenance to create added value, which derives ultimately from consumer willingness to pay for a reflected sense of virtue.

Given these insights, a question that remains is, what is the relationship between the construction of virtue-making narratives and 'actually existing virtue'? In other words, does the expansion of ethical value networks and the 'race to virtue' herald a real alternative to the 'race to the bottom' and result in fairer, more sustainable, and locally connected networks of food production and distribution? It should be clear from the locality studies in this book and the discussion in this chapter that the answer we offer is a sceptical one. Across different product networks and in different geographical settings, we have shown tenuous relationships between genuine commitments and market success, between deep socio-ecological relationships and effective virtue-making tactics. More often than not, we have argued, the largest benefits from ethical value networks are captured by actors with existing social and market power.

However, our presentation of provenancing and virtue making as an active process does not necessarily imply that it is a cynical one. All values are socially constructed, and genuine commitments to social justice, sustainability and authenticity must also be established and shared through storytelling, thus being on some level 'fictive'. Indeed, this insight can help us move beyond the expectation of peeling away all subterfuge, or of obtaining a sufficiently robust assurance that a particular product truly is ethical. What our analysis does imply, however, is a need for critical and detailed examination of ethical value networks. This means not only assessing whether particular claims to virtue can be verified but also questioning how and by whom the criteria for ethical practice are defined, how these might be contested, and what is obscured or missing from the story with which we are presented. As researchers, it leads us towards undertaking more place-based studies, which look at how the material and discursive elements of ethical value networks interact with lives and livelihoods. For consumers and the general public, we hope that these reflections might stimulate critical engagement with ethical value networks, a healthy scepticism towards marketing claims, and an interest in learning more.

NOTES

1. Virtue ethics is a form of ethics (espoused most notably by Aristotle) which emphasises the moral character of actions, rather than their consequences or their relationship to duties or rules (see https://plato.stanford.edu/entries/ethics-virtue)
2. In reality, such guarantees may involve some flexibility, in things such as the 85% (or similar) rule regarding wine in New Zealand: the use of a recognised place name allows for up to 15% of the volume of the product to come from other (unspecified) places (Overton and Murray, 2014).

REFERENCES

Andolina, R., Laurie, N. & Radcliffe, S. (2009). *Indigenous development in the Andes: Culture, power and transnationalism.* Duke University Press.

Banks, G. & Sharpe, S. (2006). Wine, regions and the geographic imperative: The Coonawarra example. *New Zealand Geographer*, 62(3), 173–184.

Barham, E. (2003).Translating terroir: The global challenge of French AOC labelling. *Journal of Rural Studies*, 19(1), 127–138.

Barker, J.P.H. (2004). *Different worlds: Law and the changing geographies of wine in France and New Zealand.* PhD thesis, University of Auckland.

Bidwell, S. (2020). *Cultivating what is ours: Local agro-food heritage as a development strategy in the Peruvian Andes.* PhD thesis, Victoria University of Wellington.

Bowen, S. (2010). Embedding local places in global spaces: Geographical indications as a territorial development strategy. *Rural Sociology*, 75(2), 209–243.

Bramley, C. & Kirsten, J.F. (2007). Exploring the economic rationale for protecting geographical indicators in agriculture. *Agrekon*, 46, 47–71.

Dogana, B. & Gokovali, U. (2012). Geographical indications: The aspects of rural development and marketing through the traditional products. *Procedia – Social and Behavioral Sciences*, 62, 761–765.

Gluck, M. (2009). *The great wine swindle: How snobs are ruining your wine.* Gibson Square.

Gómez Tovar, L., Martin, L., Gómez Cruz, M.A. & Mutersbaugh, T. (2005). Certified organic agriculture in Mexico: Market connections and certification practices in large and small producers. *Journal of Rural Studies*, 21, 461–474.

González, A.A. & Nigh, R. (2005). Smallholder participation and certification of organic farm products in Mexico. *Journal of Rural Studies*, 21, 449–460.

Goodman, D., DuPuis, E.M. & Goodman, M.K. (2012). *Alternative food networks: Knowledge, practice, and politics.* Routledge.

Hudson, I. & Hudson, M. (2003). Removing the veil? Commodity fetishism, fair trade, and the environment. *Organization & Environment*, 16(4), 413–430.

Jena, P.R. & Groote, U. (2012). Impact evaluation of traditional Basmati rice cultivation in Uttarakhand State of Northern India: What implications does it hold for
geographical indications? *World Development*, 40(9), 1895–1907.

Morgan, K., Marsden, T. & Murdoch, J. (2006). *Worlds of food: Place, power, and
provenance in the food chain*. Oxford University Press.

Overton, J. & Murray, W.E. (2014). Finding a place for New Zealand wine: *Terroir* and
regional denominations. In P. Howland (Ed.), *Social, cultural and economic impacts
of wine in New Zealand* (pp. 41–57). Routledge.

Overton, J. & Murray W.E. (2016). Fictive place. *Progress in Human Geography*,
40(6), 794–809.

Overton, J., Banks, G.A. & Murray, W.E. (2014). Waipara. In P. Howland (Ed.), *Social,
cultural and economic impacts of wine in New Zealand* (pp. 243–252). Routledge.

Urban Dictionary (n.d.). 'Virtue signalling' https://www.urbandictionary.com/define
.php?term=Virtue%20Signalling (accessed 11 November 2020).

Vandecandelaere, E., Arfini, F., Belletti, G. & Marescotti, A. (2010). *Linking people,
places and products. A guide for promoting quality linked to geographical origin
and sustainable geographical indications*. FAO.

Walker. H. (2015). *Kopi, cooperatives, and compliance: A case study of fair trade in
Aceh, Indonesia*. Master's thesis, Victoria University of Wellington.

16 Critical issues in conceptualising, researching and constructing ethical value networks

Warwick E. Murray, Simon Bidwell, Kelle Howson, John Overton and Johannes Rehner

INTRODUCTION

This book sought to uncover the extent to which commodity dependence is being challenged through the evolution of ethical value networks (EVeNs). It focused on three constellations of ethical products, embodied in global trade: social justice (fair trade), sustainability (organic agriculture) and authenticity (geographical origin). We have reported on a series of grounded locality case studies that explore these constellations – in South America, Southeast Asia, the Pacific and Africa. Although the impacts are differentiated generally, the outcomes of the adoption of EVeNs are not as progressive as the narratives that accompany such evolutions might suggest. There have undoubtedly been positive impacts. We recognise that it is usually the case that growers involved in EVeNs are better off than those who are not. However, as we argue below, ethical value networks generally represent a reform in the market that reproduces the core–periphery structure of the global economy rather than a revolution in relations of power that might re-condition it from below.

In the remainder of this chapter, by way of closing the book, we reflect on three areas of concern: (1) some common empirical outcomes observed across EVeNs in our case studies; (2) the policy prospects for EVeNs as a form of governance, a development strategy and a response to globalisation; and (3) broader theoretical reflections. This is followed by some final thoughts regarding knowledge gaps and the future of EVeNs research.

COMMON OUTCOMES IN EVENS

We have a much clearer idea of how EVeNs are built and governed and how producers enter and participate in them. Although this varies from place to place, as we clearly illustrate in the broad range of case studies presented in this collection, we uncovered a range of similarities.

Environmental and Socio-cultural Benefits

There are *common positive outcomes* across the various case studies presented in this collection. In most cases a price premium is reported by research participants and there are clearly positive environmental outcomes in most localities where fair trade or organic certification is adopted. The local demonstration effect, as well as individual and collective capacity-building impacts are generally positive. The impacts of Geographical Indications (GIs) are difficult to estimate but there is clearly potential in terms of maintaining and promoting authenticity that may bring economic and socio-cultural benefits. For example, as Bidwell shows clearly in Chapter 8 with respect to the 'gastro-boom' in Peruvian agri-food networks, it is feasible that socio-cultural benefits might flow from such certifications. There is also some evidence of wider community benefits too – for example, Howson reports on the construction of community facilities in the case of Timor-Leste coffee exporting communities in Chapter 13. There can be no doubt that ethical value networks present the potential for progressive outcomes. However, more often than not, these are accompanied by sets of problems and costs to which we turn below.

Common Costs and Challenges across Ethical Value Networks

Conventional value chain governance structures are often retained in EVeNs. The socio-economic impacts of EVeN adoption vary according to local political economy, histories and geographies. However, as we make clear elsewhere in this book, the socio-economic and environmental impacts, whilst more progressive than conventional networks, nonetheless tend to concentrate value and profit at 'higher stages' in the network. Northern retailers are able to transfer costs of monitoring standards on to the supply base, while little value is retained by primary producers through the adoption of ethical codes. For example, Howson showed in the case of coffee growers of Timor-Leste in Chapter 13, very little value (estimated at 1.6% of final retail price) is retained. From a policy point of view, there is work to be done to ensure that value does not flow out in such a disproportionate manner. In this sense, as we argue in Chapter 4 and reiterate below, EVeNs are often core–periphery in structure, and whilst not hierarchical in a strict sense, can concentrate wealth and marginalise growers and workers if not regulated effectively.

Boundaries of inclusion and exclusion in certification initiatives often privilege those producers with an existing market advantage. The cost of certification in itself, as well as the investments required in order to gain such certification, especially in terms of organic production, are more easily shouldered by larger-scale farmers and those that are already relatively well-off in terms of financial capital. This was illustrated in the case of South African wine by Howson (Chapter 6) where certification was shown to work in the interests of the agents and institutions that construct the ethical trade certification systems. In the case of wine and fruit in Argentina discussed in Chapter 10, Wald illustrated that the high costs of organic certification represents a real barrier to the participation of smaller-scale growers. There is a role for the state, together with civil society, in terms of facilitating access to capital, knowledge and technology necessary for the adoption of EVeNs in the periphery. Again, this is not very different from the challenge that faces small farmers in conventional networks.

Economies of scale are often required in order that producers can afford and benefit from the adoption of ethical trade. This leaves small-scale producers at a particular disadvantage and is an essential conundrum in EVeNs as the very purpose of their existence is to challenge such inequities. Ethical value networks are built upon 'imaginaries' of the poor and marginalised. However, in general terms these participants fare relatively poorly in terms of capturing the financial benefits. This was illustrated convincingly in a number of case studies in this collection including Chilean fair trade wine by Williams (Chapter 9), who concluded that in general the problem of corporate capture was a historical legacy of a deeply concentrated agrarian system in Chile. In the case of wine and fruit in Argentina, Wald also points to the legacy of neoliberal economic governance in the 1980s as a factor which explains the dominance of large-scale companies. This is a trend common to most Latin American countries in the 1970s and 1980s, leading to the concentration of land ownership and the disproportionate role of agri-food TNCs.

The outcomes of EVeNs for equitable and sustainable development are contingent on the local and national institutional and broader geographical context. As such, outcomes are mediated by the motivations and expectations of institutions and actors involved. Increasingly, standardised certification systems are less able to address specific issues at local levels. There is thus a tension between the consumer desire for standardisation and consistency and the need to take the geography and political economy of place into account. Generally speaking, the potential of a market mechanism – in the form of EVeNs – has limited potential to correct deep-seated structural asymmetries that plague all agri-food networks, including those with ethical value, as illustrated in virtually every case study in this collection. In the case of South African wine for example, Howson (Chapter 6) clearly shows that a neo-paternalism persists in the network derived from the structural legacy of apartheid and, arguably, in this context ethicality becomes akin to a performance. In the case of Chilean fair trade wine, the legacy of dictatorship between 1973 and 1990 has clearly discouraged collective action among growers in order to counteract the oligopsonistic and concentrating forces existing in the network, as Williams points out in Chapter 9.

Market failures including imperfect information, information asymmetries, the threat of concentration and lack of access to capital are common in ethical agri-food networks. For example, Williams showed in Chapter 7 that the GI system associated with pisco in Peru clearly favours larger-scale farmers and that the productive culture of small-scale farmers is undermined as a result. In the case of Timor-Leste discussed by Howson in Chapter 13, the role of information asymmetries, based in part on lack of training and education, clearly discriminated against small-scale coffee exporters.

There is a role for the state and public policy given the persistent challenge of market failures. All of the case studies point towards the central role of the state, and quasi-state agencies in producing public policy that creates, fosters and facilitates the equitable adoption of EVeNs and ensures fair outcomes. Left to the market alone, processes of concentration, control and resultant marginalisation are clearly prevalent. For example, this is illustrated in the case of Chilean wine studied by Williams in Chapter 9, Indonesian cinnamon in Chapter 12, and coffee in Timor-Leste in Chapter 13. As pointed out by Wald in Chapters 10 and 11, without state involvement EVeNs would probably never have been established in the first place and, in Argentina, central and regional state and quasi-state institutions have played a pro-active role in their establishment. However, there remains a crucial role for monitoring as the EVeNs continue to function and evolve.

The rationale for participation is not necessarily based on a desire to practise ethical trade. There is a general lack of awareness among producers concerning the ethical component of trade, and participation is often motivated by price rather than broader sustainability and justice concerns. In this sense the networks still remain top-down and dominated in a broad sense by lead agents and firms and the signals sent out by the consumers that they supply. This was illustrated in Timor-Leste by Howson in Chapter 13 and Indonesia by Wikaningtyas and Murray in Chapter 12, where interviews clearly identified price signals as the main determinant of participation in EVeNs.

Provenance, virtue and the creation of ethical narratives can lead to loss of diversity. All the illustrated cases of EVeNs are about the making of provenance and the weaving together of facts to make a story regarding ethicality and authenticity. This can provide much needed opportunities for growers, but it can also – as illustrated by Bidwell in Chapter 8 in the case of Andean food producers – upset traditional diversity and ossify the new narrative. This may have diversity-reducing cultural and productive outcomes.

Ethical technologies are often pursued rather than wider socio-economic ethics. In general terms, as is illustrated by many of the case studies in this volume, there has been a tendency for EVeNs to focus on the technical aspects of ethicality rather than broader issues of just and sustainable outcomes. This is most certainly the case in terms of organic certification and GI-based market mechanisms. One of the main findings of Chapter 14 concerning water in South Africa, for example, was that the technological regime associated with ensuring sustainable practice placed an emphasis on technical issues. This marginalised small growers who may not possess the capital and training necessary to pursue such technologies. Ultimately, this failed to address the dualistic nature of the fruit export sector, which can be considered a legacy of deeper structural injustices related to apartheid. It is these deep-seated structural conditions that require addressing if EVeNs are to deliver progressive outcomes. We might rightly doubt if current ethical trade regimes, based as they are on market solutions and technologies, can deliver such reforms at all.

CONCEPTUAL FRAMEWORKS FOR SOCIAL JUSTICE, SUSTAINABILITY AND AUTHENTICITY

In Chapter 4 we introduced a generalised conceptual framework for ethical value networks (Figure 4.1). On the basis of the case study material presented in this book, we now suggest three conceptual frameworks as elaborations of this basic model, each of which corresponds to a different ethical constellation. Each of these has various components in common although, as we will see, each has crucial differences, which we expand upon below.

Conceptual Framework for Social Justice EVeNs

The social justice ethical network presents some particular points of difference from the basic conceptual model. As Figure 16.1 shows, within the production sector of the network there are various configurations. Most production takes place largely within the ambit of civil society regulation and certification, as we saw in the case of Chilean fair trade wine and Indonesian cinnamon (see Chapters 9 and 12, respectively). NGOs are active in organising, promoting and certifying ethical production whilst also building connections with ethical marketing networks. However, there can be industry capture also where companies act as intermediaries and establish private schemes, often in response to, and sometimes in competition with, independently certified fair trade production. The state is usually not involved at the production end, although in some cases there may be some minimum state regulated standards – for example as with labour regulations in South Africa where state labour laws provided the basis for ethical fair trade certification.

On the consumption side of an idealised social justice EVeN, we see potentially more differentiation. Civil society-mediated fair trade networks tend to be more prevalent, overseeing fair trade branding and assurances. However, we have witnessed the emergence of more unregulated schemes pertaining to, and contained within, different industry actors – such as Starbucks in coffee and supermarkets, such as Tesco in the UK, with their own range of products. This can have the impact of weakening social justice networks due to a proliferation of options and uncertainty and confusion on the part of consumers. This is especially the case as there is little to no regulation of such networks by the state in such examples. Overall, although civil society and industry do sometimes work together, the dominant element is civil society, in the governance and regulation of the chains. We see civil society active at both the production and retailing ends, and important links between them overseeing the flow of products, profits and information and, through certification schemes, providing assurances regarding social justice.

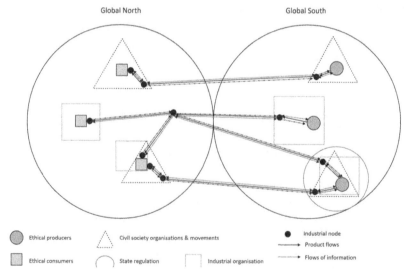

Figure 16.1   Social justice EVeNs – Fair trade

Conceptual Framework for Sustainability EVeNs

In this case we draw on organic production in order to illustrate relationships and linkages that pertain to the sustainability constellation. On the production side there is generally a relative lack of state regulation, although in some cases there may be state oversight in terms of inputs (for example in the case of water in South Africa, as illustrated in Chapter 14). There are some examples of civil society regulation and certification in such networks and there can also be state oversight, as we saw in fruit and wine in Argentina in Chapter 11. In most cases though, states in the Global South have not been active in overseeing strong regulation of organic and related standards (Figure 16.2).

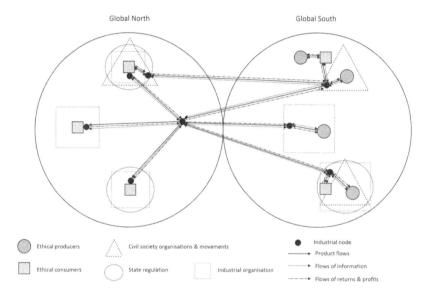

Figure 16.2   Sustainability EVeNs – organics

Unlike fair trade, in sustainability EVeNs we see the evolution of local consumption networks, as was illustrated in Chapter 7, alongside more globally-linked chains. These short local networks provide almost direct contact between growers and consumers. However, here the network is one that is generally small, unregulated and informal. In terms of the flow of products from the Global South to North, most linkages take place through conventional marketing networks – as with the trade in organic fruit and vegetables or wine. There may also be some limited alternative chains through NGOs (as with organic coffee alongside the fair trade chains). On the consumption side, there is relatively more state regulation compared with fair trade – in aspects such as labelling of food additives or monitoring of chemical residues in food. However, the majority of consumption lies within a relatively unregulated industrial context. Generally, sustainability narratives are unregulated and open to corporate capture.

Conceptual Framework for Authenticity EVeNs

In order to theorise an EVeN corresponding to the authenticity constellation, we explore the case of GIs (Figure 16.3). In this case, in the production sector, state regulation is crucial in order to define and legislate the registering and protection of place names. We also see the state involved in building place narratives – as was the case in pisco in Peru (see Chapter 7). Industry can also build place narratives, using state systems for recognition and protection, but sometimes also engaging in its own strategies of fictive place creation. Industry tends to be active in this network where certain GIs prove successful (such as pisco, wine or tequila), buying into the favoured regions and often dominating production.

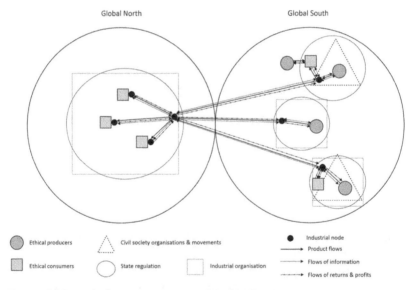

Figure 16.3   Authenticity – geographical indications

There are some local markets for GIs but it is relatively small-scale and relatively unregulated, as with local organic markets. On the consumption side there is relatively little involvement of industry or civil society in terms of regulating the ethical component compared with other constellations, given that place of origin assurances are regulated at source. Most trade takes place in conventional chains, which flow along to the retail side through supermarkets, especially in the case of wine for example. Overall, there is proportionally strong state regulation at all points in the network. This includes supra-national protection of GIs in world trade agreements. In this sense, this constellation has the highest level of globalised regulation of all sectors, and provenance and associated virtue making can become more concretised through these processes.

Core–Periphery and Ethical Value Accumulation

As noted in Chapter 4 (see Figure 4.1), the juxtaposition of the Global North and South side by side in the frameworks in the figures is intended to assist in visualisation rather than represent the true power relations existent in the networks under consideration. In reality, we argue that in all three cases the EVeNs exhibit a *core–periphery structure*, where the realisation of ethical value largely flows from the periphery to the core. It would be useful to explore other ways of representing such networks with, for example, the Global South placed outside and around the Global North or core.

In Chapter 4, *ethical value accumulation profiles* were introduced and conceptualised. A profile will vary between ethical constellations and across different products. We conceptualised six such possibilities in theory – *hyper-ethical, ethical, equitable, Southern capture*, and *Northern wholesale capture*, and *northern retail capture* based on the allocation of ethical premiums throughout the networks (see Figures 4.2–4.5)*. The distribution is dependent on local political-economic factors, the relative size of producers and their bargaining power, levels of knowledge and information. It also depends on the ability of certifiers to ensure the more just distribution of premium prices paid for ethical products and the eventual distribution of any social premium that is allocated. This distribution of premium is more explicitly undertaken in fair trade EVeNs, although it does occur in some sustainability EVeNs. However, as suggested elsewhere in this chapter, and echoing case studies in this volume, this is not necessarily the case. In general, in the case of sustainability and authenticity constellations, the flow of proportional value towards the production sectors of the networks is less pronounced. Particularly in the case where powerful supermarkets dominate the consumption sector of networks, it is highly likely that the majority of the value added is accrued there. We suggest that this is fertile ground for further research that seeks to uncover the proportional accumulation of value at each point in the networks. In some ways a more systematic evaluation of the flows and distribution of an ethical premium in a quantitative sense is urgent, with the hypothesis being that EVeNs tend towards a more equitable distribution of value.

PROSPECTS FOR ETHICAL VALUE NETWORKS[1]

In this section we focus on three questions regarding the prospects for EVeNs based, in part, on empirical reflections from this book that echo findings in the general literature. First, to what extent do EVeNs demonstrate the possibility of a private system of governance in which positive social and environmental outcomes can be achieved through market mechanisms? Second, what potential do they offer as development strategies? This question breaks down into questions about the macro- or meso-scale (countries or sectors) and the micro scale (livelihoods). Third, what is the nature of their overall relationship to neoliberal globalisation?

Ethical Value Networks as Private Governance

An important claim about all three of the ethical value constellations is that they 're-embed' (Bowen, 2010) or 'de-fetishize' (Lyon, 2006) production-consumption relations by unveiling the conditions of production and thereby reconnecting producers with consumers. While neoliberal capitalism turns human health, the environment and livelihoods into externalities in the pursuit of profit, it is argued that ethical value networks can re-internalise these concerns by providing consumers with information about the social and environmental conditions in which goods are produced. Thus, ostensibly voluntary actions by private firms and consumers can work through market mechanisms to protect the environment and improve producer livelihoods.

However, the very success of alternative agri-food movements in appealing to consumer concerns can result in paradoxical counter tendencies of disembedding or 're-commodification'. In the context of increased demand for products that are fairly traded, organic, or of certified provenance, the *specialness* of these products (Yeung and Kerr, 2011) becomes a valuable asset – what might be classed as symbolic capital. To ensure against fraudulent claims to this specialness, standards appear. These may be initially voluntary and initiated by the movement originators, but competing standards appear and this eventually leads to formal bureaucratic regulation. At this point, the way becomes clear for economies of scale to be applied and 'ethical' markets may then evolve in ways similar to conventional value chains, with increasing competition, diminishing margins for producers and dominance by powerful participants such as supermarket chains. When institutional governance does not specifically defend the position of less powerful or locally-embedded participants, the result may be captive or vertically integrated value chains (see Gereffi et al., 2005) in which large corporate participants hold most of the power.

These participants may seek to remodel ethical value chains to serve their interests, such as by increasing requirements on producers or by promoting their own watered-down versions of ethical products (such as the development of alternative ethical labels by large corporations such as Starbucks and Nestlé). An important criticism of mainstream ethical value chains is the asymmetry between demands placed on different participants. For example, in order to take part in fair trade or organic value chains, developing world producers are required to meet and document an exacting range of standards; while large retailers can choose to offer organic or fair trade as niche products and are not required to be ethical in their wider social or environmental relations. Their dominant role as market gatekeepers can allow them to extract the maximum value from the symbolic capital of ethical products, while making the minimum commitments.

In these circumstances, what remains of the 'ethical' motives of consumers and how do these moderate the tendency towards appropriation of symbolic capital by powerful interests? At least three factors weaken the ability of ethical consumption to resist disembedding forces. First, it is not possible for even the most well-intentioned consumers to have all the necessary knowledge about the social and environmental impacts of their consumption decisions (Brown, 2013; Lyon, 2006; Renard, 2005). Second, although reflexive concerns about the effects of consumption under global capitalism may be widespread, only a minority of consumers are likely to engage in conscious, political choices, while others merely seek reassurance against 'fatalism and insecurity' (Lyon, 2006, p. 456). To the extent that labels such as fair trade and organic provide this reassurance, the labels themselves become the new objects of consumption. Rather than 'de-fetishising' production and consumption, place names, organic and fair trade labels themselves become fetishised and mystified. Less reflexive consumers may be easily assuaged with alternative 'ethical' labels that allow dominant market participants to establish their own definitions of sustainability. Third, the motives of consumers are not even necessarily admirable. Consumption of ethical products may be a source of differentiation in the production of class, an expression of *habitus* whose primary role is to distinguish upper-middle class consumers from their less educated or enlightened contemporaries. Further, some authors argue that narratives and images of developing-world producers and their families in fair trade play on attraction to the exotic other, and the primary purpose of such narratives and images may be to generate 'spectacles of poverty' (Lyon, 2006), even if these are 'alternative spectacles' (Bryant and Goodman, 2004).

Ethical Value Networks as a Development Strategy

Another important claim about EVeNs in the justice, sustainability and authenticity constellations is that they offer potential as development strategies, by allowing countries in the periphery of the global economy to enter higher-value niche markets and escape from dependence on low-value commodities. Developing countries may have a comparative and/or competitive advantage in ethical agri-food markets because of their existing position as agricultural exporters, ease of transition to ethical production, or because their natural and cultural resources are particularly unique and marketable.

At a national level, there is some evidence that certain ethical value networks do provide opportunities for some countries in the periphery to gain access to more dynamic and higher-value markets. Two notable cases are the rise to prominence of the Dominican Republic in organic banana exports, and Peru in organic coffee exports (Pay, 2009; Raynolds, 2008; Shreck, 2002). However, with the entry of more participants, margins decline and niche markets come to resemble conventional commodity networks. The onus is thus on developing countries to further differentiate products and discover niches where they have competitive advantage. Geographical indications would appear to offer more potential in this respect than organics or fair trade. However, even where products gain a distinctive reputation and global prominence, the structure of their value chains can mean most of the value is captured by participants outside the Global South (such as in the case of tequila, Darjeeling tea – Bowen, 2010; Das, 2006; Giovannucci et al., 2009 – or, as documented in this book, Peruvian pisco).

At the micro level, conclusions about the effect on livelihoods of participation in ethical value chains vary widely. While some studies have shown clear benefits of involvement in ethical as opposed to conventional markets, others have not found significant differences (Dragusanu et al., 2014; Giovannucci et al., 2009; IFAD, 2003; Jena and Groote, 2012; Ruben and Fort, 2012; Valkila, 2009). It can also be difficult to separate the benefits of fair trade, organic or GI status from other factors such as land productivity, product quality and reputation, and supportive buyer relationships (Dragusanu et al, 2014; IFAD, 2003; Yeung and Kerr, 2011), although advocates would argue that fair trade and organic certification and well-managed GI regimes all work to promote these very factors. Given that improving producer livelihoods is its primary aim, fair trade has been studied most systematically in this respect. Dragusanu et al. (2014) conclude that, overall, fair trade does achieve its basic objective of facilitating (modestly) higher and more stable prices for small producers and there is no conclusive evidence of positive selection (better endowed or skilled producers more likely to access fair trade markets).

Overall, the common finding is that successful involvement in ethical value chains is associated with stable land tenancy, ability to mobilise resources and to accept risk at the family level, and effective social organisation, political presence and ability to maintain quality standards at the group level. These findings are supported by the evidence found in the case studies in this book. This raises the question of whether ethical production, at best, simply consolidates the position of relatively resilient small farmers. This is not to downplay the benefits offered by ethical premiums in increasingly competitive and insecure environments brought about by neoliberal restructuring. Rather, it suggests that instead of an escape from poverty, ethical production may primarily offer defensive measures and/or offer incremental gains for those who are already better prepared to participate in competitive markets.

It is also worth noting that many case studies that report successful outcomes of participation in ethical value chains highlight specific aspects of the national political and historical context. A history of land reform and organisation into cooperatives, with varying levels of state support, forms the background to fair trade and organic production in Mexico, Nicaragua, Costa Rica and the Dominican Republic (Fridell, 2007; González and Nigh, 2005; Luetchford, 2008; Raynolds, 2008; Shreck, 2002; Valkila, 2009) as well as Chile and Argentina, as documented in this book by Williams and Wald respectively. The marginal differences made by participation in ethical value chains may be less important than the differences between organised smallholders and landless or non-organised groups, or between these countries and others (for example, Brazil) without a history of similar political reforms.

In addition to income gains, studies provide largely anecdotal evidence of environmental improvements and the strengthening of some forms of social organisation (Dragusanu et al., 2014). However, a common criticism is that the forms of environmental protection and social organisation have often been imposed from the top down. A theme running throughout the literature is that standards for fair trade, organics, and developing country GI regimes have often been negotiated without consultation with the small producers to whom they apply. Even in cases where local groups have strategically used ethical discourses to advance their cause, the increasing bureaucratisation of certification regimes may eventually result in their disempowerment, as was illustrated in a number of case studies in this book.

Ethical Value Chains as a Response to Globalisation

Finally, comment is required on the fact that each of these three constellations has expanded rapidly over the past 30 years in parallel with the establishment of a global neoliberal regime of trade and investment. Key dates – 1988 for the establishment of the first fair trade label, 1990–1991 for the passing of

European and US legislation on organics, and 1992 for the establishment of a EU-wide framework for GIs – cluster together with watershed dates for globalisation, such as the fall of the Berlin Wall in 1989 and the establishment of the World Trade Organization in 1994. Markets for fair trade and organics – which can be more easily quantified than GIs in terms of their global value – have grown by orders of magnitude over the past two decades. What, then, is the nature of their relationship with globalisation?

One interpretation is that ethical value chains represent resistance to neoliberal globalisation or radical alternatives to it. The case for resistance can perhaps be made most forcefully for geographical indications, which have been presented – especially by European interests – as defending traditional relationships between small-scale producers and the territory they live in against the corporatisation and homogenisation of food and agriculture (Guthman, 2007). GIs have also been promoted as a means for developing countries to defend their natural and cultural resources against appropriation and alienation by transnational interests (Yeung and Kerr, 2011). Meanwhile, the movement most commonly presented as an alternative to actually existing globalisation is fair trade. Advocates argue that while engagement with mainstream markets is necessary to support producers and raise public awareness, this is just one part of a broader movement towards an alternative trading system that works 'within and against' the existing structure of global markets (Shreck, 2002).

An opposite view is that ethical value networks are simply part of a new iteration of global capital accumulation. Although the fair trade and organic movements in their original form might have proposed alternatives to mainstream markets, they have quickly become subsumed within them, and rather than resisting neoliberal globalisation, they help renew and extend it. As traditional commodity markets become exhausted, ethical products are able to enter new, more dynamic niches. As suggested in the critique of 'de-commodification' above, this market dynamism particularly benefits large corporate interests, which can use their dominant position in value chains to capture the ethical capital offered in EVeNs.

This more critical view would suggest that ethical value networks expand in conjunction with neoliberal regimes because they are in harmony with, and enabled by, such regimes. From this perspective, promotion of geographical indications by the European Union is less a defence of local diversity than an attempt to leverage a particular form of intellectual property – little different from the rent-seeking of entertainment and pharmaceutical companies with patents and copyright. Rather than defending traditional cultural resources against global capital, the characteristic action would be the attempts by EU governments to 'claw back' rents by, for example, preventing the use of wine and cheese names that have long developed their own local traditions in other settings (Battaglene, 2005).

A third, intermediate, position is that ethical movements are compatible with, and part of, neoliberal globalisation but may also play a role in shaping it. They do not represent a genuine challenge to existing power structures and may support and perpetuate them. However, by mobilising consumer concerns, ethical movements can influence what eventually becomes the regulatory framework under which capitalism evolves, and indeed represent one of the ways in which powerful value chain participants such as TNCs can differentiate and defend their position from 'irresponsible' competitors. Thus, ethical movements may contribute to certain basic labour protections, consumer information on provenance and the phasing out of some environmental harms eventually being woven into formal standards for global market transactions.

This interpretation is consistent with a view of ethical value networks as part of the 'double movement' described by Karl Polanyi, in which the expansion of markets is countered by attempts to regulate them and address their negative impact (Fridell, 2007; Raynolds, 2012). This is close to the perspective put forward by Raynolds (2012), who argues that fair trade and other ethical consumption movements are not 'private regulation' but rather 'social regulation', emphasising the role played by groups of activists, NGOs and certifying agencies in defining and enforcing standards for market exchanges. This view can be contrasted with that of Guthman (2007, p. 473) who asks whether 'there is no alternative' and whether movements that depend on individual consumption decisions 'obscure possible paths of action outside the market'.

THEORETICAL REFLECTIONS ON EVENS[2]

From a theoretical point of view, we can draw a number of conclusions from the work contained in this collection. First, EVeN formation and outcomes are reliant on the range of localities, actors and discourses which they interact with. Ethical certifications are not fixed and objective interventions resulting in certain outcomes, because they operate in fluid and relational networks which, in reality, evade or evolve faster than theory and policy. Although EVeNs deploy the tools of order and consistency – rules, audits and guarantees – they ultimately rely on the very uncertain and immeasurable factors of trust and commitment for their transformative power. This goes to the heart of the contestation in geography between the analytical frames of structure, and agency. Studying ethical certification as a structural intervention within the globalised system of economic exchange yields important findings about global trends, such as the mainstreaming trajectory of certification, but it is less able to generate knowledge about the extent to which specific ethical needs are being met, and about whether participatory governance exists in certified networks. It is also less able to account for the power exerted by agents within relational ethical value networks.

EVeNs as a framework – taking its cue from post-structuralist literatures of actor–network theory and global production networks – calls for greater attention to be paid to the distribution of agency, as well as the more material considerations of profit and upgrading in ethically-certified networks. A key contribution of EVeNs is their combination of theories of the machinations of global trade – chains, networks, governance, value – with theories of alternative development prioritising local ownership and grassroots-led development.

This book has devoted significant consideration to the historical context of the case studies contained within it, identifying ways in which the various contexts – or path dependences in an evolutionary economic geography context – have influenced the adoption of ethical certifications and their configuration as EVeNs. When taken as a whole, the body of case studies of the impact of ethical certification in various commodities and production contexts, clearly shows that outcomes of ethical certification are historically and geographically contingent. The idea that ethical certification might be more or less effective depending on context seems intuitive. However, an important extension of this is the fact that the presence of an ethical certification within a network does not automatically mean that the network is ethical. In this sense, EVeNs are both a *descriptive tool* (a network where value is added through alignment with ethical conventions) and an *aspiration* (a network where production is sustainable, distribution is just, and governance is inclusive).

That context matters seems a simple point to make, and arguably it is implicit in the conduct of case-study research in the first place. However, if we accept that a central function of the creation of EVeNs is to re-embed commodities in their territorial and social origins, and to resist the disembedded homogenisation of neoliberal globalisation, then the paradox of doing so through globalised technologies of ethics, and measuring progress towards this through empirical studies and theories that do not account for local factors, becomes plain. Ongoing critical research and political action which prioritises the bottom-up empowerment of the most marginalised is a crucial project in constructing truly ethical value networks.

Although we are arguing against the decontextualisation of EVeNs research, this book has revealed ethical certification itself to be a decontextualising process. In conceiving of ethical certification as a *technology*, a complex tool based on regimented rules, and the deployment of regulation through technical expertise and auditable metrics, we can clearly see how certification is available for utilisation by powerful actors to standardise and monitor the behaviour of other actors in their networks. In this capacity, certification becomes a technocratic tool of control. Again, this is counter to the popular interpretation of ethical certifications – that they shift the balance of power in networks in favour of producers by asserting place and context of production as something which adds value, that can be accumulated at production nodes. Indeed, we are increasingly seeing ways in which the value created by ethical certification is not in fact transferred to producers, but captured by retailers. Producers pay the costs of these technologies of control, while finding themselves subsumed into relationships of dependence, tied to buyers through new forms of indirect regulation.

Convention theory discusses how values of social and environmental good can become valorised within the existing framework of global economic exchange – essentially, how these considerations can come to attract monetary reward, thus allowing (in most orthodox economics, the irrational) concept of ethicality to become a concern of (otherwise rational) economic actors. However, within the logic of global capitalism, ethicality is only useful if it attracts profit. Therefore, it is predicated on demand and scarcity. In order to remain a gateway to lucrative premium markets, ethical certification and the generation of virtue more generally must remain scarce. However, this leaves the majority of vulnerable network participants exposed to the extractive and exploitative forces of conventional markets. The proliferation and 'ubiquitisation' of ethical certification only serves to heighten this dynamic. The end point of this process is one at which every product on the supermarket shelf carries an ethical label, allowing consumers to revert to making choices based on price and material quality/functionality. At this point, will all trade and production be ethical? Or will ethics have been fully commodified and compromised by global capitalism?

There are inherent governance struggles occurring in EVeNs which exist in parallel with the contests of driven-ness and accumulation which scholars theorise as characteristic of conventional networks. As we have identified at various points throughout this book, these struggles crystallise along a series of dichotomies. EVeNs are sites of contestation between producer and buyer governance, between local embeddedness and commodity fetishism, between empowerment and control, between the protection of smallholdings and the facilitation of economies of scale, and between grassroots visions for ethical development and globalised technologies of ethics. It is inevitable that within this ostensibly democratic contestation – the process of constant creative destruction of rules and norms – that the loudest and most powerful existing interests will prevail. Ethical value networks do not necessarily rebalance global trade processes in favour of producers, but rather have the potential to perpetuate core–periphery governance struggles.

KNOWLEDGE GAPS IN EVENS RESEARCH

We have learnt a considerable amount concerning the evolution, construction and outcomes of EVeNs. However, there is much we do not know. We have already mentioned that, in general, studies have tended to focus on consumption nodes. Furthermore, work has tended to focus on one or two lead sectors – with coffee being the most analysed. Further to this, we recommend that future research seeks to incorporate the three issues that we identify below.

Dynamic issues – What happens over time after the adoption of EVeNs? There is a paucity of studies on the medium- and long-term prospects of communities of producers that participate in such markets. We know of no time-series studies and this collection certainly does not address this shortcoming. It would be useful to build base-line studies that can be returned to after five-, ten- and twenty-year intervals.

Community externalities – We are clear that there are price and other socio-economic and environmental benefits and costs of participating in ethical value networks for producers and their families. We know relatively little about the impacts on the broader community however. As Wald points out in Chapter 10, whilst certification may confer 'ethicality' on productive aspects of export networks, the wider implications – especially when based on a backdrop of concentration and marginalisation brought about through neo-liberal regimes – may well not be 'ethical' when interpreted in a broad sense. Such studies could be as straightforward as tracing the broader destination and outcomes of social premium but might also be more complex in terms of uncovering demonstration effects and neighbourhood effects in terms of participation. Economic, environmental and especially social externalities are difficult, though, to measure. We recommend case studies that more explicitly deal with the overspill effects of EVeNs in specific communities.

Systematic quantitative studies of the distribution of monetised ethical value – The studies here are largely qualitative and this is the case generally in terms of ethical trade analyses. The studies of non-quantifiable processes and outcomes would be complemented by quantitative studies that trace the flow of realised monetary flows and profits that accrue through networks, as we conceptualised in Figures 4.2 to 4.7. The implication from all the studies reported here is that profits flow out from the margins of networks and accrue in the distribution and retail nodes that exist at the core of such configurations. Empirical studies that explore this hypothesis would be useful.

CONCLUSION

This book has provided an overview of three constellations of ethical trade: justice, sustainability and authenticity and their transformation into global ethical value networks. It has argued that while each of these movements has its particularities, they have a shared concern with the social and environmental context of agri-food production, including questions of how, where, and by whom the agri-food commodities are produced. The appeal of these movements to the 'reflexive' consumer is one of the key reasons for their surge to prominence. The other relates to the imperatives of neoliberal globalisation, which require differentiation in the name of competitiveness and, at the same time, provide new possibilities of reach and power for symbolic capital and intellectual property.

There is no single answer to questions about the ability of ethical value chains to achieve positive social and environmental outcomes, or about their contribution to development. Rather, they can be seen as arenas of political contest under the current mode of capitalism, in which greater protection and freedom is available to capital of all types and the actions of national states are constrained, but where spaces have also opened up for new kinds of local and transnational action. Ethical consumption movements can provide a focus for producers, consumers and activists to rally around, while at the same time they can be subject to appropriation, dilution and reworking by powerful interests. This is a dialectical process – even as ethical niches are colonised and transformed, new ones appear, both through the emancipatory politics of social movements and the personal politics of consumer differentiation. Despite this, theoretical debates will continue about whether market-oriented movements have as much potential to restrain and democratise capitalism.

In light of the findings in this collection we argue that there must be a greater role for government, civil society, activists, researchers, as well as worker and farmer collectives in generating new forms of policy and regulation that prioritise not only producer and labour rights, but ethical development for agri-food based communities. If new policy frameworks are responsive, participatory and bold, perhaps this change will herald a more just redistribution of power in a way that ethical value networks promise. For now, the status quo of dependent small farmers and disenfranchised labour often prevails, obscured and legitimised by 'ethical' labels on agri-food products. Our argument is that ethical certification, as a capitalist technology, has not served the urgent project of ethical development in the Global South. It has instead allowed capital to commodify fairness, to maintain the socio-economic status quo and benefit the most powerful capital interests. What makes this inherently unethical in the case of EVeNs is that the image of poverty forms part of the narrative upon which ethical claims are built. Under such a system the marginal are fetishised and commoditised in ways that deliver benefits to those – consumers, retailers, wholesalers and other intermediaries – who are relatively well-off. This process can be conceptualised as one of super-exploitation. Clearly, this outcome is neither always the case, nor inevitable – there are many examples of progressive configurations and positive spatial and social externalities that have resulted from participation in EVeNs. Ethical certification of some form is almost certainly better than none at all from a socio-economic and environmental point of view. In cases where outcomes are negative, intervention and regulation can re-construct networks from below and improve results. As such, there is nothing inherently progressive or regressive about ethical value networks; it depends upon how they are constructed, participated in, governed, regulated and re-produced.

As was discussed briefly prior to this conclusion, there is a range of areas that we would recommend focusing upon. Future research on fair trade, organics and geographical indications, value chain and commodity network approaches will continue to provide important insights, by exploring how market dynamics, institutional regulation and the ways value chains 'touch down' in different political contexts and affect the way value is created and distributed. Another avenue involves investigation of the institutional politics of certification regimes and how these have come to act as a development discourse – an example being the normative dissemination of particular approaches to social organisation and environmental management by the fair trade labelling movement. There is ample space for more micro studies of how ethical value chains interact with livelihoods, and the dynamics of exclusion, empowerment, benefit and risk that they create. Efforts to combine these perspectives or scales of analysis will be particularly useful. Researchers should consider complementing qualitative work with a quantitative analysis in case studies, which has been noticeably absent to date. As noted previously, studies that consider the broader positive externalities of ethical value networks in agri-food communities and regions would be welcome as would work that provides baseline studies to be revisited in future.

EVeNs clearly have enormous potential to flatten the development landscape, characterised as it is by persistent and unwieldy unevenness. But this potential will not be reached without supra-national incentives and structures, together with effective government regulation and promotion, blended with grassroots organisation, regulation and resistance. Coordinating and incentivising such a response is a daunting task. However, without such intervention the market will continue to exhibit the failures it does and threaten to undermine the progressive promise of EVeNs. Left to its own devices, the creation of virtue through ethical value networks can clearly become commoditised and co-opted by the market. Private concerns can and have grown to become regional monopolies and oligopsonies. In this sense, the networks that have evolved, whilst not hierarchical, top-down and linear in the traditional commodity chain sense, are often characterised by structures that are reminiscent of core–periphery systems. Whilst the difference between the extent of marginalisation at the periphery and oligopsonistic profit accumulation at the core may not be as extreme as it is in conventional networks, vis-à-vis EVeNs, the fact that such inequities continue to exist threatens to undermine the integrity of the ethical trade project. To guarantee the early promise of EVeNs we need to re-double our efforts to research, critique, politicise, reform and revolutionise them.

NOTES

1. This section draws from and builds upon a working paper by Bidwell et al. (2015).
2. This section is based upon and borrows from the doctoral thesis of Kelle Howson (2019).

REFERENCES

Battaglene, T. (2005). The Australian wine industry position on Geographical Indications. Presentation to the Worldwide Symposium on Geographical Indications. Parma (Italy), 27–29 June 2005.

Bidwell, S., Murray. W.E., & Overton, J. (2015). Ethical value chains – Latin American perspectives. *EVeN Working Paper* Series 1, Victoria University of Wellington, 44pp.

Bowen, S. (2010). Development from within? The potential for geographical indications in the global south. *The Journal of World Intellectual Property*, *13*(2), 231–252.

Brown, K.R. (2013). *Buying into fair trade: Culture, morality, and consumption*. New York University Press.

Bryant, R. & Goodman, M. (2004). Consuming narratives: The political ecology of 'alternative' consumption. *Transactions of the Institute of British Geography*, *29*, 344–366.

Das, K., (2006). International protection of geographical indications with special reference to Darjeeling tea. *The Journal of World Intellectual Property*, *9*(5), 459–495.

Dragusanu, R., Giovannucci, D., & Nunn, N. (2014). The economics of fair trade. *Journal of Economic Perspectives*, *28*(3), 217–236.

Fridell, G. (2007). Fair-trade coffee and commodity fetishism: The limits of market-driven social justice. *Historical Materialism*, *15*(4), 79–104.

Gereffi, G., Humphrey, J., & Sturgeon, T. (2005). The governance of global value chains. *Review of International Political Economy*, *12*(1), 78–104.

Giovannucci, D., Josling, T., Kerr, W.A., O'Connor, B., & Yeung, M.T. (2009). *Guide to geographical indications: Linking products and their origins*. International Trade Centre.

González, A.A. & Nigh, R. (2005). Smallholder participation and certification of organic farm products in Mexico. *Journal of Rural Studies*, *21*, 449–460.

Guthman, J, (2007). The Polanyian way? Voluntary food labels as neoliberal governance. *Antipode*, *39*(3), 456–478.

Howson, K. (2019). *Bottling the colonial unconscious: Ethical value networks and the commodification of fairness in the South African wine industry*. PhD thesis, Victoria University of Wellington.

International Fund for Agricultural Development (IFAD) (2003). *The adoption of organic agriculture among small farmers in Latin America and the Caribbean: Thematic evaluation*. Report no. 1337, IFAD.

Jena, P.R. & Groote, U. (2012). Impact evaluation of traditional Basmati rice culti-vation in Uttarakhand State of Northern India: What implications does it hold for geographical indications? *World Development*, *40*(9), 1895–1907.

Luetchford, P. (2008). *Fair trade and a global commodity: Coffee in Costa Rica*. Pluto Press.

Lyon, S. (2006). Evaluating fair trade consumption: Politics, defetishization and producer participation. *International Journal of Consumer Studies*, *30*(5), 452–464.

Pay, E. (2009). *The market for organic and fair-trade coffee*. Trade and Markets Division, Food and Agriculture Organization of the United Nations.

Raynolds, L.T. (2008). The organic agro-export boom in the Dominican Republic: maintaining tradition or fostering transformation? *Latin American Research Review*, *43*(1), 161–184.

Raynolds, L.T. (2012). Fair trade: Social regulation in global food markets. *Journal of Rural Studies*, *28*, 276–287.

Renard, M.-C. (2005). Quality certification, regulation, and power in fair trade. *Journal of Rural Studies*, *21*, 419–431.

Ruben, R. & Fort, R. (2012). The impact of fair trade certification for coffee farmers in Peru. *World Development*, *40*(3), 570–582.

Shreck, A. (2002). Just bananas? Fair trade banana production in the Dominican Republic. *International Journal of Sociology of Food and Agriculture*, *10*, 25–52.

Valkila, J. (2009). Fair trade organic coffee production in Nicaragua: Sustainable devel-opment or a poverty trap? *Ecological Economics*, *68*, 3024.

Yeung, M.T. & Kerr, W.A. (2011). Are geographical indications a wise strategy for developing country farmers? Greenfields, clawbacks and monopoly rents. *Journal of World Intellectual Property*, *14*(5), 353–367.

Index